Wired for Sound

A Guitar Odyssey

Martin Melhuish & Mark Hall

QUARRY
MUSIC
BOOKS

This book is based on authorized interviews
and original research conducted for the television and home video documentary film
"Wired for Sound: A Guitar Odyssey,"
produced by Hallway Entertainment Inc.

Images of the artists in this book are
reproduced as photographic stills
from the documentary.

The publisher gratefully acknowledges
the support of The Canada Council
for the Arts and the Department of Canadian
Heritage for the arts of
writing and publishing in Canada.

ISBN 1-55082-210-1

Design by Susan Hannah.

Printed and bound in Canada by
AGMV Marquis, Cap-St-Ignace, Quebec.

Published by Quarry Press Inc., P.O. Box
1061, Kingston, Ontario K7L 4Y5 Canada,
www.quarrypress.com

Contents

To the late Michael Bloomfield, for the musical inspiration, and to Jim Burke, Phil Cooke, Bill Cundiff, John Keith, John Kelly, and Brian Rowley, the boys in the bands with whom I shared my 15 minutes of musical fame back in the late '60s and early '70s.
—Martin Melhuish

To my family, Michelle, Jason, Adam and Nicole — the best band a guy could have!
—Mark Hall

Preface

I can tell you exactly when this guitar thing started for me. The year: 1966. The place: the second floor of Sam the Record Man's main store in downtown Toronto and an open box of records with an intriguing cover that pictured a group of black and white musicians wailing away at what appeared to be some smoky club on Chicago's South Side. The Paul Butterfield Blues Band. Hey, love the blues and these guys look pretty cool. Sold! Well, there are blues and there are BLUES. Yeah, Paul Butterfield could wail on that harp like no one else, but how about that kid Mike Bloomfield on guitar? The record didn't leave my turntable — hey, remember those? — for a month. Then I picked up the group's next album, EAST WEST, and hit the track *The Work Song* with the Bloomfield solo that defies superlatives or duplication and that was it for me. I was gone. I had played in local pop groups for a couple of years and now I was ready to trade in my four chords and a gross of "sha la las" for some of what Mike was laying down.

Bloomfield was my main man, but Toronto was a hotbed of pretty interesting and innovative guitar styles in those days, particularly in that percolating R&B scene over on Yonge Street where players like Robbie Robertson, Domenic Troiano, and Fred Keeler were cutting razor sharp into the neon glare of Toronto's nightlife. And if you ever began to get cocky about your guitar playing, you could always head over to Yorkville Village where the late jazz guitarist Lenny Breau could humble you with his mesmerizing virtuosity.

I traded in my guitar for a typewriter in the early '70s — probably not long after one of those Breau club dates, as a matter of fact — but my fascination with this instrument of a thousand voices and moods has never waned. *Wired For Sound: A Guitar Odyssey*, the television documentary, was a labor of love for all of us at Hallway Entertainment. Reliving those special moments and conversations in this companion book has been an unexpected treat. We hope you find it similarly entertaining.

— Martin Melhuish

"Blame it on The Beatles!" Isn't that the answer most people give when asked about how they got into music, especially us baby boomers who grew up in the '60s? I live in Nashville now, but I was about nine years old when the Fab Four emerged in Canada as I was growing up in Toronto. *Love Me Do* was released in March of 1963, but *She Loves You* was the first big single for them, and I can still remember hearing it for the first time on my transistor radio as I walked along Willowdale Avenue in Toronto one Saturday afternoon. That would have been in December of 1963. It was certainly previous to their appearance on the *Ed Sullivan Show*. The cool guys had a Beatles' cap and Nehru jacket in those days and you'd see them hanging around the plaza. It was definitely the era when the quarterbacks lost their hip status to the musicians. Like everybody else, I played a bit. I wasn't all that musical, though I did play trumpet in the school band and had a little rock band in which I played organ when I was in public school. I do remember that with the British Invasion and groups like The Rolling Stones, The Kinks, and all those Liverpool groups, suddenly people began to take notice of the instruments these groups were using, so, besides hanging out at the local record store after school, we used to go over to ABC Music on Yonge Street and just ogle the guitars that were hanging there. There probably weren't many Gibsons or Fenders. Most of them were Japanese knock offs that all seemed to have that classic Gibson 335 look. I had a fake Japanese Beatle bass — it could have been a Stuart or something like that — which was just like Paul McCartney's Hofner bass.

When I got out of high school, I ended up at a Toronto radio station as an operator and copywriter before moving into television where I held the position of technical editor at the Toronto-based Global Television before departing to test the entrepreneurial waters. My brother Greg and I founded Hallway Entertainment in the mid-'80s, initially doing some National Geographic style travel programs and some public affairs interviews features before we gravitated back to music. We saw the opportunity to blend music and documentaries in a way that could be really exciting, and over the last decade, working with dozens of artists over the course of more than 20 productions, that has proven to be the case.

When the opportunity arose to work with Gibson guitars on a production inspired by their 100th anniversary, we jumped at the chance. The first consideration was, how do we approach the story? Obviously, the guest artists had to have a particular liking for Gibson and their instruments, but beyond that, what was "Wired

For Sound: A Guitar Odyssey" going to be about and how would we tie all the elements together? Was it just going to be a bunch of players talking about their guitars or were we going to take it past that to some sort of linear story about the relationship each of the artists has with the guitar? We wanted to talk to artists who had a particular point of view on their connection with the guitar, whether it was Emmylou Harris, who you wouldn't normally associate with the instrument but ended up relating dozens of interesting stories on the subject, or Steve Winwood, who's usually more associated with keyboards in people's minds. Another element of the show that was important was the footage of artists like Don Felder, Peter Frampton, B.B. King, Chet Atkins, Brent Mason, Skunk Baxter, Steve Howe, and John Entwistle, among others, alone with their guitars in an impromptu performance for the camera.

It was a fun project to work on and, as you will see when you read the various artist interviews contained here, a fascinating look behind the scenes at the players and instruments that made music history.

— Mark Hall

Foreword

"**I** spend most of my time either thinking about it or just having it close by so it's always next to me," says Slash. "It drives my wife crazy, I know that, but it's what I do."

"Once in a New York hotel, I was so afraid somebody was going to steal it that I put it in the bed with me . . . but there was no physical contact," confides Steve Howe of Yes.

"There's two things in my life I hug, three, if you count the wife. One is an old Wurlitzer jukebox, which I love, and this," relates Glen Tipton of Judas Priest. "This has got a better shape to me than any woman."

Comments Tom Petty, "You know, all my life I've tried to put it into words. I don't think I ever have. I don't know how to put that into words. It's like describing sex, it's just *really* good."

"I kind of forced myself to stay away from it," reveals John Entwistle of The Who. "I'd get paranoid after about three weeks so I'd have to play one. I'd start having nightmares about rubberneck basses and all sorts of really creepy dreams and I'd have to sort of pick the bass up and make sure I could still play it!"

You have probably gathered by now that the above comments, brimming with unabashed passion, relate to the above artists' relationship with their guitar or guitars of choice.

Tom Petty is downright guitaraholic confessional on the subject. "I was bitten pretty hard at the age of eleven, then everything went out the window," he admits, with a broad smile. "I never had any interest in anything again but guitars. Even now at the age of 46, I'm trying to find something else I'm interested in. If I have spare time, I go look for guitars. Kind of sad, isn't it?"

Sad? Maybe. Understandable? You bet!

Back in 1994, as Nashville-based Gibson guitars celebrated its 100th anniversary, there was great excitement among the principals of Hallway Entertainment, a leading producer of feature length, music-based entertainment programming for television with its head office in Nashville, at the opportunity of celebrating the

Gibson centennial with a TV special that would explore the singular connection between this American icon and the artists who have brought these instruments to international attention. The result was the production of the documentary "Wired For Sound: A Guitar Odyssey" and this companion book. "Wired for Sound" was shot in the United Kingdom and across North America, primarily at the homes and studios of the artists who graciously extended their hospitality and took time from their busy schedules to sit and chat for a while about their guitars and the impact they have had on their careers.

"Wired For Sound" ultimately had its 'big screen' premiere on July 11, 1997 at the Nashville Arena as part of a Gibson-sponsored event during the NAMM Summer Session '97 convention, hosted by Raul Malo and Robert Reynolds of The Mavericks and featuring live performances by Steve Earle, Deborah Allen, Skip Ewing, Kim Richey, and Phil Keaggy, as a benefit for the National Association For Music Therapy. The show had its television debut shortly after on the MuchMusic network, originating in Canada, and was also part of the Legends series, hosted by Bryant Gumbel, on the Learning Channel in the United States.

:| |•|•|

For over a century, Gibson has defined the word "artistry" in the guitar world. From Orville Gibson and his original arched-top guitar to Ted McHugh's adjustable truss rod and Seth Lover's Humbucking pickup, this history of innovation has made Gibson guitars trend-setting instruments for the last century. These are the instruments that shaped modern music. As Gibson luthier Mike McGuire recently commented with pride in an interview with *Vintage Guitar* magazine, "From Lloyd Loar's trend-setting L5 to the classic Les Paul and the jet age Flying V, no other guitar manufacturer has influenced the art of modern guitar like Gibson."

The greatest tribute to the quality and craftsmanship of Gibson guitars is to be found in the fact that they are considered to be the most highly collectible guitars in the world and cornerstones of the vintage guitar market. According to Gibson research, an investor who acquired a 1959-1960 Les Paul Flametop in 1968 would find that his or her investment had increased in value 5,500 percent in 25 years. Had they bought a 1950s Les Paul Black Beauty or a 1939 Super 400, their investments would have grown 2,000 percent and 2,500 percent, respectively, from 1968 to 1993.

In some ways, the genesis of the Gibson guitar story stretches back in time to the Renaissance period in Europe when mandolins began to evolve from the lute family of instruments. By the mid-to-late 18th century, Neapolitan mandolins began to appear in America, having been brought to the New World by Italian immigrants. The instrument enjoyed a brief popularity before giving way to the banjo, which was being manufactured by, among others, Elias Howe, the subsequent inventor of the sewing machine.

The mandolin came into fashion in the wake of the American minstrel shows that were the rage in the mid-to-late 19th century, thanks to the popularity of artists like The Virginia Minstrels, European favorite Horace Webster, and five-string banjo pioneer, Joel Walker Sweeney.

The dawn of the 20th century was an era of unprecedented creativity and invention, and Orville H. Gibson, a part-time woodworker who had been born in Chateaugay, New York in 1856, was a young man in tune with his times. By 1881, Gibson had moved west, and from his workshop in Kalamazoo, Michigan, he set himself the task of improving the quality of the mandolin. In the process, he lent his name to one of the most enduring American icons, the Gibson Guitar.

Giant strides were also being made at the time in sound recording as Edison's wax cylinder gave way to the jukebox and a new breed of entertainer was born — the recording artist. The popular songs of the day, which included moldy old gems like *After the Ball*, *Bicycle Built For Two*, *The Sidewalks of New York*, *The Band Played On*, and perhaps the most often performed song of all time, *Happy Birthday To You*, were in great demand — but not only to listen to. It seemed that everyone played a musical instrument, whether it was solo in the parlor or as a member of one of the many banjo, mandolin, or guitar orchestras that were flourishing at the time.

Orville Gibson patented his new, improved mandolin in 1895, and seven years later, he became the first stockholder in the Gibson Mandolin-Guitar Manufacturing Co. Ltd. He would sell all his shares in the company in the summer of 1903; in 1909, as the Gibson brand name dominated the mandolin market, Gibson fell ill and was hospitalized in Kalamazoo, Michigan. A few years later, and with his health still poor, he returned to New York State, where, on August 21, 1918, he died in hospital in Ogdensburg, just outside of his hometown of Chateaugay. He was 62.

:| |•|•|

By the First World War, one of the hotbeds of musical innovation was the southern United States, where blues, Dixieland, and country were beginning their migration to the urban centers of the north. By the late 1920s, the popularity of the guitar was on the rise, though, for the most part, it was playing it coy, content to lend rhythmic support to the big bands of the day. But, along the way, the guitar found a new voice, an electronic one, and in the hands of jazzmen like Charlie Christian and Django Reinhardt, it emerged from the obscurity of the rhythm section into the spotlight as a lead instrument.

Christian, whose landmark album, SOLO FLIGHT, was a major influence on future generations of guitarists, including Billy Byrd, Barney Kessel, Herb Ellis, and Tal Farlow, died tragically of tuberculosis at the age of 24, just a year after the record's release in 1941.

Gypsy guitarist Django Reinhardt almost had an equally tragic demise in a fire that swept through the caravan in which he was living in 1928; his left fingering hand was badly deformed from the burns he sustained. He nonetheless went on to become one of the few Europeans to have an impact on the jazz world in America in the '30s and '40s.

Extraordinarily, his influence is still felt among a wide-range of guitar players today. Steve Howe of Yes recalls first encountering Reinhardt on a 10-inch record that he bought from a neighbor. "He told me: 'This is the greatest guitarist in the world; look it says it right on the back.' I put it on and instantly knew that he was right, that this guitarist was in another league altogether."

"My father had brought a Django Reinhardt album into the house very early on and I hated it to start with because it wasn't The Shadows and it was jazz," Peter Frampton recalls with a grimace. "But, each time I'd go back and look at the record collection, I'd get it out and play a track from it and all of a sudden that sort of music took over. That became very seductive to listen to."

Chet Atkins remembers meeting Reinhardt in Chicago in 1946. "I was up there without a job and I spent my last dollar and went down to the Civic Opera House and watched the show. I was way in the back and after it was over I went back and got his autograph. It's about the only autograph I ever got I think. I wanted to play for him. I wanted to so badly."

In the mid-1960s, Reinhardt's courageous battle to overcome his infirmity became the inspiration for a young rock guitarist in Birmingham, England, who had lost the tips of his fingers in a factory accident. "At first, I thought it was all over with and then somebody who I worked with — actually, the manager of the firm — came around and brought me a record of Django Reinhardt and that sort of sparked me on," recollects Black Sabbath guitarist, Tony Iommi. "I thought, 'Well, he's done it so I'm going to have a go. I made some tips out of a Fairy Liquid [dish-washing detergent] bottle and melted it down and made it into a ball. I then got a hot soldering iron and burrowed it out so that it would fit the finger, and then I glued leather on top of that so it would grip the strings. And it works."

:| |•|•|

Radio, which had first been introduced in America in 1919, was big business by the 1930s and soon became one of the main influences in the development of the guitar as it gave wide exposure to the major players of the day. Lester Polfuss, later known as Les Paul, and singer/guitarist Jimmy Atkins, Chet Atkins' older half-brother, were both heard playing Gibson L7s when they worked with Fred Waring and his band the Pennsylvanians on his radio show in the late '30s. Paul's amplified single-string solos which spectacularly cut through the band's wall of sound would later be cited as an influence on the playing styles of such noted guitarists as Tony Mottola, Charlie Byrd, and Johnny Smith.

Paul was an accomplished musician whose unquenchable curiosity would lead him to become a pioneer in the development of the electric guitar. Initially, feedback from the amplified hollow body guitar was a constant problem, and he tried to plug up the body with socks, shorts, towels, and even plaster of Paris before successfully experimenting with strings on a steel railroad track. The weight alone made the instrument impractical, and in the end he settled on a four-by-four block of wood for the body of the guitar he would dub "The Log." It was practical alright, but hardly a joy to behold.

"People hear with their eyes, and so I said maybe if I put wings on this four-by-four and made it look like a guitar, let's go back to the club and play it the following Saturday night and see what happens," Paul relates. "I did, and there was a great reaction."

With a few major design improvements, the solid body electric guitar, which would bear the Les Paul name, was born. Ironically, he had created the instrument of his own demise by which rock 'n' roll would ultimately displace his style of music from the record charts. But Les Paul's inventive mind soon had a new focus — multi-track recording.

"I met the man himself once," Rolling Stones' guitarist Ron Wood says, recalling his encounter with Les Paul. "It was a marvelous experience. I was in a studio in New York with him — and he's a lovely old man. He's sitting there and he's going, 'What do you think of this studio, Ronnie?' And I'm going, 'It's marvelous, what they can do today in the recording studio like, here we are in the control room and look at all this.' And he said, 'Well I invented that. I invented this and you see that console. That's one of my original modules that I invented.' All the outboard stuff. It's amazing. I didn't know this, he invented 80 or 90 percent of everything that's used in the studio today."

:| |·|·|

From the guitar's earliest solo flights in the hands of pioneers like Charlie Christian, Django Reinhardt, Les Paul, and the electric guitar's first showman, T-Bone Walker, in the 1930s, it was obvious that this was an instrument no longer content to play second fiddle in the band.

"When I heard T-Bone Walker playing the electric guitar in that single-string style, man, I just went crazy for that," recalls blues guitar legend B.B. King. "That was the sweetest sound this side of heaven to me. I never heard nothing that sounded like that. And then when I did see him, he had one of those big, full-bodied Gibson guitars, a big one. It had three pickups on it, and he would play it with it lying on his chest."

In the 1950s, blues and country collided head-on in Memphis with a young, truck drivin' man by the name of Elvis Presley looking on at the crossroads. They called it rock 'n' roll and music would never be the same again.

"I grew up playing classical music, but, a few years later, I started to hear this new thing called rock 'n' roll," states guitarist Randy Bachman. "I saw Elvis on television with Scotty Moore playing that big blonde Gibson and that was it for me."

Don Felder of The Eagles agrees: "Elvis Presley hit the black and white screen on the Ed Sullivan show and I was hopeless from there on out."

"Elvis was a guy who that made it possible for us hillbillies to play rock music because before then it was always keyboards or saxophone and that sort of thing," suggests Charlie Daniels. "Of course, Scotty Moore brought the guitar right into the forefront."

"Scotty added to the rhythm greatly because he played fills and played with his thumb too," adds Chet Atkins. "Elvis just played rhythm part of the time, so it wouldn't have been much without Scotty."

Of course, the next major musical revolution arrived in the form of The British Invasion led by The Beatles and The Rolling Stones in the mid-'60s. Surprisingly enough, good guitars, which were vital tools of the trade for these British musicians, were initially extremely hard to come by.

"We used to have to settle for a Burns Black Bison," laughs Ron Wood. "That was top of the line then. It had these huge horns on it. That was state of the art. And there was the Futurama with the push buttons."

"When I first started, I think there was a choice of about three different basses," says The Who's John Entwistle. "The best one of those was the Hofner Violin, which was pretty gruesome."

Explains Mick Ralphs of Bad Company, "Part of the reason that all of the bands from Liverpool had such a foot in the door really in that whole new music was the fact that they used to get stuff off the American seamen who would come into port and need some money and they would sell their B.B. King albums and The Miracles albums."

Adds Entwistle, "At a lot of the ports, people came across the Atlantic and smuggled the guitars and basses in, and the guys in Liverpool would give a friend in the merchant navy their money and they'd go away and bring back a guitar."

Recalls Ralphs, "I think in 1964 or 1965, the trade thing between the U.S. and England was modified so that you could then purchase Fenders and Gibsons and get American albums."

"When American guitars did arrive to these big, huge music shops, like Selmers, in the Shaftsbury Avenue and the Charing Cross Road area where all of the music shops were, they were all behind glass," Peter Frampton recollects. "You couldn't touch them; they were beyond reach."

There was no such scarcity in America. Former Doobie Brothers/Steely Dan guitarist Skunk Baxter jokes that he could have cared less anyway when he was a kid. "At the age of nine, I decided I wanted a brand new bicycle so I asked my parents for one for Christmas and they obliged me by buying me a guitar — which pissed me off! But, somehow or other, it kept rearing its ugly six-pegged head all through my life, and, finally, it just seemed like it was the right thing to do."

Aerosmith guitarist Joe Perry says that, like most musicians who had their beginnings in the '60s, he was influenced by the British Invasion. "Seeing what The Beatles did, you always fantasized about going through all that yourself, but I never sat there and said, 'Well, I'm going to be a rock musician and a rock star.' All I wanted to do was have a gig next week and put food on the table. Other than that, it was all gravy."

:| |•|•|

Guitar and career philosophies abound but behind all of them, as you will discover when you read on, there is always an underlying perception that each guitar, far from being simply a lifeless block of wood with strings attached, somehow has a soul and character of its own. Dave Matthews of the Dave Matthews Band talks about songs lurking beneath the surface waiting to be captured. Explains Matthews, "I feel almost as though things are just waiting there because all of the combinations of notes and all the twists and turns, they're all there in a way, it's just a matter of pulling them out."

For Billy Corgan, the sudden realization that the styles of guitar playing which he had been unconsciously developing over the years had found their perfect union in the sound of his group, Smashing Pumpkins, was a significant revelation for him. "The most prophetic moment," Corgan recalls, "was when it finally dawned on me that the things that I intuitively played when I was 15 years old, which were kind of like strange open-chord tuning kinds of things, melded with all the bad heavy metal riffs that I'd learned. That was really the beginning of what people would call 'Pumpkin sound,' this sort of strange, dense, open-chord thing. The day that all came together in my head, it changed my life really because it was the moment that everything I understood about the guitar fused together."

Chet Atkins has the last word. "I think to be a great guitar player, you've got to really love it. As Jerry Reed says, 'You've got to be eaten up with it.' I still can't keep my hands off a guitar and I've been playing for years and years — because I love it."

As you will discover, Atkins speaks for all of the guitarists featured in this book.

Enjoy!

Chet Atkins (C.G.P.)

Certified Guitar Player

Chester Burton Atkins
Born June 20, 1924
Near Luttrell, Tennessee

"The first time I heard Chet play I recall my heart thumping in my chest, my whole body and spirit being so moved and excited!" That's Australian guitarist Tommy Emmanuel, who shared playing credits on the album THE DAY FINGER PICKERS TOOK OVER THE WORLD and imparted, in his contribution to the liner notes, his unbridled admiration for the man they call "Mr. Guitar." "From the age of seven," Emmanuel continued, "I knew I wanted to play like him. I was told that he did 'recording tricks' on his albums and you couldn't really do 'all that' at once. I didn't believe that. I knew he was 'for real' and all through my young years and my teens, I spent every day listening, practicing and learning. I've 'bragged' about him all my life and shown, to the best of my abilities, the magical ways of the thumb and finger styles, that bring so many people so much joy. I've enjoyed 'turning people on' to the greatest player in history."

Chet Atkins grew up in a life of poverty on a farm near Luttrell, Tennessee, where, at the age of six, he experienced the heart-wrenching break-up of his parents. He worked the farm with his younger brother to help keep food on the table, but eventually his chronic asthma got the best of him and he moved to Georgia when he was 10 to live with his father, hoping that the climate would be more suitable. His father was a journeyman musician who played through the South in the '20s and '30s. His brother Jim was also a guitar player and worked with Les Paul in those early days. Paul became one of Atkins' earliest influences, as did Merle Travis, whose finger-picking style left a lasting impression. (Atkins and wife Leona would name their daughter Merle after the guitarist/singer).

The story goes that at age nine, Atkins traded in an old family pistol for his first guitar. In 1942 he left home to work as a musician at radio stations across the U.S. He signed to RCA Victor Records in Chicago in 1947 and the following year became guitarist for the country/comedy duo Homer and Jethro. In 1950 he moved to

Nashville, where he would be more responsible than anyone for the city's subsequent nickname of "Music City U.S.A." He arranged the first Nashville sessions for Elvis Presley, playing guitar on the tracks *Heartbreak Hotel* and *I Want You, I Need You, I Love You.* (He also played on The Everly Brothers' *Wake Up Little Susie* and Hank William Sr.'s *Your Cheatin' Heart* during this period.) From 1957 until 1982, when he retired from the company and gave himself the honorary degree of Certified Guitar Player (C.G.P.), he oversaw RCA Nashville's operations during which time he built the legendary RCA Studio B and influenced the sound and overall careers of artists like Dottie West, Jim Reeves, Bobby Bare, Eddy Arnold, Waylon Jennings, Roy Orbison, Jerry Reed, Porter Wagoner, Dolly Parton, Skeeter Davis, and Charley Pride, among others. He became the youngest artist ever inducted into the Country Music Hall of Fame in 1973 and won the Academy of Country Music Pioneer Award in 1982. His trophy case also boasts 12 Grammy Awards, one for Lifetime Achievement.

One of Atkins's closest friends is writer/broadcaster Garrison Keillor, who has marveled in print at Chet's dedication to his craft. "It's amazing to me that a man can love his instrument so much after all these years the way Chet does, but he does," Keillor once commented in a Chet Atkins Appreciation Newsletter. "Chet picks up a guitar the way other people pick up a phone or turn on the TV or pop open a beer on a hot day. Once I was at his house and we were watching a golf tournament on television and Leona was talking about seeing Bill Monroe on an awards show a few nights before and Chet reached over for his guitar and picked out a Monroe tune and went into a long stream-of-consciousness medley of country songs. It was the prettiest thing. Leona turned down the sound and Chet played this amazing string of old tear-jerker ballads — which he dearly loves, things like *Pictures On The Wall* and *Mother Dear Come Bathe My Forehead* — and Hank Williams and Lefty Frizzell and a little Django and Carter Family and a Bach chorale and The Beatles' *Lady Madonna* and *The Old Oaken Bucket*, and so forth. I wished I had a tape recorder. What a gifted and good man!"

We spoke to Chet at the house that doubles as his office on Music Row in Nashville, not far from the four-block section of South Street that was renamed Chet Atkins Place in 1991, on a day when the thunder rolled and the rain lashed down outside. At the very instant the lights were switched on to begin shooting the TV interview, all the power in that area of Nashville went off and stayed off for a couple of hours. Having determined that the blackout wasn't our fault, we passed the time being entertained by a magician, a friend of Chet's who had dropped by, and then we broke for lunch for a few hours. When we reconvened, Chet pulled out his signature model Gibson SST, which is now also played by artists as varied as Travis Tritt, Clint Black, Mark Knopfler, Slash, and Bret Michaels of Poison, among others, and settled in for a brief chat.

My first interest in the guitar came from my older brother who was about 12 or 14 years older than me. He played a Washburn guitar, which was a popular guitar back in the early '30s. He would pick and sing songs for me like *Coming Around The Mountain* and things like that. One day, he came home from school and I had his Washburn filled with dirt and I was dragging it around the yard. That was the first guitar playing I ever did, and he put a stop to that real quick.

My first guitars were of the cheap variety. In fact, I had a ukulele. It had some gut strings on it when we got it, but eventually they broke, and sometimes I'd put an old guitar string on it or just rip a wire off the screen door. It would stay in tune for a little while but, because it was soft metal, it would stretch.

As I said, we had real cheap guitars in those days. My first one was a Sears-Roebuck that was broken at the neck and the action was about half an inch high. I never got out of the first position for a long time because I was a little kid and couldn't push the strings, so I'd play it with a kitchen knife; I'd take the knife and hold it down on the strings.

I played guitar first and then I got a fiddle when I was about eight years old and I learned *Red Wing* and *Sally Anne* and *Shoot That Turkey Buzzard,* and, about two weeks later, I played a show. When people would get sick at home — a lot of people died of tuberculosis in those days — we would do a show and give the money to the family. We'd charge about ten cents.

I kept playing guitar, but also played fiddle on the side. When the war came, I heard that Archie Campbell and Bill Carlisle were looking for a fiddle player down at WNOX in Knoxville, and I went down and auditioned and I got the job. They paid me three dollars a night when we worked, and sometimes I'd sleep in the railway station or the bus station. Sometimes, when I had the money, I'd get a 50 cent room, but I was in show business and I loved it. One time, I asked Archie Campbell why he only paid me three dollars a night, and he told me it was because I wasn't a very good fiddle player, and I had to agree with him.

The first good guitar playing I heard was Merle Travis and Les Paul. My brother worked in Les's trio in the late '30s or early '40s and I hung around and listened to this great guitar player. And then I was living down in Georgia, the war had started, and I was listening to this radio that I'd built and heard Merle Travis play. I didn't know exactly what he was doing, but I knew he was playing with his fingers. It knocked me over. He was playing with his thumb and one finger, and I started to imitate that. I would listen for him every morning. The reception was bad though because it was a long way from Cincinnati to Columbus, Georgia. I played more of a stride — a piano style — but it was real exciting the way Merle played. But, back at that time, Merle was the only one doing it and I was right behind and everybody else was fighting with a straight pick. So we changed the world, I think. In fact, my new album is called THE DAY FINGER PICKERS TOOK OVER THE WORLD.

Django Reinhardt was a big influence on me; still is. That gypsy style — I love the way they play. One day a guy played me a Django record and I wasn't too impressed, but I thought he played with a lot of drive. Later on, I heard more of his records and some of those great solos, and I fell in love with him. I finally met him in 1946 in Chicago. I was up there without a job and I paid my last dollar and went down to the Civic Opera House where he was appearing. I sat way in the back and after it was over, I went backstage to get his autograph. I think it was the only autograph I ever got. But I wanted to play for him; I wanted to so badly because I thought he would like finger picking, but I didn't get to.

The Everly Brothers and I were into Bo Diddley as a guitar player. I thought that was the greatest thing, that beat, and Don [Everly] did too. When they got a record deal, I met him back at the Opry. He said, 'Will you come and play some of that Bo Diddley with us?' and I said, 'Lord, yes! Anytime!' Don would sit around and figure out great rhythmic things like Bo Diddley did, but his playing was much more sophisticated than Bo's.

Scotty Moore was also real important as a guitar player. He was very primitive and he tried to play like me, of course, but, with Elvis, he added to the rhythm greatly because Elvis just played rhythm part of the time, so without Scotty, it wouldn't have been much. Scotty played fills and rhythm with Bill Black slapping the bass and making it sound sort of like a snare drum. That rhythm was very similar to something we did three or four years earlier on some Bill Carlisle records.

I think to be a great guitar player, you've got to really love it. As Jerry Reed says, you've got to be eaten up with it. I still can't keep my hands off a guitar — and I've been playing for years and years — because I love it. I would play all day sometimes and take it to bed with me. I still sometimes fall asleep with a guitar in my hands.

Randy Bachman

THE GUESS WHO, BRAVE BELT,
BACHMAN-TURNER OVERDRIVE

Randy Bachman
Born September 27, 1943
Winnipeg, Canada

:|Randy Bachman|·|·|

Guitarist/songwriter/producer Randy Bachman was raised in the Canadian prairie city of Winnipeg, Manitoba, a hive of musical activity in those days, surprisingly. Bachman's musical contemporaries included rock legend Neil Young and the late jazz guitarist, Lenny Breau, whom he befriended. Breau was 15 years old at the time and already demonstrating the genius that would see him emerge as one of the most innovative and highly-acclaimed jazz guitarists in the world. His stylings rubbed off on Bachman as did those of artists like Bo Diddley, Chuck Berry, Duane Eddy, Hank Marvin, Chet Atkins, and the fast-picking 'country cabin jazz' guitarist, Jimmy Bryant. And Bachman was no musical purist. When he wasn't a-pickin' and a-grinnin' with a local country group, he was over at the local community center teen dance playing instrumentals by people like Duane Eddy, The Fireballs, The Ventures, and The Shadows in a group called The Silvertones. Chad Allan and the Expressions emerged from that relatively isolated music scene in the mid-'60s to become The Guess Who with Bachman at the helm and the hit song, *Shakin' All Over*. He left the group over personal differences in May of 1970, as The Guess Who's single *American Woman* hit the top of the charts across North America. That same year, Bachman released his solo instrumental album, AXE, featuring guest appearances by guitarists Domenic Troiano and Wes Dakus. A subsequent recording project with former bandmate Chad Allan evolved into the country/rock flavored group Brave Belt. This band, in turn, gave way to the heavy metal thunder of Bachman-Turner Overdrive, which reached the rock 'n' roll pantheon in the mid-'70s in the wake of chart-toppers like *You Ain't Seen Nothin' Yet* and the ubiquitous *Takin' Care Of Business*.

The years since have seen Bachman, who remains a prolific songwriter and producer, release a number of solo albums and continue to administer his two record companies, Legend and Guitarchives. The latter has become the posthumous home of

Lenny Breau and the vast body of recorded, yet unreleased, work that Bachman has uncovered during the course of his untiring research into the shambles of his old friend's career. Guitarchives also recently re-issued two of jazz guitarist Howard Roberts' classic Capitol Records albums from the early '60s, H.R. IS A DIRTY GUITAR PLAYER and COLOR HIM FUNKY, on a 2-CD set titled DIRTY 'N FUNKY.

We spoke to Randy in Nashville, where he is currently spending an increasing amount of time expanding his songwriting and music publishing activities. He arrived with one of his black Gibson Les Paul guitars with gold fixtures and a Bigsby. We shot the TV interview in an alley in Music Row that runs between the houses-cum-offices of artists like George Jones, Chet Atkins, Anne Murray, and Waylon Jennings, among others. Bachman, as you will see, was characteristically enthusiastic and voluble in discussing a subject close to his heart.

I grew up playing classical music and played violin until I was about 13. Playing classical was very strict; you had to play what was there on the paper; in fact, it was just so strict that I wanted to leave it. A couple of years later, I started to hear this new thing called rock 'n' roll and I saw Elvis on television with Scotty Moore playing that big blonde Gibson. I also listened to Les Paul, who was on the hit parade at that time. This was just pre-rockabilly. There was Les Paul and Mary Ford and you'd see pictures of Les with his little Gibson — the "Les Paul" Gibson with the Pulverizer on it. Then there was rockabilly, rock 'n' roll, and a lot of Chet Atkins kind of stuff that I was introduced to through a friend of mine, Lenny Breau.

When I had first started to play guitar in Winnipeg and I was trying to learn the Scotty Moore licks, the Chet Atkins licks, the James Burton licks, nobody in town knew how to play that. I would go to the offshoot Grand Ole Opry shows that would come into Fargo or Minneapolis or into Winnipeg, where maybe half of them would come and I got to see Billy Grammer and Thumbs Carllile and these guys just blew me away. But they were so far away; I couldn't go to them and say, 'Teach me!'

I remember going to a Les Paul show once. He was playing in Winnipeg at the Rancho Don Carlos and I couldn't even get in because I was underage, so I had to stand in the kitchen with these doors with the big round windows that swung back and forth like you see in the movies. So I peeked through the window, but right beside me in the kitchen were these eight Ampex tape recorders. Les Paul had the controls, and I'd see these things start at different times and I'd hear this incredible music come out. I watched his whole show — he was with Mary Ford and his son played drums.

At the end of the show he came into the kitchen and he just looked at me and asked me what I was doing there. I told him I couldn't get in but wanted to come and see him. I asked him, 'Could you show me one of your runs — this particular run?' and he showed it to me. [Plays chromatic lick from Les Paul & Mary Ford's *How High The Moon.*] He did it over and over for me. He just had it down pat. Actually, he came backstage and said, 'Hold this kid!' and he handed me his guitar. And I thought my Les Paul was heavy. His with the Pulverizer on it was like handing somebody a bucket of cement. So there I was holding his guitar, which was quite different than a normal Les Paul.

I met him again 20 years later when I was opening for Van Halen at the Meadowlands in New Jersey. Les Paul came backstage, and after I had my picture taken with him and Eddie Van Halen, I said, 'Les, you changed my life 20 years ago in Winnipeg at the Rancho Don Carlos.' He looked at me and said, 'Hold this, kid!' — that same line, and he told me he remembered. He's a great guy.

Also in Winnipeg, I met Lenny Breau who showed me all of this finger style that was inspired by Merle Travis and Chet Atkins. Lenny would play Les Paul songs that were originally double and triple and quadruple track, with his fingers and his hands all at once. I then started to hear Duane Eddy and Chuck Berry. I was a rocker; I was born to do that. When that came out, I knew that was my purpose in life. Lenny Breau went more into jazz, but there was a time there when he was learning by listening to Barney Kessel, Tal Farlow, and Howard Roberts and he would say to me, 'Listen to this! Listen to this!' But it was just too far out for me. I liked the three chord rock 'n' roll with the beat, but there's still a little bit of jazz in some of the things I do.

: ┆·┆·┆

It was always a dream of mine to get a Gibson guitar, but I could never afford one. I started with a Harmony guitar, then a black Sears Silvertone, the one they call the Jimmy Page model now. My first Gibson was a Les Paul, a '59, and I came upon it quite by accident. I'd had a guitar that had a broken neck and I took it in for repair and, as a replacement, while mine was being fixed, they gave me a Mosrite guitar with a turquoise sparkle finish with big knobs. The neck was quite bowed and it was very tough to play and I was just using it as a spare. If I broke a string, that's what I would use. I remember playing in the basement of a church in a place up in Canada called Nanaimo, which is on Vancouver Island. They had a rec room with a little stage about a foot and a half high where they did plays and things like that. There were about 40 or 50 kids at this dance, and it was run by the minister, who wore his white collar and the whole thing.

At one point, I was on stage and I had broken a string and our soundman — we couldn't afford a bunch of equipment techs in those days — left the soundboard and came back to change the string on my guitar. I was playing this Mosrite and a young kid came in the back door carrying a brown case. Well, the minute you see a brown case shaped like that, through decades now, you know what it is: it's a brown Les Paul case. He came right to the front of the stage and I was in the middle of the song *Tossin' and Turnin'* — I was playing with The Guess Who at the time — and he pointed to the Mosrite which, by the way, I had used on television. We appeared regularly on a television show in those days which was called at various times *Let's Go* or *Music Hop*. This was in 1967 and 1968 and he had seen this Mosrite guitar on the show. The guitar was really sparkly, and because it was black and white TV, you used anything you could that was sparkly and had knobs and everything. So he had seen this guitar on the show and he pointed to the guitar and pointed to the case as if he was asking me if I wanted to swap. This was right in the middle of the song, and I was at the mic singing and I nodded. I unplugged the Mosrite and gave it to him and he opened the case and it was a '59 Les Paul with a factory, all-aluminum Bigsby. I just tuned it up to whatever key we were playing in and finished playing the song. I played the whole night on this guitar. It had the sweetest neck pickup. I grew up playing violin and it almost sounded like a viola.

At the end of the night, I went to him and I said, 'Thank you. This has been incredible!' I went to give it back to him and he said, 'You mean you don't want to trade?' I thought he had just wanted to trade guitars for the night, but he really wanted the Mosrite that he had seen me play on television a couple of weeks in a row. I thought, 'Wow, this isn't quite right.' I had been on the road for about two weeks and I had about $75.00. I said, 'Well, I'll give you some money and the Mosrite; I'll do the trade and I want the minister to come and witness this.' So we wrote up a little thing that said that this kid had agreed to trade this guitar — we put down the serial numbers

— and I was giving him the $75.00, and the Reverend signed it. And that was that.

When we got back to Winnipeg, I started working with Gar Gillies, who was building Garnet amps, on creating the first pre-amp distortion, and that guitar fit right in. This was 1967, and suddenly I had a sound that was almost all my own. There were other guys trying this sound in England, maybe Eric Clapton and Jeff Beck, but in Canada and in America, it didn't exist. But I had that sound on *No Time* and *American Woman*, and whenever I hear it today on the radio, it still really stands out. There's something neat about the combination of that guitar, the Garnet pre-amp, which we called a Herzog, and the Garnet amp that had great big tubes in it. It was just a magical combination. That guitar became somewhat legendary. It was my *American Woman/No Time* guitar, and then I took it on into Bachman-Turner Overdrive and I was playing that Les Paul on the records.

I think seven or eight years had gone by from the time I did the trade when I got a notice in the mail from a lawyer who represented the guy who had traded me the Les Paul for the Mosrite. Because I keep all of my archives, it took me about three days to dig out this paper that we had signed. When I faxed it to the attorney, he said, 'No contest!' He had originally contacted me saying that I had stolen the guitar or taken it under unfair conditions. I had this letter on the church letterhead from Nanaimo and signed by the Reverend and he thought that was pretty legitimate. Funnily enough, only about three years ago, I was collecting some guitars and I had a call from a guy who was the brother of the guy who traded me the Les Paul. He said he lives way up in northern Vancouver Island and he's very happy. I still have the guitar, and I love it. I use it all the time.

But I also have another Les Paul with a Bigsby and there's a neat story, which I'd like to think is true, and I'm sure it is, behind how I acquired it. When I had my '59 Sunburst Les Paul, it became a little too heavy to play on stage because I was playing four or five 50-minute sets a night, six days a week and it started to wear on my shoulder. That evolved to playing that guitar sitting in a chair in the studio, because it has a wonderful sound that you can't get with another guitar.

One day, I walked into a music store in West Chester, Pennsylvania, which is just outside Philadelphia, and on the wall there was a black Les Paul guitar with a gold Bigsby, and I thought, 'Wow! That's like the one I already have.' Bigsbys were very rare on Les Pauls. They normally just had the stop tail piece. Since I had the '59 with the aluminum Bigsby, I thought, gee, this was really cool. There were two of them on the wall, one had P90 pickups and the other one had humbuckers. I said to the guy, 'I'd like to buy that guitar' and he said, 'It's not for sale. It's here with a kind of a lien on it. Keith Richards' roadie brought this guitar in for a fret job and something was wrong with the pickup. So I fixed the pickup and I did the fret job and I keep calling their [The Rolling Stones] office in New York and I never get a reply.'

I said, 'Well, if you do get a reply, see if they want to sell the guitar.' I asked him about the lien and he told me that there was a mechanic's lien. If you take your car to get fixed and somebody doesn't pick it up because the brake job or the ring job was too much, you can then sell that car to get your mechanic's wages out of it. And I said, 'Well, if this guy doesn't call you soon on this great black Les Paul [the '59], could I get it?' He said, 'Well, the odds on that are pretty slim.' But about six months later he called me and told me he'd had an answer back from an office somewhere to do with The Rolling Stones and that they couldn't be bothered to come back and get the guitar. It's for sale. I said, 'Fabulous! How much?' He said, '$750.' And that was it.

I use that guitar all the time. When I plug it in, it has that Keith Richards sound. Sometimes the pickups are loose and I stick something in there. When I took it apart, I found a matchbox cover that had been folded up from the Bag'o'Nails, which is a club in England, so I hope this is, or was, Keith Richards' guitar. In my heart, it is. I play it whenever I want to do a Keith Richards' kind of solo because he did very neat Chuck Berry stuff, but Chuck's sound was the big, hollow body guitar with pickups on it, whereas Keith played this kind of thing. I used it on many, many BTO records, and even on my new solo records, when I wanted to get two or three special kinds of sounds. They're on the Black Les Paul because all the pickups on it sound good. On my '59 Sunburst Les Paul, only the neck one sounds good. It's got that *American Woman* tone and the bridge pickup seems to be lower in output. I've had it checked and it was just the way it was wound and I don't want to touch it. So I use each guitar for its particular inherent qualities, which are great.

I like the necks on the Les Paul; they're real kind of chunky, nice necks. You can't really go wrong with them. Mine's been through the rock and roll wars. I look at the prices now. Almost every guitar player's got a story about a '59 Les Paul and what he paid for it and what it's worth now. I have a very similar story. Mine was just done on the trade for the Mosrite, and even when I got my black one, it was for $750. What they're worth now, because they've been played on famous records and been in videos and movies that I've done, I don't know.

It's funny, I think I have about 14 or 15 Gibsons and every single one of them is a '59. I didn't purposely do that, but in looking at them and trying to date them . . . I've got the TV model, the blonde one; a single cutaway; a Melody Maker; a great big L5, that my wife bought me, and they're all '59s. I love the blonde ones. I was lucky enough to get what I call the Chuck Berry model. I don't even know what it's called. It has two black P90s and a sharp cutaway and a very thin body and it's blonde. I got that from my cousin in Winnipeg when I was there, who bought it at Winnipeg Piano. When that guitar came in, guys lined up to see the first Gibson that came into Winnipeg because it had that coolness about it because it looked like a Scotty Moore guitar or a Chuck Berry guitar. We could only see those guys when Chuck Berry was on *American Bandstand* or when Elvis was on *Ed Sullivan*. So to actually see the guitar ... well, every guitar player came into town to see this blonde Gibson. My cousin bought the guitar in 1960 and I was lucky enough to get it from him on the tour we did with Van Halen in '87. He was in Detroit and told me that his son wanted a guitar but he wanted one like Eddie [Van Halen]. He told me he'd trade me the Gibson for one like Eddie's, so now I've got my cousin's blonde Gibson and it's a prized possession.

:| |•|•|

I've had a number of hits in my career and people often ask me about the formula. The only answer I can give is that there's something about a combination of elements that if I knew what it was, I'd do it every time and have 50 hit records. Sometimes in my life, I have been lucky enough to be a part of a bunch of guys or musicians, in a room with the right gear — it could be a terrible piece of gear — with the right song and a magical thing happens. *Shakin' All Over* was one example of that. It just stood out head and shoulders above the other material that we were recording at that time. It was a British hit earlier by Johnny Kidd and the Pirates and in the early Guess Who, we weren't confident enough in our own writing, which was quite terrible when we started as anyone's is. We wrote lovey-dovey kinds of songs with amateur kind of riffs. All the British bands were copying old American R&B standards, so we thought, gee, we'll copy some British standards. A couple of friends in England would send us two or three-year-old singles when they were done. We loved them because they already had centers in them — remember those centers in the 45s? We had this one that was Johnny Kidd and the

Pirates' *Shakin' All Over*. I thought, 'Wow, this really rocks!' It has a guitar with an echo and I had a tape recorder that made the echo so we just did that song. We recorded it late one night in a television studio in Winnipeg with, I believe, one microphone and all the instruments going through Jim Kale's Fender Concert amp, which was two channels and two inputs in each channel. We had a little black pickup that we stuck in the back of an upright piano and my guitar went through the tape recorder, which gave it an echo, and into one channel, and the bass went into the other channel. So everything was in this one amp, which became our mixing board. There was also one microphone that Chad Allan sang into and a set of drums. It was done in a television station in a big room that they used to dance in like *American Bandstand*. It was also a concrete room which gave the sound a liveness. The mic was in the center of the room, so somehow, through an accident, we managed to get everything. I remastered that song recently because I re-released the old Guess Who material on three different CDs, and the song really sounds great. There's not a great bass sound; there's not a great anything sound; but together, there's a good sound.

The song *American Woman* actually started as an improvised lick when Burton Cummings was late for a show. That was on that Les Paul I got in the trade for the Mosrite. I only had one guitar at the time. I think we were playing a three or four hour dance in Kitchener, Ontario in the arena and I broke a string, which meant we had to take a break. So the band had gone in different directions, and Burton went out into the parking lot to meet friends of the band — we had all kinds of friends all over Canada and every time we'd play a dance, they'd come and visit us. I remember putting on the string and tuning it up; hitting a note on the piano and tuning to that and out of the blue I started to play that riff.

It had been so boring. We'd been on a tour for about three months before that playing a set of about 18 minutes featuring *Shakin' All Over, Tossin' and Turnin'*, two other songs and then *Shakin' All Over* again. In the old days, when you had one hit, you had to open and close this little set with it. We were on tour with the Kingsmen, who did *Louie Louie* twice and the Turtles did *It Ain't Me Babe* twice. That's all you had was three or four hits and it was so boring and repetitious that, when I started to play this new riff, I saw Jim Kale, our bass player, and Garry Peterson, our drummer, come out of the audience and come on stage as I was doing that riff. [Demonstrates riff from *American Woman*] They came up and I couldn't even say change chords. We were just playing, so we played this riff endlessly and then I did a solo over it. Somebody apparently — I heard this later — went to Burton out in the parking lot of the Kitchener Arena and said, 'How come you're not on stage?' He didn't recognize the song. Back then, when you took a break, they played records, so he just thought it was a record. In an arena, the sound is bad anyway so you don't know if it's a record or the band. I remember Burton running up on stage and saying, 'What are you doing?' I said, 'We're jamming in E, play something!' And he played the flute and he played the piano and he played harmonica and I did another solo. I didn't want to forget this riff. We didn't have any tape recorders in those days. You didn't carry a cassette like you do now. And I ran over to him and yelled out, 'Sing something!' and the first words that came out of his mouth were, 'American woman, stay away from me!' I think he sang that line four times, we soloed, he sang it again four times, I soloed. Now the song was eight, nine, ten minutes long; it had just been a long jam and it brought the crowd in. They could sense our excitement and the chemistry and when it was all over we just went, 'Phew!' We knew that something had happened. The next set, we did it again so that we wouldn't forget it. Then came the realization that we had to make some sense of the *American Woman* lyrics, which kind of meant to us the [Vietnam] war, the Statue of Liberty...it wasn't the American woman on the street. Rather than saying Uncle Sam stay away from me...we had toured the States in the late '60s and they had tried to draft us a couple of times and, as true Canadians, we crossed the border and went back home. It was kind of an anti-U.S. song, which I think if it had come a couple of years earlier, would have totally bombed. By the time it came out in late '69 or early '70, all America had turned around; they wanted to get out of Vietnam. They wanted to get out of the war; they just wanted it over. And this song just kind of came at the right time.

You Ain't Seen Nothin' Yet was a reject from the third Bachman-Turner Overdrive album. When I was producing the band, we would rehearse a lot for two or three weeks, for four or five or six hours a day, running through the arrangements but never really staying on one song for hours to get it worn out and tired so that you were sick of it. We ran through it two or three times just to make sure it was taking a different shape, and then, the next day, we'd go through it again and try to change the tempo until we found a groove for it. When I went into the studio, I'd like to get sounds so I'd run in and out of the studio and be moving drum mics and trying different placement of mics and run in and listen to a playback with the engineer and say, 'No, I don't like the bass drum sound. Let's try a different snare!' or whatever you're doing when you're producing.

So I had this work song which we would play over and over five or six times with terrible sounds and then I sang a rough vocal over it and that was put away never intending it to be on an album. I knew it was never going to be on an album so I stuttered and stammered through it and I thought I'd send the track to my brother, who used to manage the band before we made it really big. He kind of stammered and it was just intended as an in-joke between brothers. I was going to send him this track and only he would have it. It wasn't to tell the world that I had a brother that stuttered or stammered. He has since overcome that, but it was a family joke.

When the head of our label [Mercury] came in to hear the album . . . we had had a slow rise from the first album. The second album had *Let It Ride* and *Takin' Care Of Business*, and the head of the label wanted to hear a magical song that was the icing on the cake that would take us to the top. We played him the whole third album — the NOT FRAGILE album — and he said, 'It's really a great album, but I don't hear a single. I don't hear a magical thing there; I want to hear a magical thing!' I said, 'That's it! We've got eight tracks and we're back on the road in two days.' And the engineer poked me and said, 'Play him the work track!' And I said, 'You've got to be kidding!' And the head of the label says, 'What work track? What work track?' So we played him the work track and he literally jumped out of his chair and fell over backwards and said, 'That's a monster!' I said, 'It's terrible! The guitar's out of tune and the sounds aren't great; they don't sound like the rest of the album!' This all happened at about two in the morning and I said, 'I want to come back tomorrow and sing it.'

So we came back at noon the next day and I tried to sing the song and it was so square when I sang it straight. It sounded like Bill Murray doing a *Saturday Night Live* thing. It was like Frank Sinatra. He said, 'Well, just leave it the way it is. There's a charm to the way it is.' And I said, 'Wow, I've got a bad throat. I'm not a great singer to begin with. I've got a head cold. The guitar is out of tune.' He said, 'Leave it! This has happened to me before,' and he named about four or five other things that he had heard that became a smash. One was *Hey Baby* by Bruce Chanel and another was Rod Stewart's *Maggie May*, all of these songs that shouldn't have been hits but were hits because there was a magic of the moment. So I squeezed *You Ain't Seen Nothin' Yet* onto the third album; it was the only album we had nine tracks on and it became what it became.

:| |•|•|

I used to write with a guitar all the time, but in trying to keep things simple, I can now write without one. I can write country songs in my head. I know the three or four chords so I don't need a guitar there all the time to lead me. I can just write a song on an airplane or something. Somebody might say something . . . the pilot in taking off might say something that I would jot down and basically block out a whole song. I need a guitar to finish it, but initially I can kind of sketch it out in my head. With really complicated, chordy, jazz kind of things, I do need a guitar. Once in a while, I'll even write on a piano.

But I couldn't go too long without a guitar, though sometimes I've taken a vacation with my family and you just can't take a guitar along. You just can't haul a guitar with you if you're hiking in Scotland or Japan. But I would wait two or three days and go into a music store — a little local mom & pop store which might be in Tokyo or in Glasgow — and ask if I could play an acoustic guitar and just sit there and play for an hour. Maybe a crowd of two or three would gather but at least I'd get to do some playing.

Sometimes I go through a period where I figure I'm really a slug as far as playing guitar, that I'm not fast enough or not good enough. I see these young kids play and they're unbelievable. My own two sons can play better than I can. Luckily, these days, you can get videos and things in tablature, which is something you couldn't do when I was growing up. Now, I can just call one of these services, which are in all the vintage magazines, and order four or five videos and set up an intense two or three hour practice for two or three weeks where I then come out of it feeling like at least I've sat down and studied some guy, be it Chet Atkins or Michael Hedges, or some guy that's really on another plane of guitar playing, or some Celtic stuff, some Duck Baker and things like that which I really like, which are different tunings. Afterwards, I just feel that I've learned something. I've played at Celtic-style "Open Mics" all around Vancouver and Vancouver Island. It's kind of scary to go out there and play solo acoustic guitar, but then, when I do pick up an electric again and get on stage . . . I can't keep practicing *Takin' Care Of Business* over and over and playing it over and over; it's not something I play in my spare time. I just find that it keeps my fingers fluid doing these . . . about once a year I'll do a crash course of playing two or three hours a day for two or three weeks of intensive study and learning something.

I don't think my style has changed that much at all. I believe when people come to see me live, they don't want to hear all the latest licks I've learned. I'm really not like an improvisational jazz kind of guy.

They come to hear what's etched in their mind, what's etched on that piece of vinyl or now burned into a CD. They want to hear that *American Woman* solo; they want to hear that *Takin' Care Of Business* solo; they want to hear the *Blue Collar* solo, so I pretty much replicate exactly what's there and maybe I'll lengthen the solo and put something new on the end. In other words, I've stayed true to my style, which I was lucky enough to fall into. On my own, I play all kinds of finger style and jazz and Celtic tunings and things like that that's really keeping the dexterity in my fingers going and keeps my interest going in guitar, which is the most marvelous instrument with so many styles and guys adding every day to it.

My style is pretty much simplicity. When you do a guitar solo — I learned this from Lenny Breau a long time ago — sing it first in your head, then figure it out on the guitar, which means someone else can figure it out in their head. I try to just play melody. I'm still playing violin, in other words. When you're playing violin you're not really playing chords, you just play single notes. I even think the vibrato I use in my left hand is somewhat of a violin thing. I'm not really quite sure about my style. I have not analyzed it and nobody has analyzed it for me.

Jeff 'Skunk' Baxter

ULTIMATE SPINACH, HOLY MODAL ROUNDERS,
STEELY DAN, THE DOOBIE BROTHERS

Jeff Baxter
Born December 13, 1948
Washington, D.C.

:|Jeff 'Skunk' Baxter|·|·|

By the time that Jeff Baxter joined his first "hit" band, Steely Dan, he was already gaining a reputation for his guitar work as a member of a number of late '60s groups like Ultimate Spinach and the Holy Modal Rounders, both of which had regional followings in the United States. Originally a communications major from Boston University, Baxter joined keyboardist Donald Fagen and bass player Walter Becker in the group Steely Dan, with whom he recorded three albums, CAN'T BUY A THRILL, COUNTDOWN TO ECSTASY, and PRETZEL LOGIC, between 1972 and 1974, and on which his guitar work was showcased to best advantage on tracks like *Reelin' In The Years* and *Do It Again*. By the summer of 1974, Becker and Fagen had tired of touring and would limit their activities to the studio for the next three years.

Baxter had already toured with the Doobie Brothers by this time and opted to join the group full time in 1974. When guitarist/vocalist Tom Johnston fell ill during 1975, Baxter suggested that the Doobies recruit ex-Steely Dan vocalist/keyboardist Michael McDonald. McDonald's impact on the group's sound would prove significant, as first demonstrated on the album TAKIN' IT TO THE STREETS and tracks like *It Keeps You Runnin'*. In 1979, as the group's MINUTE TO MINUTE album and the accompanying single, *What A Fool Believes*, was climbing the charts on the way to a five-week stay at number one, Baxter departed to pursue his production and session work in Los Angeles, where, over the past two decades, his contributions to a wide range of projects, from film and television scores to commercial jingles and artist recordings, have become a thing of studio legend. In a recent publication issued by Gibson guitars, with whom he has worked over the past few years in their Epiphone division in developing a couple of guitars that bear his name, he also revealed another dimension to his current activities. "I do work as a defense analyst and a consultant to U.S. Congressmen on military defense and national security issues, mostly in the area of missile defense," Baxter revealed. "In regards to the technology of music and defense, a lot of the hardware is basically the same. It's just the software applications. Doing so much R&D for different musical instrument companies led me down that path." We spoke to Baxter in Los Angeles at his home in the Hollywood Hills.

I started playing guitar when I was around 10 while growing up in Mexico City. I started taking piano lessons when I was about five, and at the age of nine I decided I wanted a brand new bicycle so I asked my parents to buy me one for Christmas. They obliged me by buying a guitar, which pissed me off, so I hung it on the wall and kind of looked at it. A few apartments down in the same building, a friend of mine, Kirk Bundy, had just started taking guitar lessons, so he showed me a couple of chords and I said, 'Wow! This works for me.'

Of course, in Mexico it was very difficult to buy instruments. They were very expensive, probably three or four times more than the price in America, so I would press my nose up against the glass of the music stores and look fondly at the Gibsons and Fenders. They were way out of my price range, but that's how I started. My grandmother bought me my first electric guitar and a copy of *Green Onions*. She was pretty hip; a very cool lady, God bless her soul. So that's how I got started. I just started playing in bands. In Mexico, the rules and regulations that govern underage people and their presence in bars and drinking establishments and other places are rather lax, so I started playing strip bars and other places when I was 11 and 12, and got a tremendous amount of experience playing rock 'n' roll.

In Mexico, rock 'n' roll was a big deal. Mexican rock 'n' roll bands certainly weren't vocally the same but instrumentally, they were incredible. I got together with Abraham Laboriel and Fito De La Parra and some of the guys I grew up with. We played in different bands, and 25 years later I walk into a recording studio and there's Abraham Laboriel, the number one call on bass. Small world, but that's how it all got started.

Radio was very different then. There was a two-hour program on Radio Mexico with a blind gentleman, who was the deejay for American rock 'n' roll. The rest of the radio was a combination mariachi, Cuban and Brazilian music, both of which I dearly love, actually. It was kind of eclectic. One minute it would be jazz and the next minute it would be mariachi and the next minute it would be classical and the next minute it would be some German band. It was very international. Most of the music that I got a chance to listen to were either records that were brought back by friends of mine or their parents or listening to Wolfman Jack broadcasting in 50,000 watts up there near the border.

Maybe subconsciously I was preparing to be a professional guitar player all along. Certainly I went to school. My parents sent me to a boarding school. I went to the British school in Mexico City and I went to college for a couple of years at Boston University, all with the intent of pursuing a career that I'd talked over with my father. But somehow or other the guitar just kept rearing its ugly six-pegged head all through my life. Finally, it just seemed like the right thing to do.

One of the wonderful things about Mexico was the fact I could get recordings of some very different stuff. I even got the first recording of *Apache*. A lot of people think this song was done first by The Ventures or The Shadows, but it was really a gentleman by the name of Jorgen Ingmann, who was a Danish-born guitar player — a sort of Danish Les Paul — who would overdub sound on sound. The drum part on it, I believe, is his wife using his hollow body acoustic. But I heard all kinds of different guitar players and certainly Django Reinhardt, Charlie Christian, and Kenny Burrell, guys like that, who were on my father's recordings. My father was a big fan of artists like Ella Fitzgerald, the Jazz All Stars, and Louis Armstrong, so I'd hear a lot of the older guitar players on his records.

But I guess my biggest influence was a gentleman by the name of Howard Roberts. When I was eleven years old, I believe, somebody gave me a record called HR IS A DIRTY GUITAR PLAYER and COLOR ME FUNKY, the two first albums that he did with Burkley Kendrix, Paul Bryant, Chuck Berghoffer and Earl Palmer. And I listened to these records and I was blown away because I couldn't believe a guy who was ostensibly a jazzer could burn. I mean this stuff was on fire. So naturally I learned every note, practiced every thing, learned every single thing. Later on, I met Howard Roberts when he was at the Guitar Institute of Technology and basically said to him, 'You are my mentor. You and Bob Bogle from The Ventures are the two guys that have influenced me the most.' I wrote a letter to The Ventures actually when I was 10 saying I wanted to be a guitar player. I got a very nice hand-written letter back from Bob Bogle who explained to me what kind of guitar I should buy and what I should do. Later on, when I started producing albums for The Ventures, I showed him the letter, which my father had saved, and he actually remembered it. The Ventures are very, very sweet guys. So between Howard Roberts and Bob Bogle, those were my influences, but Howard was the guy, and God bless his soul, that man was an incredible guitar player. I miss him.

I also listened to a lot of Be-Bop Jazz and a lot of saxophonists, and that influenced me a lot. I think it was good growing up in Mexico because you weren't over inundated with Top 40 radio; there were so many different influences all the time. I don't know whether it worked with my later session work, but it helped stylistically. I did take two guitar lessons from Sal Salvador, and this is no reflection on Mister Mel Bay, but when I took my Mel Bay books into see Sal Salvador and said, 'I'm ready to go!' he tore them up and dropped them in front of me and told me I was going to study out of clarinet, saxophone, and trumpet books. That was a positive thing for me because the saxophone players I had listened to, like Charlie Parker and Eddie 'Lockjaw' Davis and Dizzy Gillespie on trumpet, had already influenced me because of my father's records. I had always looked at melody kind of from a horn player's point of view, so it seemed I had found a friend here. Really it was the trumpet and saxophone players that influenced me.

In terms of session guitar playing, you just jump in there with both feet. Luckily Tommy Todesco was around. Tommy is a wonderful man who helps everybody who's first getting into the recording scene. Tommy was there for me to help me through some of the Scylla and Charybdis of the L.A. recording scene. Basically, the session thing is just getting a shot at it and having somebody give you the opportunity and taking the opportunity and then showing you can provide the services and the musical depth that they need.

I'm sure my style has changed somewhat over the years. I know when I was very young I loved to bash — three chords was good. [Demonstrates] If I could do that for an hour, I was a happy man. Most of the instrumentals at the time were very simple. I remember things like *Tall Cool One* and *Wild Weekend* and a lot of The Ventures stuff. The Duane Eddy stuff, and the whole 'surf' genre, too, that influenced me. A lot of the kids in Mexico were rockin'. The bands were really rockin' hard with things like the Eddie Cochran stuff. The guitar playing and the drumming was always, I think, much better than that of their American counterparts. So my style of music was rock 'n' roll but rock 'n' roll with somewhat of a little learned edge. I would come at it like this [Plays standard rock riff] but I had also maybe just finished learning *Girl From Ipanema* or

Black Shiny Stockings from a Howard Roberts record.

I know I've improved, in terms of my 'vocabulary,' my ability to express what I want to express because I have a greater depth of what I call 'vocabulary' — or what other people might call 'chops' or whatever — to pull from, but I think my style has always been kind of horn-oriented.

Then there's the matter of emotion. I know quite a few guitar players who are wonderful players in terms of their ability to execute tremendously difficult and otherwise scholarly riffs, but there's something missing. I'm not putting it down, it's just that the really great players, I believe, mix that with emotion. I mean, let's face it, Bo Diddley certainly is not the chop master from hell, but I could hear that guy play that riff for hours and not get tired of it. So there must be something else involved besides just ability. So I'm a big believer in heart. I've played with guitar players who do not have a lot of chops, but I'm so in awe of their raw, gutsy ability that it touches me. Heart and gut feeling is an integral part of being a guitar player.

:| |•|•|

Playing with Steely Dan was a lot of fun. The music was new and fresh and challenging and I really enjoyed it. Playing with The Doobie Brothers was slightly different. The music was not as challenging on one level; it was really gut music. It was music that was so much fun to play. And I guess maybe I brought a sort of a scholarly element to it. Not that these guys weren't great players, because they certainly were, but just a different way of looking at things. And maybe bringing Michael McDonald into the band and looking at it from more of a recording sense brought the band to the point where we could do the MINUTE BY MINUTE album, which, I think, is the high point of the band.

But I like playing with everybody and playing sessions lets me work with varying styles of music. I've played with all kinds of bands. Some of what I think is my best work has been with bands that probably nobody has ever heard of like Brooklyn Dreams and people like that where you go in and do sessions and you come back and go, 'Man! I played that! Wow!' I love playing varied styles of music. I love to go at nine o'clock and do a country record until noon and then maybe have to do a quick classical piece for Taco Bell and then off to play some R&B with Donna Summer and then spend the rest of the evening playing rock 'n' roll. Again, the fact that I grew up with so many different influences probably gave me the basis that I needed for that because I know a lot of people and some wonderful guitar players but they're very one dimensional. Now it's very hard to get exposed to that. You have to go out and specifically go to the record store and buy Django Reinhardt and Link Wray and The Ventures and B.B. King; you have to find those things as opposed to just hearing it over the radio. Armed Services Radio is great too; I listen to a lot of that. That was very eclectic. They always had many different kinds of music. A couple of my friends in Japan who are guitar players benefited heavily from Armed Forces Radio because of its tremendously eclectic mix of music. I think maybe radio now has kind of lost its way. Maybe it'll find it again; we hope.

The solos I play on sessions depend on what is called for at the time. If somebody has a suggestion and I'm working on a project for somebody and they say, 'Would you try this?' I'm all ears because as a studio guitar player, one thing you want to do is please the people that you're working for. If they don't have any idea what they want or they're saying we want you to decide, then I'll approach it in a slightly different way. Certainly, there are some basic things, or milestones, that you can start from. The melodies of the song itself give you a good place to start. Melodies that are common to us as we grow up are great places to start. Certainly, as you're roaring along at lightning speed and maybe if for two seconds there you're not really sure what you can do, you can always whip up some kind of melody that will get you from Point A to Point B. But it's hard to say. Usually, I find that the best solos I play are the first takes because when you're put on the spot and you have to think on your feet, usually that's when you do your best work. If you start to think it out too much, you can lose that delicate balance between brains and brawn. If you start playing it too many times, you start to overthink it. So I guess the best way to do it is just to jump into it feet first.

I'm not sure having a background in production matters when you're a studio musician. Being a stomp box guy, which most guitar players are, once you get something that has a 'goes-inta' and a 'goes-outa', you plug it in and out of things maybe where it's not supposed to be so you begin to develop a sort of a working man's, journeyman's knowledge of production. I know that's how I started and a lot of my friends did. Most of the really good guitar players that I know have some production skills simply because you get to a point where, about 15 or 20 years ago in the mid-'70s, when the actual recording technology became available like a four track machine that had synch on it so you could overdub. A lot of my friends began to draw knowledge from that, and you used it to do demos and other things like that, and then getting into the commercial jingle world, you had to have some knowledge of that because sometimes you did it by yourself. But I don't think as a session guitar player that is really important. I think that the only production knowledge that you really need is studio etiquette, knowing enough about how the studio works, both on a technical level and on a social level, so that you stay within the paradigm and you don't piss anybody off. There are probably people who would disagree, but as a studio musician your job is to the best of your ability to execute either someone's idea or to offer, on a musical level, input to their creative process. You may say, well you might want to try this effect on it or that effect on it, but I don't really think it's important.

:| |•|•|

If you are serious about taking up the guitar, one of the first things you certainly need to do is examine your motives because there are guitar owners, guitar players and guitarists. Being a guitar owner is no problem. You plunk down your dough and you are now a guitar owner, but getting to the next step as a guitar player is a long, long step. That's not to say that you have to become a Larry Carlton or a 'Skunk' Baxter or somebody like that. You can play three chords and have a wonderful time and that makes you a guitar player. But if you're looking at it as a part of your portfolio along with hair extensions, leather pants, the limousine, and a charge account at The Rainbow, I'm not sure it's going to be fulfilling. I think you'll be disappointed.

But if you want to play the guitar, there's such a wealth of material out there. There are some great books like Ted Green's *Chord Chemistry*. Of all the books I've ever dealt with, I would say that's the most exciting and the most fulfilling and the most in depth. With the advent of the CD and companies going way deep into the archives, you can find music by Little Beaver and other people who wouldn't normally be in the mainstream. You can listen to a Link Wray record. There's a lot to be gained by listening to that stuff... and then learn to sing because I've noticed that if you can sing it, you can play it. I'm talking about melody. Probably the best method and the fastest way to teach yourself how to play the guitar, the best method to practice and the best syllabus to follow, is your own and tapping into those melodies in your head. The easiest way to do that is to sing. That doesn't mean you have to be an opera singer and have to be able to stand up there and croon, but learn to sing. There's something about the connection between the voice, which is the instrument you practice with every day, and the motor skills that somehow connect to your fingers. [Plays guitar and sings scat-style] If you can sing it, eventually you can play it. You may only be able to play 20 percent of what you sing, but three months from now you'll be able to play 40 percent and then 60 percent and by the time a year comes around, there's nothing that you can hear in your head that you can't play. That's kind of a treat. If you listen to Oscar Peterson playing the piano, you can hear him grunting and making noises. He's not singing, but he is connecting vocally.

There's something about the connection with the voice which you practice with every day because you use it every day, and the little storehouse of melodies in your head. You know how to do it. Your fingers might not know how, but you do somewhere inside. The question is forcing your fingers to learn what's already in your head. So if you sing and play at the same time, if you can sing it somehow or other, this will find its way into your fingers. The caveat to that, obviously, is that you still need to practice your scales — you still need to arm yourself with the tools that you'll need — but if you're looking for a place to go, there are so many melodies that you can pick out of the sky that you already know. Learn the Star Spangled Banner, but just try it once, then find another melody, whether it's the music from a Cheerios commercial or some great jingle or Beethoven's Sixth Symphony. Just pick melodies out of the sky and eventually some of it will stick.

:| |·|·|

This guitar [Gibson Super 400] was actually given to me by Gibson. It's kind of a star-crossed instrument. Some of the guys knew that when I was on the road with the Doobies, I loved to hang around the Holiday Inn and try to find a band that could play some standards. It was always hard to find guys who could play that kind of stuff. It just wasn't something that was part of the rock 'n' roll genre. I took an old Harmony guitar with me on the road in case it got busted up. Mr. Johnson, who was working at Gibson at the time, said, 'You need a Super 400!' I said, 'Well, I certainly do.' So he had Gibson send this guitar to me. When it arrived, the head stock was broken off, so I sent it back and they fixed it again and they sent it back and it was broken again. I guess they must have really beaten it up in the mail. I sent it back and this time they must have done a monster job because it's the only one that has a pearl inlay in the back of the instrument. It was pretty nasty back there so they tried to make it a custom instrument.

I love this instrument [Gibson Super 400]. I love going to clubs and playing it. Actually, I used it on stage sometimes because it's so much fun to play. And it's like any instrument having a certain dynamic, being constructed in a certain way, it makes you think and you sit down and you definitely want to play the sweet stuff. [Plays some cool jazz] That's really what this instrument wants you to do, although it's a great country & western instrument, too. It's got that great twangy sound to it. [Plays country riff] It's got a little green on it, but it sounds wonderful. I've recorded with it, and as a matter of fact, I've just done a record about six or seven months ago with an Argentinean band who are very popular in Argentina and in the whole Latin American music scene. I was helping them with the production of it, and they had one song where they wanted some wild, crazed be-bop. This guy's a great guitar player in the band, but his template is slightly different. So I unsheathed the old Super 400 and went in and whipped off a few scales at break neck speed and it sounded great. I plugged it in direct. I didn't even use an amplifier. But I've used it on a lot of dates. It has a certain sound that interprets the music, especially on rhythm; it's a very nice rhythm guitar, but the jazz thing is really what turns me on about this instrument. [Plays jazz riff] Something about this guitar makes you want to play that stuff. I love it because it speaks to you. It says, 'Play me! Play me! Play some jazz!' It's a beautiful guitar. The Super 400 has always been one of my favorite guitars.

I actually have a Signature model acoustic guitar with Epiphone with a little 'Skunk' inlayed on the 12th fret. I have a beautiful Les Paul, but it's a bastard child of a whole bunch of stuff because I used to be a guitar repair guy and build guitars, so I found a body and put it together with a whole bunch of different pieces and I use it specifically when that sound is called for in the studio. I love that guitar. I've got a Firebird, which always intrigued me. It's a very interesting guitar. I love the way it sounds and love the way it plays. I've also got a Gibson Lap Steel guitar, which is really old. It has a wonderful growly sound. It's a great slide blues sound. For this new Blues Brothers animated TV series, I'm going to be using it a lot because it sounds like the '40s. Actually, I've always wanted to play a pedal steel guitar with a symphony orchestra, and interestingly enough, an opportunity I believe has surfaced with the Orange County Philharmonic, so I think I'm going to get a chance to do that. For me, one of the first things that I learned on steel was Beethoven's Ninth Symphony. It just made sense. The basis of the pedal steel is very mathematical, and to me it lends itself to classical music. That's a style I've never had the chance to play — classical steel with an orchestra. Other than that, I've managed to find myself in positions from playing on mariachi records to Wayne Shorter to Steely Dan to Donna Summer and Barbra Streisand. I've done a lot of country music and played with Linda Ronstadt and Dolly Parton and even did a quick stint on steel with Charlie Rich. I just want to do more of it because I love playing the guitar. It's my favorite thing.

Orville Gibson knew what he was doing. He certainly was a luthier. I think he approached building instruments with the same kind of philosophy that Stradivari and D'Angelico and guys like that, who built incredible instruments. And you look at the way these things are constructed and the way they're designed and they're works of art. They're not just playable, but also fun to look at. Look at this! [Holds up Gibson Super 400] This is beautiful.

Kix Brooks

Leon Eric Brooks III
Born May 12, 1955
Shreveport, Louisiana

:|Kix Brooks|·|·|

Brooks & Dunn are simply the most successful country music duo in history. In a broader musical sense, as a duo, they are second only to Simon & Garfunkel, as far as record sales success. Since the 1991 release of their debut album, BRAND NEW MAN, which remained on Billboard's Top Country Albums chart for over five years on its way to becoming the number one best-selling album by a country music duo in music history, they have had no less than 15 number one singles and have won every country music award on offer. Oh, and for good measure, you can add a 1996 Grammy Award in the category of Best Country Performance By A Duo Or A Group for their single, *My Maria*, to their list of honors. They have also been featured on the front and back of over 20 million Kellogg's Corn Flakes boxes, which depicts them in action on the stage with Brooks wielding one of his Les Paul guitars of choice. Co-headlining with fellow country superstar Reba McEntire, they undertook the largest grossing tour in country music history in 1997, an experience that both parties enjoyed so much, they re-packaged the tour in 1998 and set out on a similarly successful excursion.

All in all, it hasn't been a bad decade for the two singer/songwriter/musicians who were introduced over a platter of enchiladas by Nashville record executive, Tim Dubois. Brooks, whose a bit of a Tasmanian devil on stage, comes about his wild stage antics honestly from his dues-paying days playing Texas and Oklahoma dance halls. When they first met, Brooks was already building a considerable reputation as a songwriter on Music Row, while Dunn had just won a major national talent contest. Speaking of their first reaction to each other, Brooks has said: "I was wanting him to move around more on stage and he was wanting me to calm down. We finally said, let's just do what we do. For whatever, reason it works." They have since discovered their mutual passion for car racing and now drive in and sponsor an eight-race series, the Brooks & Dunn/Sport Design Summer Legends Shoot-out which features 5/8-scale replicas of early NASCAR racing cars powered by motorcycle engines.

We spoke to Kix Brooks in Nashville where he arrived for the interview proudly bearing a couple of his custom Les Pauls, one with an alligator motif and the other with the classic oak and acorn design.

Our family's always been musical. When we were in the car riding somewhere, as long as I can remember, we were singing and carrying on. I think my cousins, who were all girls, played piano. Of course, like most boys, I was wanting to play guitar, but I was probably about six years old and really couldn't hold on right. My grandmother, whom I lived with while I was growing up, got me a ukulele when I was about six years old. I remember getting it in the mail. That was when I learned to play chords and sing songs and kind of figure out how all that went together. Strumming was just something that I was into. I guess I turned six when my father bought me my first guitar. I started putting bands together around the sixth grade and went on with it from there.

I'm from Shreveport, Louisiana, which is home of the *Louisiana Hayride*. While I was growing up, both Hank Williams and Johnny Horton lived and hung out in my neighborhood. After Hank died, his widow Billy Jean married Johnny Horton and they lived right up the street from us. Their daughter was my age, and some of the first gigs I played were parties at her place. They were always having parties in their garage, and they'd hire my little band to come over there and play. So that was the first time I saw gold records and those nice guitars hanging on the wall. That'll really make an impression on a kid.

I think it's real important as a player to try and dig up the stuff by the old masters and at least experience what they were doing so those names just aren't words in your vocabulary but it's music that you're familiar with. Then, in the end, you've got to find your own voice and play what you feel. That's where people like Hank Williams had a ton of impact. He was very blues influenced, but he was a serious country guy, and that mixture has a lot to do with where country music is now. And in our music you'll hear a lot of rock influences as well as blues influences. You can't help but pick up on that growing up.

:| |•|•|

I fell in love with Gibson guitars through the Allman Brothers. Duane Allman was such a great player — him and Eric Clapton.

There was just so much great music with great energy. It was all there: the great picking, the great slide, and those grooves were too cool. At that time, there were a lot of Les Pauls floating around, and that's when I got hooked. Even Charlie Daniels on the country side was playing a Les Paul, and I was a big Joe Walsh fan. Walsh, Clapton, Duane Allman, Steve Miller, they were just great pickers, and they always seemed to be holding a Les Paul. So it just kind of goes together. You want to do what those guys are doing. I don't think I ever reached that music level, but it was great to be holding a Les Paul. It kind of made you feel cool.

You can put any pickups in a guitar you want, but traditionally they [Les Pauls] have got that growl and that bite. The first time I saw Billy Gibbons of ZZ Top I went, 'Man, that sound moves something down there.' A Les Paul just sounds like that. There's other guitars that are good for other stuff, but I'm into that 'chunking' kind of thing, especially rhythmically, and I just love the sound of them. They've got that sustain and that bite. Nothing else sounds like them.

I have a couple of custom-carved Les Pauls, one with an alligator motif and the other that has a motif that looks like leather with the classic acorn and oak leaf design. The Les Paul with the alligator motif was made by my buddy Bruce Kunkel at Gibson. He's kind of their master carver. It was an idea I had because, as I said, I'm a Louisiana boy, and I wanted to do something with an alligator. I kind of told him how I wanted it to be with the alligator curving around and his mouth chomping on the guitar knobs. He went to the library and did a lot of research, and when I saw the blueprints, I knew he was into what I was talking about. On the fret board, he's got the design of a gator from overhead swimming in the swamp with the water moving and a little frog up on the guitar head that he's chasing kind of running for his life. That inlay incorporates 329 pieces of mother of pearl. At first he was going to leave the alligator natural on black, which I'm sure would have been very hip, but I'm way too gaudy for that. I begged him to paint it, which I'm glad he did. He did a really classy job. I love it. It plays good; it's real thick at the top. It's not what you'd call a great lead type guitar for the upper frets but it's got a great sound to it and I would say from seven frets down, this really doesn't effect your playing too much. I can't wait until Jimmy C. Newman sees this guitar. He's going to be very jealous.

He [Bruce Kunkel] also built a guitar called the "autumn guitar," which was the first time I had any experience with a guitar that had been carved at the back of the neck. This guitar is about the same shape as a regular Les Paul. I'm really into saddle carving, and this is a classic design called Acorns and Oak Leaves. This entire guitar is carved. Most people that see it think it's leather, but it's not; it's wood. You'd think on the neck this [carving] would really slow it down, but it doesn't. It's cool and it plays great. When I saw that, I said, 'Let's take that gator tail [on the other guitar] all the way up the back; it'll be okay.'

And speaking of some of my favorite guitars, I was down in Mexico once and I didn't have a good gut string. I had several guitars that I played, but I really wanted a gut string to write with. While I was down there, I did some detective work. I was in Zihuatanejo, which is south of Puerto Vallarta, and I asked around shops where I could get a guitar. Finally, I ran into this mariachi band and I approached the guitar player there and told him that I wanted to buy a gut string. There's a town in Mexico where they make 90 percent of the Mexican guitars. He started telling me about a Senor Gonzalez, who makes these small guitars with a bright sound. Then he told me about a Senor Juarez in the same area who makes the big jumbo guitars with a big sound. He went through about nine different guitar makers and what they all did, and I'm writing all this stuff down. Finally, at the end he stops and says, 'You know, if I were you though, I would buy a *Geebson*!'

When I first started playing down in Louisiana, I was into a lot of blues. I had a lot of small Robert Johnson-type guitars. In college, I started playing electric and I was chasing Allman Brothers licks and stuff like that. I've been in bands with guys who could run circles around me playing and I've been in bands where I had to be the guy and my playing tended to fit wherever I was at the time — whatever I had to do.

:| |•|•|

Keeping the energy up in our live shows and playing guitar is tough and that's why I tend to cheat more now that we've gotten on a lot bigger stages and we move around a lot more. I see Angus [Young] of AC/DC and people like him who are real active on stage. My guitar player, Charlie Crow, is real active, and I can't really play on tough stuff like that and be running across the stage at the same time, so I've sort of leaned back into more of a rhythm role; I'm 'chunking' most of the time. When you're singing, it's really fun to find or make the groove. I can rock pretty good and keep the groove going, but I've passed off a lot of the leads. It's not laziness; you just kind of get into doing a different thing and, being a front man, some of that [playing lead guitar] suffers. I can see where some guys prefer to pass those duties off and just stick to business or be still on the stage. That's the integrity of a great player, but it's just not my deal.

It's just like communicating. When you have a conversation with somebody, when you say something, you hope it's meaningful, but if you just talk all the time, people just stop listening to you. I've always chased the emotional thing. I've always been really into songwriting, so chording is kind of the way I've always leaned. Phrasing of chords and that kind of thing tend to inspire you lyrically in a way a song's put together.

I tend to write a lot more rhythmically with guitar because that's just kind of what I've always held on to, but sometimes if I feel I'm getting into a rut as far as the songs I'm writing, I'll write six or seven songs, then I'll write something on the piano. I tend to get more melodic with my writing on piano. But I've probably written 10:1 songs on the guitar.

I still love doing my demos. I'll play everything on work tapes at the house and I really enjoy the creative process. When we go to make records, I'll turn Brent Mason loose on something that I've done and he'll just take it to another level. I appreciate my limitations as a player. Brent Mason is my favorite guitar player. I'm a realist; he's so imaginative and so musical. When I hear him do something, it's like: 'I'd have never thought of that in a million years!'

I think at some point in your career you look back and see a 20-year hole in your resume; all you've ever done is play guitar. It's funny, a lot of people come to me now and say: 'Who do I need to talk to? What do I need to do? How do you get started?,' but I don't remember a starting point and I hope there's not a finishing point. It's just something that you do because you love it. When you walk into a room, you pick up a guitar and you sit down and start noodling. I don't know if it's nervous energy or wanting to be like other people . . . or if it's because music's in your blood. You can't explain to somebody what the shortcut is because there's not one. It's just something you love to do and all the awards and stuff that goes with it, that's just sort of a by-product from something that's a part of your soul. Even when I sing a song on stage, I've usually got a guitar hanging off me. I feel awkward without one. When you go that many years hanging onto one, you feel weird to let it go.

Mark Bryan

HOOTIE & THE BLOWFISH

Mark William Bryan
Born May 6, 1967
Silver Spring, Maryland

: |Mark Bryan| · | · |

The late '90s continue to be a pretty heady time for the four members of the group with the unlikely name of Hootie & the Blowfish. Within a year of the release of their multi-million selling debut album CRACKED REAR VIEW MIRROR in the summer of 1994, the group made their first appearance on the David Letterman show, undertook their first tour of Europe, picked up an MTV Video Award in the category of Best New Artist for *Hold My Hand*, and appeared on the cover of *Rolling Stone* in the wake of their chart-topping CD. The following year, as the accolades and awards continued to roll in, including two Grammys, an American Music Award, and "Pop Writers Of the Year" honors from ASCAP, the band even had the time to found their own record company, Breaking Records, release their sophomore album, FAIRWEATHER JOHNSON, which also went to number one on the *Billboard* charts in April of 1996, and take part in Farm Aid in Columbia, South Carolina with Willie Nelson, Jewel, and John Mellencamp, among others. Obviously favorites of U.S. President Bill Clinton, Hootie played at the Union Station Inaugural Ball in Washington, D.C. in January of 1997 and, in July of 1998, even had the honor of trying out some of the material from their third album, MUSICAL CHAIRS, on the President at a gala evening at the home of actors Alec Baldwin and Kim Basinger at the Hamptons on New York's Long Island, organized as a fundraiser by VH1 in conjunction with the Democratic National Convention.

Of course, all this is a far cry from Pappy's, a fried chicken-wing shack in Columbia, South Carolina where Bryan and Darius Rucker once played as an acoustic duo covering songs by Simon & Garfunkel and The Commodores. At that point, Bryan had already paid some dues as a musician in a band known as Missing In Action with Hootie bassist Dean Felber back in their high school days. Rucker's credentials were more a matter of right place, right time.

Bryan once heard Rucker singing in his dorm room and, duly impressed, approached him with an eye to a collaboration. In the fall of 1985, Bryan and Rucker were known as the Wolf Bros., but by May of 1986 had become Hootie & the Blowfish and had hit the road "to play music for people who like to have a good time."

Mark Bryan's opinion on the appeal of the band is fairly basic. "We're only a rock band, which is why we appeal to many different people, so many different types of listeners," he has said. "We ourselves have had so many influences that we don't fit into any one category. We're not 'grunge'; we're not 'alternative'. We just play rock and roll."

We spoke to Mark Bryan on the afternoon before a Hootie & the Blowfish show at the University of Tennessee Arena in Knoxville, Tennessee.

If you come and see a Hootie & The Blowfish show these days, I'll be playing the three different Gibsons that I own. One of them is a Country Gentleman, which I use for more mellower songs like *Let Her Cry*. The Gibson 335 is another hollow body guitar I use, but it's for more groove type songs and more up-tempo funky type songs. It's got a brighter feel to it. And then I use a Les Paul for the power chord type stuff, rockin' songs like *Drowning* and *Honeyscrew* and stuff like that. So it really just depends on the song. Each has a different feel and different tone, so that's basically how I play it.

My first guitar was an Ibanez Blazer that my mom bought for me from Harmony Hut at Lakeforest Mall in Maryland. I sold that and a little plastic practice amp to some kid for $150 and bought my first Les Paul when I was 15 or 16. I still have it. It's a 74 Cherry Sunburst. So I really call that my first guitar, even though it wasn't officially. But that's the one I've had the longest. And as I got a little better and began delving into some more diverse sounds, I began to like the hollow body just as much as the Les Paul, so that's why I've been playing this Country Gentleman and the 335. They just give you a different tone. I've played Gibsons ever since getting that Les Paul, which was exactly like the Jimmy Page model. He [Jimmy Page] was another influence on me.

When we started playing back in '85-'86, Darius [Rucker] wanted to learn how to play guitar. He was sort of intimidated by electric guitars, so he learned on acoustic and kept playing acoustic. So what that did was it made it very concisely Darius on rhythm, Mark on lead, and I guess from that I learned a lot of techniques where you can be a rhythm player and a lead player at the same time, sort of like Peter Buck from R.E.M., who plays a lot of arpeggio type of stuff. Pete Townshend [The Who] and Mark Knopfler [Dire Straits] were big influences on me, as well as George Benson and Chet Atkins. I've never been able to learn the finger pick style the way he does it because I was always more of a rock guitar player, but I've always been pretty fascinated by it nonetheless. Where Darius would be strumming, I would do the kind of things that would off-set it. And I guess we developed a style together from that; he and I playing off of each other like that.

I also learned a lot of what Paul Westerberg from the Replace-ments was doing back in the '80s, like the octave slide and that kind of thing. And I ended up doing a lot of melodic-type licks over chord changes that Darius would be playing on songs like *I'm Going Home*. He's on acoustic and I have a lick, just a melodic thing, going on over top of his chords, but the two parts work really well together. Being the only electric guitar player in the band has given me the opportunity to come up with some different styles.

If you've ever seen The Who movie *The Kids Are Alright*, there's a scene where they're doing *Won't Get Fooled Again* and Townshend's playing a Les Paul through a Hiwatt amp. The tone that he got was just perfect. I never went and got a Hiwatt, just because I really like the Mesa Boogie amp. It gave me the same great tone that he was getting. It has the perfect amount of distortion. I always go for that sound where you can get a good power chord sound but still sound sort of clean. I get that with my Gibsons through the Mesa Boogie amps. I just go with that because I like it. I use it on the albums and I use it live. It's just the tone that I've always gone for.

My solos always start as improvisation and then usually, by the time they get recorded, I've come up with some parts that I like bet-ter. But it always starts with just jamming, and then, while I'm jam-ming, I'll just retain whatever little lick that I like. 'Oh, I like that a lot,' I'll say to myself, so I'll keep that and memorize that and then eventually I'll build a solo. Once it gets to the album, it's written.

Everybody writes on their own and then, when we write together, we bring our own parts in and the other three guys lay their part down with it. Soni [Jim Sonefield] will pick up the guitar and say, 'This is what I've been working on!' and he'll show me and I'll do whatever variation on that that I feel like. Dean [Felber] will write his own bass line, or I'll bring in a guitar part, and they'll sit down on their instruments and write. Everybody just jams and it's a lot of fun.

A lot of times I'll spend more time actually writing songs than I will doing scales. But I'm into being a better guitar player and a better songwriter, trying to do it all at the same time.

I have a lot of guitars now, but the main one I have, that I carry with me, is a baby guitar that's easy to travel with. I take it with me everywhere I go. I'll write my songs on that when I'm traveling and going to hotel rooms and stuff. When I'm at home, I have an old 1963 J45 Gibson that I write on. And on the road, when I'm at the show, I usually just pick up the Country Gentleman or my J100 and mess around on those. But when I have to fly away from the band or away from home, I carry that little guitar to write with so I always have one with me.

For me playing the guitar and writing songs is the perfect outlet. Whenever I get stressed out — if I'm bored or whatever — I can always turn to a guitar to pass the time. Whether it's just to sit down and practice licks or whether it's to write a song, if it's not there, I go crazy. I just like playing it, I really do. It gives me a good feeling, whether it's on stage or whether it's sitting around and writing a song or whatever. It just feels right to be playing guitar for me.

Jack Casady

JEFFERSON AIRPLANE, HOT TUNA, JEFFERSON STARSHIP

John Casady
Born April 13, 1944
Washington, D.C.

:|Jack Casady|·|·|

When they finally write the definitive history of the music of the Psychedelic '60s, Jefferson Airplane and the nascent San Francisco music scene of the mid-to-late '60s will certainly command a fair share of the content. "One pill makes you larger and the other pill makes you small," the Airplane observed, and you knew that weren't talking about some new-fangled diet regimen from Weight Watchers. The group, and their little White Rabbit buddy of legend from one of their earliest hit songs of the same name, urged you to "feed your head," and that was certainly a precursor to the dietary preferences of the Flower Power Generation during that Summer of Love in 1967. The music of the times was as cerebral, given to long, flowing, stream-of-consciousness jams. It was into this musical land-scape that Jack Casady wandered, being summoned to the west coast by his old bandmate Jorma Kaukonen, with whom he had played in the group The Triumphs in their hometown of Washington, D.C., back in the late '50s. Kaukonen was playing guitar in the Jefferson Airplane at the time and the group was in need of a bass player.

In late 1965, Casady dropped out of Montgomery Junior College in Maryland and headed cross-country to join the group. Having renewed their musical collaboration as members of the Airplane, Casady and Kaukonen formed the splinter group, Hot Shit, in late 1968, which under the quickly revised name, Hot Tuna, has pre-vailed for more than 30 years and 15 albums. Over the years, Casady's chord-based, melodic bass playing has also been heard in a number of off-shoot bands from the Jefferson Airplane, including the Kantner, Balin and Casady Band, also known as the KBC Band, and Jefferson Starship. The Jefferson Airplane was inducted into the Rock and Roll Hall of Fame in January of 1996.

We spoke to Jack Casady in the newly-constructed studio in his home in Beverly Hills, California one Hallowe'en afternoon. It was, according to Casady, the first event held in the new facility, which also houses an impressive collection of rare bass guitars and Mandobasses, including the Gibson Les Paul bass he held and played during our chat.

I was born in Washington, D.C. and grew up there. I left Washington in 1965, but prior to that I was lucky enough to have the opportunity to listen to all kinds of music: blue-grass, R&B, jazz, folk, blues. Through different periods of influence from age 12 to 21, I had the chance to delve into all of that, and it was a lot of fun.

I think, like a lot of bass players, I started out as a guitar player. I was playing guitar by the age of 12 and discovered the bass at about age 16. The first time I actually saw an electric bass, I was about age 15. I saw a Fender bass being played in an R&B club with my partner Jorma Kaukonen. At that time, he played rhythm guitar and I played lead guitar. In order to keep the songs together, he chose a guitar on stage and I chose the bass at a jam one evening. I was a little confused by it at first, but later on, as I got more work playing the bass, I became intrigued by the instrument and what it could do. I switched permanently to playing the bass when I came out to California in 1965 to join a young group called The Jefferson Airplane.

In those early years, I played with Jorma Kaukonen in a high school band. He's a couple of years older than I am. When he went off to college, I did a lot more bass-playing work. And then we hooked up again through a friend in Washington, a bluegrass banjo player. I asked Jorma what he was up to and he said he had just joined a band called Jefferson Airplane. I said, 'You the purist, joined a rock 'n' roll band!?' He said, 'Yes, and they could use a good bass player,' and he asked me what I was up to. I said, 'Playing bass.' He said, 'Gee, I thought you were playing guitar.' I said, 'No I've been playing bass for the last couple of years.' He said, 'I'll call you right back.' He did that and I came out to California in October of 1965.

At that time the San Francisco 'scene' was was pretty much beginning. This was October of 1965 and The Jefferson Airplane had formed in July. I think a lot of the musicians who had their back-ground mostly in acoustic guitars and folk music were sort of dis-covering the electric guitar and all that went with that. I spent a lot more time in R&B bands that had three saxes and piano and all that kind of stuff, so that was a little more familiar territory to me than for a lot of those guys.

Learning to play the bass has been pretty much by self discovery. There were very few electric bass guitar players at the time. This was about 1959 or '60 and most of my influences for bass came from jazz circles and bluegrass circles. Although they were influences, they didn't have any practical reality in the music I was playing at the time, so I guess it was just self-discovery.

I got a letter from an old acquaintance who had heard me play with Danny Gatton. Danny Gatton was a guitar player out of Washington, D.C. during the years I played there, who has since passed on, and he said, 'You know, I remember you playing bass back then and you always changed the lines around from the recording and added more melody and moved the lines around more.' I guess I've had a melodic style from the beginning. Although I didn't record back in those days, I did a lot of playing and we went through a lot of different kinds of material. I do remember us changing tempos and changing songs around from the way they were recorded back then. That fit in quite nicely when I joined The Jefferson Airplane. Everybody was writing their own material and had so many drastically different influences, it actually gave me an opportunity to develop a more melodic style and not be yelled at for straying from the norm.

In the Jefferson Airplane, we developed lines for the songs pretty much on the spot, and with a lot of rehearsal you'd work it out. Jorma's influences from the finger-picking style freed me up considerably from traditional bass lines because he would have his thumb rolling on the bass parts on his guitar as well, so we could trade off melodic lines from bass player to guitar player. That was unique in that it changed from the regular format of a guitar player either playing a lead and then playing a rhythm and the bass player and drummer playing the backup part. That worked out quite well.

In the beginning, recording was quite intimidating. For the first few records for RCA, you went to where the company was and we went down to Sunset and Ivar here in Los Angeles and recorded at the big studio A there. I'll never forget hearing the technique of my playing back in all its horrific form for the first time, then going immediately to a place to woodshed a lot to clean up my technique and work on such things. It was very exhilarating and frightening at the same time, but a lot of fun.

A bit later on, I played on a Jimi Hendrix session. Jimi had also come out to California, and our paths had crossed many times from Monterey Pop to The Fillmore. At the time, we were doing a lot of rehearsing at The Fillmore when Bill Graham was our manager.

There was a lot of hanging out in those days; the pressure wasn't on quite as much as later on so we got to meet people and I got to meet Jimi Hendrix and Mitch Mitchell and Noel Redding. Mitch, Jimi, and I struck up a good friendship, and I had an opportunity to play a song called *Voodoo Child* very early one morning in New York. It's basically a minor blues tune. He had the idea for the song, and we ran over it once and recorded one half a track and he broke a string and then we recorded the final track that ended up on the record. Stevie Winwood was there and Mitch Mitchell and myself. Again, that had stemmed from hanging out after a show we [Jefferson Airplane] had done in New York. We were at Steve Paul's Scene and Jimi had come down during a break in recording. Actually, that was his first venture into producing for himself and that song was a break from the norm. You didn't really put a long blues number on an album at that time. It worked out okay. I was real happy. I didn't know it was going to end up on the album until months later. There was just one night and we were in the middle of a tour and we went on with our tour.

Hot Tuna formed around 1968 and resulted from us having time on our hands. The Jefferson Airplane would go on tour and then there was a lot of writing time. During these times, we started doing a few blues-oriented numbers that didn't fit in with the Airplane set. One thing led to another and we started doing a few shows on our own and then Hot Tuna was formed. It was also necessary at the time to move on with the music. You're a young musician and you're trying to progress and challenge yourself. The Airplane was a very creative format and it seemed to be intensely creative for a period of time and then nothing would happen for a long period of time. Then it would be intensely creative again, usually around the albums. The in-show performances sort of took on a momentum of their own with the politics of the times later on, so in the late '60s, we figured there had to be more than this and more playing to be done. A lot of the songs that Jorma played and songs that he and I were interested in had more of a blues orientation and free form to them that just didn't fit into the format of the Airplane which had so many singers and writers in it. There was only so much you could get done in one night.

I've always felt a connection with the blues dating from my very first record collections when I was 12 and 13. The blues was something that I would listen to and discover late at night from radio stations far away in New Orleans and Texas and locally in Washington, D.C. It just struck a resonant chord and pulled me into that style of music.

:| |•|•|

This Les Paul bass is quite unique for Gibson. It's an f-hole, semi-acoustic. It doesn't have a block down it. It's hollow back in front of the pickup, which in my mind gives it a little more resonance, and it has a full-scale 34 inch neck. I've played other basses, particularly during the '60s period, that were f-hole basses but shorter scale. I listen to them now with the digital remastering and whatnot and can hear a lot more of what those basses did then with the old vinyl. What they did for me was to allow me the use of a lot more chordal structure to songs for a bass player to play — two or three note chords. It also has a resonance that would not come out of a solid body bass, though I love solid body basses. I had Fender basses and still do have a couple of fine ones, but there's just a certain resonance that my style began to develop and open up more with an f-hole bass. This Gibson is one of those that does it. I use it now a lot with Hot Tuna, and it allows me to play in an electric format as well as a more, shall we say, acoustic — to use the term loosely — format, and it gets nice chordal sounds. That's why I like it.

My very favorite recording technique lately is flat and in the board. I like a nice tube pre-amp, and there's a variety of them out there that are pretty good. I like a nice warm tone to it and pretty much straight. I use a variety of amplifiers, but they have to have that good, clean, warm, direct sound. I try to go through, like I said, a tube pre-amp.

The Les Paul I've been using since 1987 I discovered in a music store next to the Chelsea Hotel — the famous, or infamous, Chelsea Hotel in New York City on 23rd Street. I've used it on almost everything I've recorded since then: a bunch of Hot Tuna stuff, a bunch of Jefferson stuff that we've done in the last few years. When I want a good, clean, warm sound and the music allows enough space in it for the tone to come out, it's great. I have other basses for the times you have a full-blown rock sound and there's keyboards and there's really a lot of low end from other instruments. For those situations, I've got a few other instruments in my arsenal that just cut through a little better.

But the Les Paul is my favorite. I've got a special case made for it, and, yes, you do tend to be a little possessive with your guitars and your women. The nice thing about these Gibsons is you can play chords and they sound nice and full and rich.

The Mandobasses are also interesting. The one I have suffered a little accident in the back, but it's about to go off to Boseman, Montana, to the Gibson acoustic factory, and be put right again. It is a 1911 Mandobass and I got it in Palo Alto in about 1967 along with a bass Balalaika. For those who know Balalaikas, they'll notice that it's a four string now; it has a tremendous tone to it. I had my friend Rick Turner do a conversion on that and change it over to four strings. I got both these instruments in Palo Alto from a gentleman named Dante Profumo, who was an Italian gentleman who got conscripted into the Danish army and ended up on the Russian Front during the Second World War and somehow talked his way through three or four different armies before ending up in Palo Alto with 200 instruments. The guy must have been quite a talker.

The Gibson/Epiphone factory in Nashville is going to put out the Jack Casady model, and I'm working on the pickups now. We're after a good, pure, simple-sound, single-pickup bass to begin with. It will be the first full-scale f-hole bass out on the market.

:| |•|•|

To me, being inducted with the Jefferson Airplane into the Rock and Roll Hall of Fame was great. There are some that sort of *poo-poo* it, but all of my heroes when I was a young lad are there, like Lester Flatt and Earl Scruggs, pickers that were out of bluegrass. Charlie Mingus, I admired greatly, and Eric Dolphy; various players that really took me to a new place and had that craft ethic that I admired. They just loved to play all the time and that's what I like to do. It was nice to be recognized and to have the opportunity to mix it up and see all these other folks, too.

I try and play everyday. When you're home, of course, there's a lot to running a home, which I do with my lovely wife, Diana. We've just built this studio here with its new pine floors and I hope to get a lot more action going up here in my home than I have in the past.

When asked about hearing my influence as a bass player in others, I can only say I hear it a little more when bands play with us in person or something like that. It's really hard for me to tell, but I have had other bass players come up and say they have listened to my stuff over the years. Hopefully, I'll keep cranking it out here.

Billy Corgan
& James Iha

SMASHING PUMPKINS

Billy Corgan
Born March 17, 1967
Chicago, Illinois

:| Billy Corgan & James Iha |·|·|

If the emergence of Seattle-based "grunge" bands like Nirvana and Pearl Jam ushered in the so-called "alternative" music movement, then it must be said that Chicago's Smashing Pumpkins guided it the remaining distance to overwhelming mainstream acceptance through the mid-to-late '90s. Hmm, "mainstream alternative" — an oxymoron by any other name — but back in the early '80s, Pumpkins co-founder Billy Corgan was having no such thoughts about musical classifications. He was listening to bands like The Cure, Judas Priest, Black Sabbath, and Cheap Trick and pondering life as a rock star. He ultimately worked in a band in Chicago known as The Marked, which showed some gumption when they fled the local "goth-metal" indie scene to base themselves in St. Petersburg, Florida in 1987.

Corgan returned to Chicago after a year and subsequently teamed up with a young, Japanese/American guitar player by the name of James Iha to play some local club dates. Soon, augmented by D'Arcy Wretzky, a classically trained musician from Michigan, and drummer Jimmy Chamberlain, who departed the band in the summer of 1996, Smashing Pumpkins was born and their debut album, GISH, was released. It was their sophomore CD, SIAMESE DREAM, released in the summer of 1993, that brought the group widespread attention and multi-million CD sales. They became the raving point of the Lollapalooza tour across the U.S. in 1994, and that acclaim has followed them, through subsequent SRO tours and recordings like PISCES ISCARIOT; *The End Is The Beginning Is The End*, their chilling contribution to the soundtrack of the film *Batman & Robin*; the best-selling double CD, MELLON COLLIE AND THE INFINITE SADNESS; and ADORE, their latest opus. James Iha recently released his debut solo album titled LET IT COME DOWN, which gives more than a passing nod to some of his earliest musical influences, including Gram Parsons and Neil Young.

We spoke to Billy Corgan and James Iha of the group at the Union Station Hotel in Nashville as they passed through on tour.

Billy Corgan

My father was a musician who played a lot of blues and R&B, so I don't ever remember a time when there wasn't music around. I can't remember life without it, but I didn't start playing until I was about 15 years old. At that point, it was your typical girls, cars, guitars.

I have a very distinct memory of the first day I got a guitar. It was a Les Paul copy, because I couldn't afford the real thing, and I remember sitting in my basement playing and it was just like an immediate sensation. I felt as comfortable as you'd feel breathing. I just felt like I understood it, and that was it. I started out wanting to be your classic guitar hero, you know, fast solos and long hair. It wasn't until I was about 18, when I was in a band, that one of the guys in the band encouraged me to start writing my own songs and singing my own songs. Once I did that, it all seemed to make more sense. Music became much deeper for me than just how well I was playing or how well I played a solo. It was much more about song construction and composition and texture. And all the practice that I'd done suddenly made a lot more sense in the context of songs as opposed to one shining 30-second moment.

Up until recently, I always wrote with the guitar, but I started playing piano as well, so I go back and forth. Sometimes, when I'm writing a song, I'll play it for a while on guitar and then play it on the piano and then hear it differently and go back and forth all day. For me song writing is always about chord structure and the movements of the chords against the melody. My poor piano playing brings out something different as opposed to my slightly proficient guitar playing.

I play a Stratocaster most of the time, but I actually own a lot of Gibson guitars. It's always interesting to me, as far as electric guitars go, that the Fender sound versus the Gibson sound is almost the dual polarity by which we work in Smashing Pumpkins. The Gibson sound is a deeper, richer tone, and the Fender sound is almost more like a voicing. So, it's the combination of those sounds that we always put together. I play a lot of Gibson acoustics like a Southern Jumbo and a '60s J200, and I would use those a lot to write songs. I bought a 1972 ES335 in Nashville and I played that on a number of songs, including *Tonight Tonight*.

Co-producing our albums is always an interesting challenge to find out how things go together. The thing I like about my Gibson 335 is that it produces a strange combination between the richness that you normally associate with the Gibson sound and yet it has more of a chord voicing, a little more of an edge, a B.B. King classic kind of cutty solo sound. It's not quite as cutting as, say, an Albert King or Albert Collins; it's somewhere in between, and that's what I like about the 335.

I've often thought that songs come from guitars, and a good example of that is the Les Paul Jr. I have. Once we were playing a show and there was a music store down the street where I bought a guitar, took it home, wrote the song *Where Boys Fear To Tread*, then went and played the show. The song came immediately from the guitar. I always look at guitars as good luck pieces, and every guitar that I have has a song, or many songs, attached to it in my mind. Every time I buy a new guitar, it seems that a new song seems to come with the guitar.

Being in a band with two guitars, you lose a lot of the freedom to express yourself as an individual voice, where people will hear you in a single context, where you can articulate subtle things. The subtlety gets lost with two guitars, but you can create this mountain of sound. And so the albums that we have done so far have always been about this kind of overwhelming wall of sound — a sonic denseness — trying to combine extreme amounts of distortion with kind of complex chord arranging.

When people used to ask me about guitar playing influences, I used to cite people like Jimi Hendrix and that kind of stuff, but these days I think my influences are much more the Delta Blues kind of guys like Son House. I've been listening to Blind Boy Blake. I'm really impressed by their chord work and the bass movements underneath the chords. I'm kind of in an interesting position because I'm moving back towards what would be a singular guitar style, but I play in a band with another guitarist, so, personally, I want to move towards more subtlety in my playing. I think a lot of the subtlety in my playing gets lost because its going to get lost against another tone or texture.

When you listen to something like Son House, Muddy Waters, or Howlin' Wolf, it sounds just as powerful — if not more powerful — than anything I could create with modern day technology and physical rock power. It sounds like a cliché, but I'm trying to understand what's powerful about it. I know certainly the emotion and the context in which the music was made has a lot to do with the power of it, but there is a physical force. Hubert Sumlin, I think, was the guitarist who played with Howlin' Wolf. If you listen to the original Sun recordings with Howlin' Wolf, they didn't even have a bass player, so he's alternating between lead and chord work. It was just unbelievable and just the physical force of the guitar against Howlin' Wolf's voice was incredible. I've so fully explored density with guitars that I think I'm naturally gravitating back towards something simple.

At an early age, I was attracted to music for its sonic qualities, and so I was attracted by anything from Jimi Hendrix to The Beatles to Black Sabbath because it was the physical property of the sound that was being created that drew me in just as much as what they would be singing about. When I was eight years old, I didn't know what Black Sabbath was singing much less The Beatles. It was the sound of the music that drew me in, and I think that when I became older and I started to draw the intellectual parallels, I started to realize that the actual physical properties of sound are just as attractive to the human ears as the smell of a rose. It's something that we intuitively understand and we don't intellectualize it. Certain vibrations, certain chords attract us more so than others. So I think there's a science in there somewhere, by creating moods and texture you can get right to somebody's heart much quicker than you could with a lyric or a cool drum-beat or something.

Originally, when we first started approaching the reality of two guitars in the group, like I was saying about the Strat and the Les Paul, it was trying to create this sonic density where all parts of the frequency spectrum would be covered by the guitars and then we'd figure out a way to get the bass underneath that. Over time, it has evolved into this thing where it is kind of unspoken. We know when to clear out of each other's way and where to play on the neck. If somebody's playing here, then you want to go here. There's not as much dialog about it as there used to be.

I haven't practiced the guitar since I was about 19 years old. I'm 29 now, so I need to start practicing again. I've pretty much played variations of the same things for ten years and I'm kind of bored with my playing. I heard James talking about the same thing. When you're on tour everyday, the guitar almost becomes your enemy. We play so hard and so physical that the guitar almost becomes ... it's like picking up a gun or something. It becomes this thing, it's no longer just a guitar. It's like a weight and a weapon and a ray gun. It gets kind of weird for me to the point that I just don't want to deal with that. I don't know if I can explain that any better. I have to wait until I'm happy and content and drinking tea to get to the point where I want to play because I want to play not only because I have to be on stage at 8:30. I love to play guitar and I love being a singer. I think I have even more appreciation for the guitar because there's such a close resemblance to the human voice in frequency and your ability to emote out of it. Eric Clapton did an amazing job of creating a symbiosis between his guitar playing and his singing.

The most prophetic moment for me in considering my relationship with the guitar was when it finally dawned on me that the things I intuitively played when I was 15 years old, which were kind of strange open chord tunings, and melded that with all the bad heavy metal riffs that I'd learned, that was really the beginning of what people would call 'Pumpkin Sound,' this kind of strange, dense, open chord thing. The day that all came together in my head, it changed my life really, because it was the moment that everything I understood about the guitar fused together. Since that point, I think I've made strides sonically, but I don't think as a guitar player I've made any strides. I'm flattered that people think I'm a good guitar player and I'm flattered that people emulate my style and things like that, but I don't think I'm as good a guitar player as I could be. I don't think I've really dedicated myself to the guitar like I could have. A lot of that has to do with mainly focusing on songwriting.

James Iha

James Iha
Born March 6, 1968
Elk Grove, Illinois

James Iha

The first guitar I ever had was a Cort guitar. It was horrible, just horrible, but it was okay at the time. I was into heavy metal music and 'New Wave', groups like The Pretenders and Iron Maiden. Those were my first records.

Generally, most of our playing these days for the Pumpkins is pretty much whatever the song requires. We used to do a lot more solos on our early records, but it seems kind of pointless now. We're just into playing good parts for whatever the song calls for. If the song just requires one rhythm guitar just playing bar chords or open chords or whatever, that's fine if it sounds okay, but if a song needs 30,000 overdubs, we'll do that too. Whatever makes the song better.

When I look back, I guess my playing has gotten better. [Laughs]. We used to use certain kinds of chord formations and chord changes. I guess on our new material [ADORE], we're going for more simple and direct songwriting and more simple and direct guitar parts as well but trying to stay away from clichés and less obvious things.

Unless you're into the guitar purely to solo, after a while it just gets so mundane. I like to play the guitar, but I like to play songs more than just diddling around. Anybody can pick up a guitar and just screw around, but to play a good song and to play the right guitar part for that song, whether it's a fast solo or just one note like B.B. King, that's ten times better.

My main influences are songwriting bands. Early on I was really into The Edge from U2 and Peter Buck from R.E.M. The older I get, I'm more into guitarists like Mick Taylor and Eric Clapton.

My history with the Gibson Les Paul goes back to our first record and our desire for a classic rock sound, and Billy, our singer and other guitar player, played a Fender Strat. His Strat was a cutting, more trebly kind of guitar, and I was more rhythmic and heavier, more bassy. To us, it was the classic rock sound. You've heard it on a hundred records. It's a flexible sound. It can be heavy. I just always think of Boston and Tom Scholz.

I don't tend to make any modifications to my guitars. In the studio and on stage I pretty much play Les Paul Customs. I'm pretty sure they're stock. I don't think there's very much done to it. I have one that's an '88 and one that's a '77. They both sound pretty smooth and pretty heavy and bassy, once again, kind of like Boston.

I dug that, so that's our sound — the unknown sound.

When working up the arrangements in the studio, the individual contribution depends upon the song and what kind of song it is, whether it's a rock song or whether it's more of a singer/songwriter song. We put down the drums and the bass, sometimes together, and then just record rhythm parts all the time. Generally, one of us would sit in the room with the tapes and a bunch of guitars and fuzz pedals and just overdub stuff over and over and then sift through it and take out the bad stuff.

We don't improvise much in the studio. We've done one or two things, but most of it is pretty much planned out. We record it to make it sound like it's improvised. Generally, the parts for our songs are written out so that it feels like the right part. We try to go for those performances where it doesn't sound too over thought out or analyzed.

As far as playing the guitar every day, I don't have an edict in that regard. All we do is tour, so we generally play for a couple of hours every night. When we don't tour, there'll be some days when I just play guitar during the day and at night I won't even think about it. I have to go grocery shopping or something. On tour, after about three shows in a row and having toured over the course of a year, my hands can't play anymore. I just think it's a good idea to take a couple of days off. In the studio, we really don't have that luxury so we just keep going at it.

Touring and recording are really two different things. Recording is the best, but it's also the worst just because you realize just how inept you are when you're recording. On the other hand, it's the best in that you come up with new stuff and lay it down. Live is just live, full of mistakes and imperfections, but it's also much more spontaneous and I guess that's how the songs really should be heard.

I have a Gibson J100 Extra which I played on a couple of songs on the last record [MELLON COLLIE AND THE INFINITE SADNESS]. It's a totally great guitar because it has a lot of bass, but it also has a lot of definition. It's really balanced. It looks cool, too. All my references are pop culture references. It looks like something Keith Richards would have played. It's just got a great sound, kind of like a country guitar.

Charlie Daniels

THE CHARLIE DANIELS BAND

Charles Edward Daniels
Born October 28, 1936
Wilmington, North Carolina

:| Charlie Daniels |·|·|

T*he Devil Went Down To Georgia* is The Charlie Daniels Band's unmistakable signature tune, a little ditty in part inspired by a poem, titled "The Mountain Whippoorwill," by Stephen Vincent Benet, that Charlie Daniels had read in high school back in North Carolina. It's about a young country boy who challenges the devil to a fiddling contest, and there's more than a hint of Daniels' own dream of musical conquest to be found between the lines. The track appears on the group's 1998 release, FIDDLE FIRE: 25 YEARS OF THE CHARLIE DANIELS BAND, that celebrated the group's silver anniversary, but the Charlie Daniels's story actually has its beginnings more than three decades ago as a young Daniels began to show a remarkable talent for music. He could play guitar by the time he was 15 and then gradually mastered the fiddle and mandolin as he began playing part-time in a local bluegrass band known as the Misty Mountain Boys while still working in the creosote factory where his father and his grandfather had worked before him.

By the late '50s, Daniels had made the decision to go into music full-time and was playing gigs with a rock 'n' roll band called The Rockets, who would subsequently change their name to The Jaguars and base themselves in Washington, D.C. The group recorded their first record [JAGUAR] in Fort Worth, Texas in 1959, working with producer Bob Johnston, who would later be instrumental in introducing Daniels to the world of studio work in Nashville and sessions with Bob Dylan, most notably on his NASHVILLE SKYLINE album. In 1963, Elvis Presley recorded one of Daniels's songs, *It Hurts Me*.

After guesting on a number of other artists albums and producing The Youngbloods' ELEPHANT MOUNTAIN record in 1969, Daniels had his debut solo album, TO JOHN, GREASE & WOLFMAN, released in 1972. The Charlie Daniels Band's HONEY IN THE ROCK came out in 1973, and Daniels inaugurated his annual charity event, the Volunteer jam in Nashville, the following year. Five years later, in 1979, the band's popularity took on international dimensions with the release of the album MILLION MILE REFLECTIONS that contained the song that would prove to be the turning point in Daniels' career — *The Devil Went Down To Georgia*. That year, having raised their profile to star status in North America and Europe, Daniels and the group picked up a Grammy and three CMA awards, among other honors, for their work on the album and accompanying tours.

We spoke to Charlie Daniels in the studio of his home in Mount Juliet, Tennessee.

Bluegrass was the first music I played in a band. When I was first learning, I just fell in love with Bill Monroe, Flatt & Scruggs, Reno and Smiley and those guys. We had a little bluegrass band, but we couldn't call ourselves the Foggy Mountain Boys because that was already taken by Lester [Flatt] and Earl [Scruggs], so we called ourselves the Misty Mountain Boys. [Laughs]

I learned my music basics on guitar rather than the fiddle, and then I fooled with a mandolin for a while; fingering on a mandolin and a fiddle are the same. I'd probably been playing guitar, maybe a year and a half or so, when I went to the fiddle.

My earliest musical heroes were people like Bill Monroe, Flatt & Scruggs, the Lonesome Pine Fiddlers, Jim Eanes, anybody who had a banjo and a fiddle and a mandolin and a bass and a guitar in the band. That was the standard bluegrass instrumentation at the time and those people were my idols.

I came from a very rural part of North Carolina and I never saw a picture on a TV set until I was 15 years old. We didn't have hardly any place for a professional musician to work then, and it was not a very prolific profession at the time. There was a time when all I wanted to do was to make a living playing music, but I didn't have any idea how to go about doing it. Then finally I found out that they pay you money to play your music in beer joints. I started as a full professional in 1958.

I soon got real interested in rock music. The first electric guitar I ever had was a Gibson. I'm not good at quoting the numbers and stuff but it was one of the archtop open body guitars. I was playing in a country band and I went and got this guitar about the time Elvis Presley came along. Of course, he just turned the world upside down. He was the guy that made it possible for us hillbillies to play rock music, because, before him, it was all keyboard and saxophone and that sort of thing. Scotty Moore brought the guitar right into the forefront — and Carl Perkins cannot be given enough credit for what he did for early rock music. I wanted to play that music so I lay my fiddle down for several years and started playing rock music. I soon found that rock was the most commercial thing to play and it was the music they really wanted in the beer joints because it was what the people were listening to.

I went to Washington, D.C. in 1958 and jazz, as a real popular form of music, had been big in Washington. It was kind of in its death throes in so far as being a monster of a music because rock was really starting to move in, but some of the guys were still playing jazz and there were some very good jazz players around. I had never really been exposed to it before but I discovered it, I enjoyed it. We had a couple of horn players in the band that were into it and I learned quite a bit from them, so I got to the point where I really respected good jazz. I still enjoy jazz and I still enjoy jamming from time to time. I probably played more jazz at that period of my life, in the early '60s, than I ever have. And when I talk about jazz, I'm not talking about the real abstract stuff that doesn't have a rhythm to it or that you can't snap your fingers to or that you can't discern at least some part of a melody. The jazz that I liked was by people like Louis Prima, and I got into a lot of the big bands. I loved Count Basie, that shuffling, swinging sort of stuff that you can jam to. I never really got into the real esoteric type of jazz. I respect it, but it's not what I choose to listen to. If you can't snap your fingers to it, it doesn't mean anything to me.

I came to Nashville in 1967 and worked as a session player until about 1971. A lot of people thought that I played too loud, and I did. I had a different music philosophy than what was going on in Nashville at the time. I came off from playing bust-head music for 11 years or so in clubs. In Nashville, you'd sit in a studio and instead of having your amplifier on 10, they wanted it on one; they wanted a mellow sound rather than a rough sound. And I did play too loud. I was the proverbial square peg in the studio at that time, except for a few sessions. Some sessions it worked real well on. I'm very proud of the three Bob Dylan albums that I worked on. I'm also real proud of the work I did on some of the albums that people have never heard of because the weren't successful. I never was a first-call session musician. There were just certain things that I fit on and could contribute to. I mean, I could sit back and tinkle along on an acoustic guitar, but there were a lot of people who did a whole lot better than I did, but there were certain times and certain things that I had a feel for. A lot of Nashville pickers had a feel for stuff that I didn't have a feel for and I had a feel for some of the things that they didn't particularly have a feel for.

This is back in the folk days and the folk music of that time. The [Bob] Dylan/[Leonard] Cohen type of music, they didn't want it too smooth; they didn't want it too put together. You've never heard a slick Dylan album in your life. Some are slicker than others, but I don't even like to use that word with it because I don't consider it to be slick. Some are less rough sounding than others, but there's always that edge there because Dylan never wanted to do a song anymore than he had to. Maybe he'd leave it after a first take or maybe after a second or third take or whatever. Of course, NASHVILLE SKYLINE was a little different than that. We worked pretty hard on the arrangements and stuff for that, but that kind of music, that folk/rock type of thing, was not a slick type of music where people who played perfectly didn't necessarily play the music in the studio.

I did a solo on the track *Country Pie* on NASHVILLE SKYLINE with Bob Dylan that I was really proud of. [Demonstrates] Something like that. I was real proud of that and, every time I hear it, I feel good about it. Some of the stuff that I've done on our albums — I can't really remember specific cuts — but after listening back two or three years down the line, I'm quite happy with the stuff that I did.

I don't usually map out a solo ahead of time. We've got three guitar players and we do a lot of three-part guitar harmonies. Of course, that we need to practice. We practice rhythmically, but as far as playing lead is concerned — unless there's some specific reason that there's a riff you've got to stay with or something like that — it's totally improvised. It wouldn't be fun, or like reading music, if you had to do it the same way all the time. Guitar players love to jam; that's what they live for. We have stuff, though it's a certain number of verses and choruses and that sort of thing, where there's room for jamming. We have four people that play lead. We have a keyboard player and three guitar players and everybody likes to get their licks in so I try to throw in a couple of songs a set where people get a chance to kind of show out a little bit. I'm just as bad as they are. I love it too.

There's something funny about 'Southern Rock' music, though I've never considered it to be a genre of music because all the bands are different. The Allman Brothers Band was a blues band, still is, and a good one. Marshall Tucker Band was kind of leaning a country sort of way. They weren't a country band, but they had that kind of feel. The Lynyrd Skynyrd Band is as pure a rock band as you can find anywhere in the world. The Rolling Stones are no purer a rock band than the Lynyrd Skynyrd Band is. We were off in the middle somewhere. I don't know what we were. We used some elements of all of it. But I think the thing was, and what people saw most of all, you had a bunch of guys from admittedly different parts of the South but basically with the same accents, the same attitudes, and raised in basically the same religious/economic/social type of situation. We made some good friends. I think the similarity to me was in the people more so than in the music, but radio loves labels and the music industry loves labels, and the term 'Southern Rock' came up. There were basically four bands that were lumped into that group: The Allman Brothers, Marshall Tucker, the Lynyrd Skynyrd Band, and us. But I've never considered it to be a genre of music. It was just what a whole bunch of Southern boys brought to the table when they started writing their own music.

What gave the Charlie Daniels Band a unique sound was all the years that I had listened to other people's music, music that I had admired. It was all kind of run together. We did songs that had jazz influences, songs that had bluegrass influences, songs that had straight out rockabilly influences, just all different things. Sometimes we'd mix two or three different styles together at the same time. That made for whatever uniqueness that we brought. But, as I said, all the bands were different. Their was some sameness and similarities, but I could tell each band apart much more so than I could San Francisco bands or a lot of the bands that were in what they called 'a movement.'

I kind of go through different phases with my guitar playing. I get hung up on stuff. I really get in to listening to one particular type of music for a while more so than I do others. I've gone through a blues phase the last little while — of course, I never get very far away from it. There'll always be the blues, and it will always have a revival once in a while because, whatever happens to be defined by the ambiguous term of 'rock' that we use nowadays, that's where it started; that's its roots, its basis. When rock goes so far that it kind of loses direction after a while and everything starts sounding the same, everybody goes back to the blues again to find out where they came from. So you go back home and you start out again and you go in another direction. It happens periodically. It happened back in the early days when bubblegum rock was around. A lot of people had never heard of B.B. King because he'd been playing the chittlin' circuit all that time. The same with artists like Albert King, Freddie King, Lightnin' Hopkins — all of those people that had been very esoteric and kind of secluded to a certain type of fan and they became almost mainstream artists at that time. It seems to me that every few years the blues come back in a big way, and I think it's just people kind of going back and getting their feet under them again. Blues is as basic as it gets. You've got three chords and that's all that anybody operates with and you've got to do what you're going to do in those three chords and it kind of gets your head back straight again.

:| |•|•|

This is one of my "older newer" guitars [holding a Gibson Les Paul], older in that it was made in 1954, and newer in that I just got it a few months ago.

When I started playing music, Gibson set the style for string instruments. I was involved in acoustic music. The mandolin that everybody wanted was a Gibson. The banjo that everyone wanted was a Gibson. The Gibson Jumbo guitar was a great instrument and they kind of set the style for quality. If you picked up a Gibson instrument, you could always count on it being a quality instrument. My '54 Les Paul guitar was made back in those days. Its really like no other guitar that I have ever seen. When Les Paul put this together, there was a Fender slab and there was the big thick open body F-hole guitar. When he came up with this concept, it was like he put those two things together and you got the best of both worlds. You got the mellow sound and you got the hard driving sound that you could get with a slab type guitar. I have no idea what made it great; I'm not a guitar maker. I don't know anything about it other than it is a great guitar. When we got this guitar, we were working on an album, and when we plugged it in, it almost blew the speakers out because it's so hot. Its a very hot guitar.

I always write with a guitar, unless I'm writing something specific for the fiddle, and then I might take the fiddle out, but 90 percent of the time I write with the guitar.

I try to do a bunch of scales every day. I've got a Rockman that I'll plug in and I've got a system that I can plug a drum machine in and play along with it. I try to do that in order to keep my fingers in good shape. I try to keep my sense of rhythm and timing in shape by playing along with the drum machine. I despise playing scales, but I've got to admit it's a great way to keep your fingers in shape. It's like pumping iron or something.

John Entwistle

THE WHO, JOHN ENTWISTLE'S OX, THE JOHN ENTWISTLE BAND

John Alec Entwistle
Born October 9, 1944
Chiswick, London, England

:| John Entwistle |·|·|

The Who had its beginnings in Shepherd's Bush, London in the early '60s with three grammar school friends, Pete Townshend, Roger Daltrey, and John Entwistle. Townshend and Entwistle would become members of a traditional jazz band playing banjo and trumpet, respectively, but ultimately joined Daltrey, who had been kicked out of school for smoking in the boys' room, in a group called The Detours. That group, with Townshend on guitar and Entwistle on bass, would evolve to the High Numbers and then to The Who, which, with the addition of Keith Moon on drums, would explode onto the international pop scene in the late '60s, first as a part of the so-called British Invasion with the release of their first major U.K. hit, the youth anthem, *My Generation*, in 1965, and then in the U.S. with their show-stopping appearance at the Monterey Pop Festival in 1967.

It's hard to imagine the history of rock 'n' roll without The Who — the near-mad genius of guitarist Pete Townshend, the iconoclast, the spiritualist, and, early on, destroyer of guitars; the well-documented eccentricities of the late Keith Moon and the anarchical bombast of his drumming; Roger Daltrey, the paradigm of the rock front-man and singer, with his Olympian poses and soaring vocals; and bass guitarist John Entwistle, the stoic anchor to the group's sound, who revolutionized rock 'n' roll bass playing with his singular approach to the instrument and his unique fingering and chording techniques.

In looking back over Entwistle's career, one finds something of a renaissance man, who, though he chose for the most part to stay in the background, also contributed to the group as a songwriter (*My Wife*, *Whiskey Man*, *Boris the Spider*, *Happy Jack*, etc.), French horn player (*Tommy Overture*) and, at one point, image-maker. A critically-acclaimed artist, Entwistle's original pen and ink drawing of the band members was featured on the cover of the group's

1975 hit album, THE WHO BY NUMBERS.

Inspired by his previous efforts at songwriting and having created a backlog of material, Entwistle was the first member of The Who to step outside the group and undertake a solo project beginning in 1971 with the album SMASH YOUR HEAD AGAINST THE WALL. He subsequently formed a number of groups with whom he recorded and toured, including, Ro-Ro; Rigor Mortis; Ox, his own nickname in The Who; and finally, The John Entwistle Band. His first major solo break-through came with his 1981 project, TOO LATE THE HERO, on which he worked with Eagles guitarist, Joe Walsh. In the mid-'90s, besides touring with his own group, Entwistle also joined Ringo Starr's All-Starr-Band on tour, which also featured Randy Bachman (BTO), Felix Cavaliere (The Rascals), and Mark Farner (Grand Funk Railroad). Of late, Rhino Records has released an anthology of Entwistle's solo material.

We spoke to John Entwistle at his "Quarwood" estate in Gloucestershire, England as he and the John Entwistle Band (which at the time comprised Steve Luongo on drums, Godfrey Townsend on guitar, and Alan St. Jon on keyboards) worked on songs for a new album, MUSIC FROM VAN-PIRES, prior to Entwistle leaving for The Who's North American Quadrophenia tour. The session was being engineered by Bob Pridden, The Who's head roadie and long-time monitor man, who also runs Entwistle's "home studio," which had originally been located at the Shepperton film studios when The Who owned part of the facility. We set up next to the impressive room-length bar next to the studio above which were suspended more than a dozen, exotic, deep-sea game fish that Entwistle had hooked during various fishing expeditions in the past. Surrounded by just a small part of his renowned vintage guitar collection and holding an old Gibson Thunderbird bass, he chatted about his ongoing relationship with the instrument that has made him an icon within musicians' circles.

At first, before I picked up the bass, I played the trumpet and then the piano, but none of the rock 'n' roll bands wanted the trumpet, so I took up the bass. It had the longest neck — it was the most phallic looking thing — and I liked the boomy sounds that it made. Initially, I made my own with a little screw-on pickup that screwed to the finger board, a real rubbish bass that lasted about three months before the neck just gave way. I had the Fenders and then I bought myself an Epiphone Rivoli bass, just like the Gibson one, but slightly different. I played that for a while, but it got a little bit too boomy and I went back to Fender for a little while. I had one of the two-pickup Gibson solid bodies. I used that on *Substitute*.

I changed to Thunderbird bass guitars in the '70s because I had slightly clichéd myself with using so much treble on the Fenders and I wanted to completely change my playing style. I thought I was stuck in a rut, so I changed. I used a Thunderbird on QUADROPHENIA. It went pretty well for the next couple of years and then I went back to the treble again. I got a little bit bored.

Back in the days when I was starting out, there was an embargo on American basses. Cliff Richard and The Shadows had Fenders and there were quite a few really good guitars around Liverpool and other ports, because people came across the Atlantic and smuggled the guitars and basses in. The guys in Liverpool would give their friend in the Merchant Navy their money and he'd go away and bring back a guitar. When I first started, I think there was a choice of three different basses that you could buy, and the best one of those was the Hofner Violin, which was pretty gruesome. The first [Fender] Precision bass I got from an Irish guy who had got hold of it from a friend he had in Liverpool.

When I started out, there was really only one influence and that was Duane Eddy . . . [Plays a couple of Duane Eddy licks] . . . all that kind of stuff; all of that sinister kind of music that he was playing back then. I changed my sound to use treble to try and get it to cut through the rest of the band, and also to add the other melodic instrument that we needed because there were only two guitars and drums with The Who. Playing bass as a sort of solo instrument kind of developed on from that. When Pete Townshend played a power chord, I'd have to do the stuff over top. Also because I played the trumpet and the piano and French horn, I'd been used to being the soloist.

Being stuck on the bass really wasn't my cup of tea, so I set out to change the position of the bass within a group context. I was lucky enough to be in The Who to be able to do that. A lot of the high melodic stuff is a little bit country, but I was using a sort of French horn solo technique. The high parts always sounded like French horn parts. It kind of came from that, but we also had a drummer in one of my first bands whose drums weren't very loud, so I developed a sort of slapping technique, like hitting the snare.

If I'm doing a speech on a stage, I'm very insecure, so I hold an invisible guitar. I felt a lot closer to my basses when I first started. When I got my first Fender bass, I kept it at the end of my bed, and when I woke up, I'd sort of wave to the bass. I force myself to stay away from it sometimes, but I get paranoid after about three weeks and I have to play one. I start getting nightmares about rubber neck basses and all sorts of really creepy dreams. [Laughs] I have to pick a bass up and see if I can still play. I just play as fast as I can up and down the neck to make sure I can still play it.

:| |•|•|

As far as modifications to my guitars go, I change the strings, but, basically, I just try to get the action as low as I can. It's pretty high on this one [Thunderbird] because it had been standing on the landing for about 10 years. I also try and make sure the neck is perfectly straight. Now, I get all my basses [Buzzard model] made and they're made out of solid graphite with no wood and the action stays where I put it. The pickups and the circuit are to my specifications anyway, so I don't really have to do anything with them.

Gibson made a bass for me, which ended up as the RD Artist model, but I wanted them to make me up a bass that was similar to an Olympic, and they got Moog in to do the electronics but instead of extending the tone range, they put these two silly little effects in it. I never actually took them up on it. They sent me a couple of prototypes, which I still have. They made a two-octave neck for me on the prototype and then it got stolen from the factory.

I made the decision to start keeping some of my old instruments when I sold the first Precision, that I was talking about earlier, to Marshall's Music Store for £50. As soon as I sold it, I missed it and wished that I'd kept it, so from then on, I decided I was just going to keep all of the basses that I used. By about 1975, I had built my own studio and I wanted to get some guitars for it so, Robert Johnson, the guy who was playing with my band Ox, was an avid guitar enthusiast and he found me an old '58 Gibson Explorer and I bought that in 1975 for £3,750. God knows how much it's worth now.

I started collecting from then on. I've always liked the Fender Stratocaster, so I found a good one of those and now I've got 13 of them. You just keep finding better examples of the one you've got or you start collecting different colors and different rare models or one-offs. It just goes on and on and on. I had guitars hanging along the staircase and everywhere for the film, but my cleaner wouldn't dust those every day. She'd quit. [Laughs] There's about 30 guitars out on stands in the studio and there's a store room next to the studio. The majority of them are upstairs in a safe room.

:| |·|·|

The number of basses I take on the road with me varies. With my own band, because I use an eight-string on a couple of songs, I have to take two eight-strings with me. Usually I take three of my stage guitars and that usually takes care of it. If it's a particularly tricky Who gig, where I have to use different tunings — some basses I use tuned down to C for certain songs — I'll take four or five. It's usually on average five.

When I first started, I played like everyone else with my thumb ...[Demonstrates] ... then I saw a guy on stage using his index finger ... [Demonstrates] ... and I thought, that's pretty neat because you could go [Plays] with two fingers. I had played the piano and trumpet and French horn, so my fingers were adept enough. I met the guy a couple of years later and he said to me, 'I love the way you play!' I said, 'Well, you play like that as well, don't you?' And he said, 'No. I play with my thumb, but I got a big blister on it so I had to play with my finger and I got a blister on that one so I swapped over.' So, I guess we invented this finger style. [Laughs]

Don Everly

THE EVERLY BROTHERS

Don Everly
Born February 1, 1937
Brownie, Kentucky

:|Don Everly|·|·|

Few artists have had such a lasting impact on the development of rock 'n' roll over the years than The Everly Brothers, whose precise harmonies have influenced generations of rockers, including fellow legends of the genre, The Beatles, The Beach Boys, The Hollies, Simon & Garfunkel, The Byrds, and The Mamas and the Papas, to name just a few.

The country-rock duo's parents, Ike and Margaret, were country singers of some repute, and it was their father's thumb-picking guitar style which greatly influenced Merle Travis who in turn shaped Chet Atkins's style. It was not a style that rubbed off on the young Don Everly, who his father recruited as a rhythm guitar player when they were playing radio stations through the South in the early '50s. In fact, as Don Everly once told writer/editor Brett Ratner, his father actually discouraged any of his flat-picking, guitar-hero ambitions telling him that "the singers make the money, forget about guitar playing." Ike had actually given up the perilous rigors of his work as a coal miner to move to Chicago to sing with his two brothers.

Don would ultimately team up with younger brother Phil to form The Everly Brothers, who would head out on their own. By the mid-'50s, they had a record deal, a management contract with Music Row legend Wesley Rose, access to the songs of the chart-topping songwriting husband-and-wife team of Boudleaux and Felice Bryant and country music icon Chet Atkins producing many of their recording sessions. From 1957 until the early '60s, when the duo did a service stint with the U.S. Marine corps, the Everlys regularly topped the pop charts around the world with pop classics like *Bye Bye Love, Wake Up Little Susie, All I Have To Do Is Dream, Bird Dog, Problems, Cathy's Clown,* and *Walk Right In.* The relationship between the brothers had soured by the early '70s, and on July 14, 1973, they announced that they had played their last concert together.

Over the next decade, the brothers pursued solo careers with varying degrees of success, and in June of 1983, The Everly Brothers played a reunion concert at the Royal Albert Hall in London. Three years later they were inducted into the Rock and Roll Hall of Fame.

Don Everly, who continues to write, tour, and record with an all-star band whose members include guitarist Albert Lee, steel player Buddy Emmons, and keyboardist Pete Wingfield, spoke with us in the courtyard of the townhouse offices of Hallway Entertainment on Music Row in Nashville. He brought with him an ebony Gibson Everly Model acoustic with the historic Everly double pick guards and the rosewood "moustache" bridge.

My first memory and contact with music would have been through my father when we lived in Chicago. He took me down to the Kitty Kat Club where he worked on a street that had a whole bunch of nightclubs. It was really a pool hall with a bandstand in the back. The reason I remember it so well is because I was very, very small and he wanted to use the pumpkin that had been given to me for Hallowe'en for the 'Kitty Box', which was used for people to drop their money in as tips and things. So I was down there and I remember rolling the pool balls around. My father was working in a band, and that's when I first realized that there was something unusual going on — my father worked in a band. He had also worked in a spice factory, I think. I remember that vaguely, but it was at the Kitty Kat Club that I first realized that he worked in the music business.

As a guitar player, my father had a unique picking style. He's older than Merle Travis. He came before Merle. Him and Mose Rager were the ones who influenced Merle and in turn Merle influenced Chet Atkins. Arnold Schulz influenced my father and, strangely enough, also influenced Bill Monroe in Kentucky.

Dad sang with his two brothers even before the Louvin Brothers. Dad and Chuck Leonard were the original Everly Brothers. They sang three part harmonies, but, hey, they didn't get along all that well, so they split up and one worked in one club and one worked in another club. Dad was familiar with the harmonies and duets and he worked with a fellow by the name of Rick Green on a station in Chicago as a duet known as the North Carolina Boys. He was quite familiar with that stuff [vocal harmonies] and that's how he passed that on to Phil and I.

When we first came to Nashville, I was writing songs. We were working as the Everly Family in Knoxville, Tennessee, and Chet Atkins came through on a show. Our dad had been corresponding with him, and so we went out to see the show. Actually, we didn't really see the show, we just sort of stood backstage. Chet was there and we talked to him and Dad told him we wrote songs. Phil hadn't written yet, I don't think. He was only about 15 and I was about 17 and I had written a couple of songs. So Chet, out of being kind and courteous to my father, gave him his home phone number, so immediately, the next holiday, we were in Nashville calling him at his house. We went over and sang some of the songs, and he took an interest in one called *Thou Shalt Not Steal*. He told me I needed to do this and move this here and write a bridge there. So I went back to the motel and tried to follow his instructions and took the song back the next day, and he said, 'Yeah, if I get this recorded, I'll publish it.' We said, 'Sure! Of course!' Well, lo and behold, we're back in Knoxville and this letter arrives that Kitty Wells had recorded it. I almost fainted.

I just couldn't believe that Chet Atkins had taken us under his wing when we first came to Nashville. He, of course, got the first song recorded, and then we auditioned for RCA. They turned us down and then we auditioned for them again, I think, and they turned us down again. Chet would help us and send us to people that would listen to our work. He believed in us. People would say, 'If Chet likes them, there must be something there.' Phil and I looked a little different and sang a little different than most people that come to town, and I can see why they would be reluctant. We had long hair. We were just not your typical country boys, I guess. Chet's nod of approval was really important, and we finally got there and he could say, 'I told you so.'

It wasn't an overnight thing, though. *Bye Bye Love* had been turned down by everybody. That was a good thing, I guess. You know, it's one of those things where people say, 'Oh, I turned down this song' or 'I turned down that song.' Sometimes it's the treatment of the song; it's not necessarily the song; it's the treatment and the timing. Those things all come into play. It just worked for us. We had an arrangement on another song called *Give Me A Future*. It was kind of a rock 'n' roll arrangement really and we put it on that song and it just worked. That really set us up for the next one.

On the recording session for *Bye Bye Love*, Ray Eddington played a regular acoustic. I was using a G tuning that Chet had showed me, because I really had a big interest in Bo Diddley and rock 'n' roll at that time and different sounds on the guitar. The guitar was miked while I was singing, and that G tuning was so full. I liked it when we were singing and playing and that's the arrangement that went on *Bye Bye Love*. It was a G tuning. There weren't many electric guitars on that session. There was just Ray Eddington and myself. Like I told Chet, I really love that Bo Diddley rhythm. It was a real earthy rhythm rather than just one-two, one-two. I always loved the rhythms in music. I followed that with the G tunings and then on to the regular tuning. We had a lot of rhythmic patterns in our music. There weren't that many instruments on our early records.

The fusion of rock 'n' roll and country that resulted wasn't intentional, it really wasn't. It wasn't like, 'Oh, we're going to do something that's going to cover both fields.' We were looking to get a recording contract, so we were trying to please the people at the labels too. The first thing we recorded on Columbia Records was pure country. Maybe we just weren't suited for pure country and there was a lot of luck, a lot of timing, the song and the arrangement — it was just the right time.

Till I Kissed You was just a song that came around for me on the way back from Australia. It's just one of those songs that fell into place, and we decided to bring in the Crickets to play the rhythm section. I remembered the 'paradiddles' on Buddy Holly's *Peggy Sue*, and I wanted Jerry Allison to do something, not like that, but something similar to it. So I said, 'Try using a drum fill rather than a guitar fill here.' So he tuned them to where it sounded really good, and it was so effective. I still get a kick out of it, singing it on stage, because of the drums.

Cathy's Clown marked a particularly special time in our careers. Everyone was looking at us and saying, 'Well, you're changing labels and maybe that will be the jinx,' so we needed a hit badly to redeem ourselves. Warner was a new label that had never had a hit single before — I think that was the case. *Cathy's Clown* was it and it was a great sound. We had put reverb on the drums for a kind of an echo slap effect. We wanted it to sound like a march. It was actually taken a little bit, believe it or not, from the *Grand Canyon Suite,* and it worked. It was unique and different at the time. I was just relieved. We had just made the label switch and it worked.

In the studio, we always had arrangements of the songs. We went into the sessions with everything pretty well figured out and we knew what we were going to do. The musicians were so excellent, players like Chet Atkins and Floyd Cramer, Ray Eddington, Buddy Harmon. It was wonderful and it worked so well. It was at RCA's

Studio B, which is just down the street from here. You'd walk into that place and hope that you'd come out with something because you could take an acetate home with you and play the record that they were going to hear. That was a miracle, man. Go in for three hours, come back and there was the record. It was wonderful.

In those early days on the road, you played two or three songs at one venue and then you went back on the road. When playing the New York Paramount, you did five shows a day: you'd go back and forth across the street from the hotel to the theater, do two songs, go back, wait for the next crowd. And then traveling ... of course, we traveled with so many stars from Bo Diddley to Little Richard, Laverne Baker, just everybody, The Crickets, Buddy Holly, Jimmy Bowen, Buddy Knox, everybody. If you had a record, you were all together traveling on the road.

But it all happened pretty quick and was over with real quick. The crowd was screaming and yelling so loud, you could hardly hear anything. In fact, Phil and I were playing the Opry at the time and that was the audience that would listen to you and then yell and scream and applaud at the end, which was really sometimes more rewarding. In fact, maybe, that's the way I like it.

From those early days, I can hear Buddy Holly's influence in other music. There's a real stamp that you put on something and people say, 'That's derivative or derived from that.' Yeah, I hear it with our stuff, too, and it's a compliment really.

:| |•|•|

We were a Gibson guitar family. Dad played an L5 up in Chicago with a pickup. In order to get the crowd to come into the club, he'd put the amplifier outside the door and on the street. People would hear that music and here they'd come.

The biggest thing we used to do on the road in the Everly family was "three on one guitar": Dad had this thing figured out where I would play the rhythm up here and he would play down here with all three of us standing there, and the audience loved it. It probably would still go over.

We started with Gibson guitars. I had a Southern Jumbo that I had acquired when my dad and I went down to the Gibson place in Knoxville, Tennessee, when I was about 17. It was time for Don to have his own guitar. I was using the L5 until then and Dad was play-ing the blonde Gibson cutaway. It's in the Country Music Hall of Fame now. So we picked out this Southern Jumbo, and that's the guitar that I wrote on, recorded with, and still have. It's still probably one of my finest guitars and I will probably take it into the studio soon again. It's a wonderful sound. It's lightweight. It's just everything.

When we went on the road, we got us a couple of Jumbos and we would just tear them up, wailing away on them and lift them to the mic. Those were the days when, if your guitar was all scarred, you just said, 'Hey, let's get a new one. It's not supposed to be looking like that.' We finally said, let's design one. We ordered a black guitar and we had designed the pick guards so we wouldn't eat 'em up. Those were the days when they weren't miked or anything. Somebody was singing on one mic, you'd back up, and, bang, we'd go. You played and your fingers were hurting and bloody sometimes. Gibson did that for us [put on black pick guards] on a three-quarters kind of a cutdown version of the Jumbo and it worked. It was a lot easier to get to the mic and it had a punch to it. Right now, they are a kind of collector's item, the ones from that period. This is the new one that Gibson has. I just got it a year ago or so and I think it sounds better than the original. It's a pretty thing, I think. When we said we wanted a black guitar back then, it was a ready-made. You can't see the wood. We didn't think about that. We just thought it looked cool.

:| |•|•|

I've become a better player over the years. I think you get better. I just got off the road and I can play that [rhythm] really well right now, but the other stuff, I have to get back into the mode of writing and finger-picking and things like that. It's not that easy a change. If you're playing everyday, though, you keep your chops up.

I find that in working on the road, I can't sing without playing the guitar now. I've been doing it so long, if I didn't have a guitar in my hand, I don't know where the singing would be, and especially the up-tempo stuff. It just drives me, and you find little places to accentuate and kick the song forward. I always write with the guitar. After I've got the melody set in my head, I can do the lyrics in my head as well. To find the melodies, though, I find them on the guitar.

I'm particularly fond of what we're doing now. Buddy Emmons works with us on steel guitar and that has really charged me up. The steel guitar has so many possibilities. We haven't really ever used it on records as effectively as I think we can now. We'll go back in and do what we always have done and add the steel. We've been playing with steel on records for years, of course, but nothing that really anybody has ever heard.

Don Felder

THE EAGLES

Donald William Felder
Born September 21, 1947
Gainesville, Florida

:|Don Felder|·|·|

"**F**elder is a 'Guitar God,'" writes fan Daniel E. Smith on an Internet web page he has devoted to Don Felder. "He is one of the most accurate guitarists in the world; if he wants to play it, it will come out right. While he only sang one song (*Visions*), his talents have been exploited elsewhere. He has incredible speed while playing and he writes awesome guitar parts for songs — check out *Too Many Hands*, *Get Over It*, or *Hotel California*. He was a great addition [to The Eagles] in '74. Don, I bow my head and pray to you every night."

Glowing praise indeed for the musician who, by his early teens in his hometown of Gainesville, Florida, was already making a name for himself playing in a local group, The Continentals, with Stephen Stills (Buffalo Sprngfield and Crosby, Stills, Nash & Young). Tom Petty, who was from the same area and had been taught music briefly by Felder, says that he was always the best guitar player in town.

After graduating high school, besides working and teaching at the Lipham Music store in Gainesville and working in a number of local groups, Felder joined future Eagle, Bernie Leadon, in a group called The Flow, which actually released an album in 1970 on the CTI label. Over the next few years, Felder toured with David Blue in his band and spent some time as Stephen Stills's fill-in with Crosby, Stills & Nash before being asked to join The Eagles in 1974 after contributing slide guitar on the track *Good Day In Hell* during the sessions in L.A. for The Eagles' third album, ON THE BORDER.

Speaking to *Rolling Stone* as part of a cover story on the group in 1979, Felder talked about how he saw his position within the band, which was enjoying international acclaim at that point. "I enjoy being anonymous," Felder contended. "I spend my spare time with my wife and kids. Don and Glenn have no anchors like that and they handle being rock stars well. Everybody in the band is a different piece of the puzzle. I'm a musical catalyst. I can't worry or be political, so back when Randy [Meisner] quit and everything was real insecure, I just recorded a lot of tracks in my home studio and gave

Glenn and Don each a 90-minute cassette to work with. No vocals, just music, because they sometimes need a scene to paint their lyrics on. That was the start of this album [THE LONG RUN]. I see myself as an offensive lineman, who has to take out the middle linebacker so Don and Glenn can make the big play."

By the end of the '70s, The Eagles, for all intents and purposes, had ceased to exist. Felder, who has his pilot's license, recorded a solo album, AIRBORNE, in 1983. A decade later, shortly after the release of COMMON THREAD: THE SONGS OF THE EAGLES, a charity album to benefit Walden Woods, which featured a number of top country artists performing the group's hits, The Eagles reunited with a new album, HELL FREEZES OVER, an accompanying tour, and a couple of chart-topping hits, including *Get Over It* and *Love Will Keep Us Alive*.

The Eagles were inducted into the Rock and Roll Hall of Fame in 1998. During the induction ceremony the past members of the group re-united to perform a couple of the big hits, *Take It Easy* and *Hotel California*.

We spoke to Don Felder in the living room of his Malibu, California home on an afternoon when he was preparing to go flying with his son.

I grew up in Gainesville in north central Florida, home of the Fighting Gators, and, when I was about 14 or 15, I snuck into a bar to hear B.B. King. He impressed me so much in the way that he was able to affect the audience with the way he was playing. There were people crying and women hollering out and just really getting it on. I went backstage after it was over — it wasn't much of a backstage — and when I talked to him he was just the nicest guy. I was working in a music store at the time trying to build up enough credit there teaching guitar and selling guitars so I could order a guitar for myself. After seeing B.B. King, I ordered a new cherry red Gibson 355, and I guess I worked about a year or a year and a half saving up the money and waiting for that guitar to come. It finally came and I was probably the happiest kid on the block.

I was in a band at the time with a guy by the name of Bernie Leadon, and we were down auditioning for small clubs and hotels down in South Florida in the Fort Lauderdale and Miami area. We had gone in and done an audition, and when we were carrying our gear back and forth to the van afterwards, I set that guitar down beside the guy who was loading the van. I went back in to get something else and came back out and my guitar was gone. Somebody had stolen it, and it just broke my heart after working that long and waiting that hard to get it. To have my guitar stolen like that just destroyed me.

When I finally went through the Gibson factory a couple of years ago with Henry Juszkiewicz, I told him that story and he said, 'Well, you gotta come over and meet the guy that builds these guitars and puts the bindings on. He probably built the one you originally ordered.' I went over and, sure enough, the same guy that's been working there in the factory doing that same job for however long was still making 355s. I gave him a handshake, congratulated him, and told him how much that guitar had meant to me, so they built me another one to replace the one that was stolen. It's kind of a youth memento for me here and I play it on stage now on *I Can't Tell You Why*, which is kind of a romantic song. It kind of brings back a lot of those feelings for me when I switch it on.

Poverty was the reason I picked up the guitar in the first place. [Laughs] Like I said, I grew up in Florida on a dirt road and in a white clapboard house. I think a lot of the attraction was just the fun and thrill of playing music to begin with. My father loved music. He bought a Voice of Music tape recorder, since we couldn't afford to buy records at the time. He'd take it over to people's houses and copy their records and he'd have all this music in the house. I think his influence on me, just how much he cared about music, really led me to pursue music, and when I started playing he encouraged me and helped me along. To begin with, I ended up with a couple of pieces of junk with some nice tall half-inch action on them that really gave me some good calluses and some strength in my hand. I struggled through that, and, about that time, Elvis Presley hit the black and white screen on the *Ed Sullivan Show* and I was gone. I was hopeless from there on out. That was the end of it for me. I was sold.

I started playing when I was 10. I don't know how my parents ever put up with me. I was always thrashing away on something. There was nobody there [in Gainesville] that taught. I just had to seek out people in my neighborhood who knew a few chords. One guy would know *Red River Valley* and I'd learn that. Somebody else would know something in the key of G and they'd teach me that. I just started learning songs, and with my dad's tape recorder, I was able to sit down and do studies of music, stuff I'd hear real late at night on WLAC out of Nashville, Tennessee — John R's Record Company. I'd get copies of those and I'd also record the radio, and then I'd sit and study them as much as I could and try to mimic them. As I said, there was no real music school in my area, so I was sort of self-taught at the time and I wound up playing all my school functions, my own senior prom, my junior prom, every little women's group and all the dances. And fortunately, in Gainesville, the University of Florida was there with all these fraternity parties every Friday and Saturday night. Thank God! They kind of kept me in business and I would always have some band that I would be playing in.

Stephen Stills and I had a band. I guess we were about 13 or 14. He and I and a couple of other guys put together a band to play frat parties. We went over to play the strip at Daytona Beach during the summer when the frat parties were over because college was out for the summer. We'd lie about our age and say we were 18, though we were barely shaving at the time. There was a little blonde-headed guy named Tom Petty who was also around then. He had a band called The Rucker Brothers and I used to teach him guitar. I just wound up being attracted to the whole music industry.

I had made a couple of records in bands before The Eagles, but before I ever recorded, we would go out to the local radio station in Gainesville and we would set up to play live at night. A disc jockey there turned out to be our manager, which is how we ended up getting on the radio so much. He would make tapes for us while we were there in the radio station and he would continue to play those tapes during the course of the week until it got to the point where there was enough of a following where people wanted to buy records. So we went down to a local studio and recorded a couple of songs, made some demos, and we were selling them off the front of the stage and from out of the trunk of a car, anywhere we could sell those records.

I really had very little experience making records by the time I moved to New York. I moved there with a different band, a kind of a jazz fusion band. I was signed to a jazz label there called CTI, which had people like Quincy Jones, Freddie Hubbard, and Hubert Laws as artists. I think we made our album in about a day and a half. Everything was already rehearsed and we went in and set up and played it and it did okay. We played a lot around New York. I then moved to Boston, mainly because my now wife, then fiancée, lived in Boston, where I got a job working in a recording studio eight hours a day as staff guitarist, staff engineer, staff producer, staff broom guy. Anything that had to be done, I was elected. I made records eight hours a day for about two years. I really learned how to make everything from basic tracks through final overdubs to mixing and editing before I moved to Los Angeles, California.

When I got out here, I started making contacts with people

through Bernie Leadon, who at the time was in The Eagles. I was like every other guitar player on the street, but I met some people and played for them and wound up being invited to play on some of their records, artists like Joni Mitchell, David Blue, Bob Seger ... a lot of the people that were out here recording at the time. I was invited down to play slide guitar on an Eagles record called *Good Day In Hell*. Although I played slide guitar, it wasn't my absolute ultimate forte, but I had worked it up after I had run into a guy by the name of Duane Allman, who was working the strip over in Daytona Beach with his brother Greg in a band called The Allman Joys. They were doing club covers just like our band, and when everybody got off work at about two or three in the morning, we'd go and get breakfast together and hang out. We'd wind up over at his mom's house and he'd play slide guitar. I was absolutely fascinated by it, so I decided, well, hey, that's something I should learn to do, though I never learned to play it as well as Duane. I don't know if there are many people who can or ever will ever play like him, but I'd learned to play it well enough so that when The Eagles asked me to come down to play slide guitar on this track, I said, 'Okay I can do that.'

I got a call the next day from Glenn Frey, who asked me to join the band. At the time I was subbing for Stephen Stills in the Crosby, Nash show. I was playing and singing all of Stephen's parts with David Crosby and Graham Nash. It was a really good paying job for me, while The Eagles were still playing really small auditoriums — 2000-seaters — on college campuses. I had to think about this for a minute, but I finally said, 'Well, alright, I'll quit a good paying job and join this band.' Shortly after, I joined the band, I realized that I had joined a band that was constantly in the process of breaking up. From day to day, somebody was breaking up or quitting or mad about something. It was constant turmoil, but that was really part of the creative process of that band, everybody fighting for what they believed was the best music, the best track, the best lyrics and singers. I think that's what made the Eagles who they are.

Everyone in that band has a certain expertise. Don Henley is just a brilliant lyricist as well as a great singer. At the time Bernie and I were appointed to the job of musical arrangement, and Glenn was kind of the supervising arranger. We used to call him the Lone Arranger. He'd go off on these tangents, but he's really brilliant at it. The philosophy of that band is the less you do on a record, the better it is. The less is more theory, so everything you play and every little piece that's on that record really gets ultimate scrutiny, not only as far as the composition, but also the lyrics and the sound of each instrument, the choice of each instrument that's on the record, how it's played, the sparsity of the notes, where they're placed. There is a great deal of scrutiny put into those records. That's the key, less is more, to be really selective about what you play and not to overplay. So many records that you listen to have somebody who has to show how much he can play or how fast he can play and drummers who want to play all fancy stuff. That's just not part of this band.

It's a very simple, very selected, almost calculated part-by-part, piece-by-piece, arranging of these tracks. So far it has worked, but it makes it really difficult as far as performing those records, which span quite a few years and a lot of different styles, everything from country to R&B to rock and to *Hotel California*, whatever style that is. It's difficult to be able to perform all that live on stage.

I wrote the track to *Hotel California* on a four-track TEAC tape recorder in a bedroom in a beach house I rented, and it was completed with everything but lyrics and vocals. Almost all the solos were done. The little double harmony parts were all kind of done. I just spit this thing out and then we finally went in and recorded it. When it came time to play it live — it had about 11 or 12 guitar tracks on it — Joe Walsh and I ended up layering the harmonies and all that stuff and playing the solos. We asked ourselves, 'How the heck are we going to do this on stage? Have we created a monster for ourselves?' It wound up that I was forced to play two parts, one which is a 12-string part that I played on the record and then the electric guitar part, which we doubled on the solos. There was only one way to do it, which was to use a double neck guitar.

I wound up getting a Gibson double-neck guitar, and we wired it as if it were two guitars put together with two different output jacks and two different amps. The 12-string goes through a Leslie and an echo, and the 6-string goes through a Marshall so that I can do all that solo stuff. I have to switch between two guitars through the course of that performance. It was a difficult task to figure out how to go about presenting that song to make it sound like the record. The choice of all the instruments that go into that show, except for maybe two or three songs . . . I think everything I play on that show is a Gibson guitar.

With the solos for *Hotel California*, writing them followed the same methodology as when I write other material for the group. When I write, it's like writing a script for five different characters. You kind of know how Glenn's going to play and I kind of know Joe's style and I know how I want to play, so in all the things I write, I try to write for that band. I can't write something that's too complex and ask Glenn to play it or I can't write something that doesn't fit with the characters that are there. For *Hotel California*, I had pretty much written that track, those instrument parts and those solos and everything pretty much as they are, with the exception of some of the stuff that Joe changed on the solos, which was fine with me. It was kind of a sketch. It was like a screenplay. 'Here's the idea! You say this and I'll say this and you say something like this' and kind of get the feel of how the pieces would go together. Sometimes that works and sometimes people say, 'I want to change the script! I don't like what I'm saying here!' That's pretty much how it came out.

My prior musical experience and my subsequent versatility with various music styles served me well. When I was growing up I was forced to play a variety of styles, everything from country and western music to jazz. I had a bluegrass band with Bernie Leadon; we played Wednesday and Thursday nights. I think the guy that played mandolin and sang in the band actually worked for Florida Fish and Game. On the weekends, we had a cover band and I played nylon-stringed guitar in a bar before playing movie themes, which was a great deal of help later when we did this acoustic version of *Hotel California* for the Unplugged MTV video. Don Henley said, 'Well, we've got to do an acoustic version of *Hotel*. How in the world do you do that?' So I was handed the task and challenge of coming up with the parts and arrangements and putting together an unplugged version of that song. I used my past experience playing jazz and a classical music or gut string approach to playing jazz and country. That's really what this band does. The Eagles have a very wide variety of instrumentation and expertise and approach to writing songs. I think that's been part of our longevity.

I actually played bass on the session for *One Of These Nights*. We were recording in Miami and Randy Meisner was the bass player in the band at the time. He was living in Nebraska and he got caught in a snowstorm there and couldn't get out. We were all set up to track that song and so I started playing bass, because I'd played bass on sessions and in studios forever. I made up that bass line in the song, and by the time Randy got there, we had almost cut the whole track, except for his bass part, which I had sort of been forced to play by default.

Actually, there's a funny story from that period. During the time I was playing the parts for *One Of These Nights*, I was sitting in the studio [The Record Plant] with Bill Szymczyk one night when Don and Glenn were over doing a live FM radio broadcast as guest disc jockeys who were invited to sit in and kind of take over the station there for a while. One of the things they wanted to do on air was to phone into the studio and see how the session was going. Knowing they were going to call in, as a gag, Bill and I made this solo up that had loads of mistakes in it. It started out sort of like the one on the record [*One Of These Nights*] and, about three or four bars into it, you hear one little clam [mistake] and then a few more bars into it you hear another clam and then pretty soon, by about halfway through the solo, it's just gonzo. So they dialed up live from this FM station and we started running this screwy bass solo and we got a pretty good laugh out of it. We played the real solo when we went on the air.

:| |•|•|

Everything I do is based on the guitar. I'm a cripple on keyboards, to be honest with you. There are too many things over there that I don't know. I feel more comfortable writing on guitar, although I do use some synthesizers to sketch with in my studio. I leave keyboard arrangements to Glenn and Joe, who both play keyboards a lot better than I do.

The Les Paul has probably been the key to my success in the record business, only because I have developed a relationship with this instrument like no other instrument. It has such a wide ability to translate into a lot of different types of music, and there are a couple of sounds that I just really love that come out of this instrument that you can't get out of any other guitar around, period. As well, when you pick up an instrument, after all the instruments I've had in my hands and played, it should feel like something that is a real piece of quality work. It shouldn't feel like Fisher Price or it shouldn't feel like sort of a Chevy — nothing against GMC. It should really feel like the best quality instrument you can get, and after having struggled for so many years in my youth playing all sorts of nasty instruments, I really prefer to have a Les Paul and a Gibson instrument in my hands at every opportunity

I have different pickups put in for different songs, like the 12-string [double guitar] that I use for *Hotel California*, I took out those pickups and put in some hotter pickups for the 6-string part of it, because I had used a real 1959 Les Paul when I recorded that through a little Fender Tweed Deluxe at the time in the studio and it just screamed. To get that same sound out of the instrument on stage, we had to change that around. I don't do a lot of custom wiring on the instrument and I never refret. A lot of people like to take them out, change the curvature of the neck and refret. I think that what Gibson makes almost right off the assembly line is such a quality instrument that you can just take it off the store shelf, plug it in, turn on, and go. I don't do a lot of customizing.

I play slide on the Les Paul. Lowell George and Bonnie Raitt were first to break through with slide Stratocasters, because it's such a silky kind of sound, but having been impressed so much by Duane Allman in the past and seeing and hearing what a Les Paul does with slide, that was really the timbre that I preferred over a Strat.

I use the Gibson ES 335 on one or two things. I use it on a blues-oriented track, where I would try to the best of my ability to mimic a sort of B.B. King approach, which is kind of what we did on *I Can't Tell You Why*. I tried to do a little tribute to B.B. on some of those solos, not quite as bluesy as B.B., but sort of in that era. Or I would use it on something that was a little more jazz-oriented. Actually, there's two thin-line Gibsons on that particular track. One of them is a kind of jazz chord, major 7th type approach to a rhythm guitar, if you listen to it, and then the solo is just straight ahead B.B. King. So it really suits those idioms quite well, a jazz mode or a blues mode. That's really what it's designed to do.

I go through periods where I play anywhere from three to seven hours a day. If I'm on the road, we do a three hour show and then I'll try to play in the hotel room at that date before we go on. Then there are times when, honestly, I just get sick of it. I want to do something else in life besides play guitar. I know that sounds strange, but it's the honest truth. I think it's almost like a love affair or a relationship. If you're strapped with something everyday, day in and day out, you not so much take it for granted, but when you get inspired to go back to it and get inspired to pick it up and play, it's fresh, it's new, it's exciting, as opposed to something that's just a routine. I try to get myself periods away from playing. Going back to it is like seeing an old friend or seeing an old lover or something that you're back in touch with again. It keeps me inspired that way. That seems to work for me.

Radney Foster

Radney Mackleroy Foster
Born July 20, 1959
Del Rio, Texas

: Radney Foster |·|·|

Though country singer/songwriter Radney Foster has a great affinity for the guitar, you'll never have trouble mistaking him for a guitar hero. He has said as much in the past when asked if he was a "guitar kind of guy" by writer Thomas Goldsmith in an issue of *Country Guitar*. "Yeah," answered Foster, "though I'm no designated terrorist and never will be. I learned a long time ago that I was never gonna be a lead guitarist. And yet, I write a lot of hook riffs and teach them to the other players."

No designated six-string terrorist, maybe, but mention the word "guitar" to Foster and his enthusiasm for the subject knows no bounds as you will note in the interview that follows. This keenness is also reflected in a logo that often accompanies a stylized graphic of his name. It's a line drawing of Foster in his rocking-the-country mode and pose, holding a big-ass acoustic guitar — probably his favored Gibson J100.

Foster, who grew up in the Lone Star state but first made his way to Tennessee to attend university, began playing clubs during those college years and was sufficiently encouraged by the reception he got to consider music a full-time occupation. Of course, already being in Tennessee and with music now a growing passion, what's a poor boy to do but give into the magnetic attraction of Music City U.S.A.? Foster subsequently took a year off from university and headed for Nashville. It's hardly a unique story, but Foster actually landed on his feet in shorter order than most, signing on as a writer at MTM Music Publishing in 1985. Within two months of joining the company, he became friends with fellow staff writer, Bill Lloyd, and the two began writing together. Within a year Sweethearts of the Rodeo had made a hit of one of their collaborative efforts, *Since I Found You*. In 1987, as a duo, Foster & Lloyd signed to RCA Records for which they recorded three albums. Their eponymous debut and their sophomore set, FASTER AND LOUDER, did very well on the strength of hit singles like *Crazy Over You, Sure Thing, What Do You Want From Me This*

Time, and *Fair Shake.* The third album, VERSION OF THE TRUTH, didn't fare as well, and by 1991, the duo had split up. Foster released a debut solo CD on Arista Records the following year titled DEL RIO, TEXAS, 1959, which produced a number of hits, including the memorable *Nobody Wins.* His second solo album, LABOR OF LOVE, was released in 1995, and at the time of writing, a third, SEE WHAT YOU WANT TO SEE, was on the release schedule.

Foster has made many fans over the years but perhaps none as influential as perennial pop chart toppers, Hootie & the Blowfish, with whom Foster has actually collaborated as a songwriter. "We've been huge fans for a long time — his albums got us interested in country," the group has commented. "He never ceases to amaze us. Radney Foster is light years ahead of anybody else in country music."

We spoke to Radney Foster in a loft at the Music Row townhouse offices of Hallway Entertainment in Nashville.

My dad played guitar and, as a matter of fact, he had a gut string Epiphone guitar made by Gibson. There were always guys coming over on Saturday afternoon BBQs, bringing their guitars around my family's house, so it was pretty natural for me around the time — I was 11 or 12 years old — to pick up a guitar and start playing it. Then I started playing in local garage bands and at church and every other thing that you could think of. Any chance I would get to play it, I would.

Being a kid growing up in the '60s, The Beatles and The Stones were my greatest influence, particularly The Beatles, as well as a lot of country artists, people like Buck Owens, Waylon Jennings, and Merle Haggard. I remember wearing out a MERLE HAGGARD GREATEST HITS album that was on Capitol. Waylon Jennings made an album called HONKY TONK HEROES, and when I first started writing songs, I was really impressed with that record. It was all Billy Joe Shaver songs.

I loved singer/songwriters in general, and especially people like Neil Young. Later on, when I got into college, I started to find out that Kris Kristofferson had written all these songs for all these country acts. So, the singer/songwriters were my main influences.

I think the reason that so many singer/songwriters came out of Texas is because there's nothing to do out there. [Laughs] Or at least west Texas. Guy Clark is from far west Texas — Marathon — which is about as far west as Del Rio is, just a lot farther north. He is a lawyer's son from a little tiny town just like me. We swapped a bunch of stories and they seem to be the same stories, even though he's about 15 years older than I am. He was doing the exact same thing as I was in that little town just about 15 years before I was.

There's a great dancehall/beerhall tradition in Texas music that's been around for a century; in fact, one of my favorite places to play is a place called Greenhall, the oldest honky-tonk in Texas. It's still standing, but it doesn't have any air conditioning. The sides of the building just go up and there's screening so it looks like a cotton barn for the most part. Honky tonk bands and dancing is such an important deal that people really don't tend to clap much, but if they're on the dance floor you know they like it because they'll go nuts at the end of a show wanting you to play some more. They're way into dancing, and it's not the new-fangled, line dancing crud that you're seeing in the whole modern country deal. It's a guy dancing his girlfriend around the dance floor doing the two step. It was a lot of fun just to grow up in that tradition, but I remember it was also nerve-wracking as a musician. The first time Foster and Lloyd had ever played in any of those places down there, we were so used to people pounding their beer bottles on the front of the stage and that kind of thing. To go from that to seeing people just dancing in a circle sort of flipped out the whole band.

Most of my music is really acoustic guitar driven. I've always thought that truly, in both rock 'n' roll and country music, my favorite music always has been guitar driven. Even if you think about the Everly Brothers or The Beatles or The Stones or a ton of country records, that driving force behind it all is an acoustic guitar. A lot of times people will have in their memory this big, rocking record and they think its a stack of amplifiers and a bunch of electric guitars that are creating that energy, but the reality is that it's just that acoustic pounding — and Gibsons in particular. I have a theory about this: if you think about a lot of the early records of the Everly Brothers and The Beatles, they were playing Gibson guitars on those records for the most part and there's a bark to the strings, especially if the strings are a little dead. They just didn't pay that much attention to how bright the strings sounded 30 or 40 years ago, so you hear the bark of each string before you hear the ring of the string itself. I still try to use that in the studio. I'll sometimes keep one guitar with really bright strings for a real swishy sound and keep another guitar — almost always a Gibson — with sort of dead strings on it, so they bark along.

The only way I write is with the guitar. I know there are guys who go in and create a whole track and then write around that track, but I've always been a guy sitting in his living room, or anywhere really, with a guitar, coming up with some melody line. I think different guitars have different songs in them. The cool thing is, for some reason, you can take a guitar and play it and play it until you decide you want a different sound or feel and you'll go and pick up a different one and, all of a sudden, I literally think that guitar has a different song in it. You tend to come back to old favorites, having gone through a lot of changes. It's a process that is more felt than understood.

As I said, when we're in the studio, I'll even keep two different guitars. I'll keep one guitar strung with brand new strings on it to get a real feathery, swishy sound, but I'll generally keep a Gibson in particular so that it enhances that bark of each individual string as you stroke the guitar. It has that particular sound that you heard on those early Beatles records and early Everly Brothers records.

About four or five years ago, I felt that I was sort of hitting a wall and not improving. I started discovering a lot of different tunings and how you could tune a guitar in other ways than the standard method. I then tried to use those tunings with a capo in addition to that to get completely different sounds. The shear fact of having to fumble around again, not knowing what you're doing or where you're going, was sort of exciting and took you in different places than you had been before. Sometimes, not having the ability that you have for a while can be a big asset to you as a songwriter. It's a matter of making the most of your deficiencies, so to speak.

I've written a song with Hootie and the Blowfish and I've still got my part to do. I think it's going to end up on a soundtrack somewhere, but we're not real sure yet. I've just been real fortunate in that those guys were fans of my songwriting and the records I made and they had already covered a couple of my songs as B sides. They are some of the nicest guys you'll ever meet. I've really been able to do a lot of fun stuff with them. I think they're a wonderful band in that they truly are a band.

That's the best compliment I can give anybody — when the whole is so much larger than the sum of the individual parts. You add four guys up together and it ends up being something altogether more than you would think that four guys could create, and that's fun. They're a rock band that's driven by acoustic guitars. I think you're finding that more and more with them, and bands like Toad the Wet Sprocket and several other bands, they're getting back to realizing the fact that acoustic guitars drove so much of rock 'n' roll because of the country influence. There was always the blues and R&B influence on rock 'n' roll, but the other half of that equation really was country music. No Hank Williams: no rock 'n' roll. I really believe that. And that's a pretty cool thing to me because I've always been driven and obsessed with music that was driven by acoustic guitars.

In the studio, I play mostly acoustic guitar. If I'm playing any electric guitar, it's usually just a rhythm part. I tend to paint myself in a corner. I've had several producers who've said, 'Well, you have to go play that on the track because no one else can play that particular stroke that way. It's so bass-ackwards.' I think part of that has come more and more recently from using so many whacked out tunings that if you want that particular sound on the record, the only way you're going to get it is to play it yourself. The only other alternative is to teach somebody to do it who's awfully versatile and good at picking up things quick on something that actually becomes something other than a guitar for him because you tuned it so whackily.

Any guitar playing above the 7th fret is unskilled labor on my part. I think that any guy on his porch just about anywhere, if he thinks about it long enough, can play one of my songs. They're not that tough, and I think that's something that's wonderful about country music. It is poetry for the guy who rolls his sleeves up and goes to work for a living. That's really a goal to pay attention to — good music doesn't need a very sophisticated level of playing. There's a beauty in simplicity and you have to pay attention to playing things simply and not losing sight of how amazing that can be. It's sort of like the joy that you got the first time you strapped on an electric guitar and played an E chord as loud as your amp could possibly rattle your parent's garage. That sense and feeling was overwhelming when you were 13 years old, and there should be a part of music, no matter what age you are, that tries to re-create the overwhelming feeling of that E chord ringing around in your head.

:| |•|•|

My Gibson J100 guitar was one of the first ones to come off the line when Gibson bought the Flatiron factory out in Montana. At that time, Gibson was making J100s with the straight bridge rather than the moustache bridge, which is like a 200. And that bridge, being smaller, actually soaks up less sound, so this has got real fat low end on it and it really reverberates well and sounds great. A custom guitar shop that I once visited had a real old Epiphone with these bowtie inlays for the fret markers, and so I asked them if they'd put those bowtie inlays in my J100. Other than that, it's just a stock J100. It's been on a ton of records of mine.

When I first started getting into recording, I wondered how The Stones got that particular sound on *Street Fighting Man*. It turns out it was actually a Gibson acoustic plugged into a tape player. 'That's cool, I thought, I've got to have one of those.' You pick them up and you hear them and they have such a distinctive sound all their own. There's that bark that I was talking about. Each string barks out. With a lot of other acoustic guitars, you tend to have a sort of swishier sound and not hear the thunk of each of the strings. But with most of the Gibsons, you still have that feathery sound, but you're going to get the attack as well. I guess that's from the way they make the bracing. I'd love to talk to the guys at the factory and see what it is exactly that makes the strings bark out that way.

I actually have a guitar that Gibson made for RCA. One year, RCA gave all its artists a guitar as a Christmas gift. I thought that was the coolest thing in the world to actually give musicians something that they could use and enjoy. They had them custom-made. It was a J30, but they made it without a pick guard and with the RCA logo and the Nipper dog printed on the truss rod cover. It's one of my favorites because the lack of a pickguard makes it ring a little differently. It's a cool looking guitar. It's all black. There are probably only 30 guitars in the whole world like it — maybe 50 at the most. I'm now on Arista Records, but during the time I was with Foster & Lloyd, I was on RCA and they gave us one.

There are times in this business when you feel like you're on top of the world, when you really do own the town. There are other times that you feel that absolutely no one is listening and you're completely spinning your wheels — and yet you can't escape the heart and soul of making music. To me, it's the greatest job in the world. It's an obsession and sometimes it will own you rather than the other way around.

Peter Frampton

THE HERD, HUMBLE PIE, FRAMPTON'S CAMEL

Peter Frampton
Born April 22, 1950
Beckenham, Kent, England

:| Peter Frampton |·|·|

Though Peter Frampton would go on to become something of a '70s rock icon, his initial notoriety came in The Herd, the South London pop group he left school to join at the age of 16. The group had a zealous following among teen girls, but, though the adulation no doubt had its moments, Frampton had reason for the odd second thought about the direction in which his musical career was headed. "I realized that some people seemed to care more about how I looked than what I was playing," he once commented. He was dubbed "Face of 1968" by a number of fan magazines.

You might say, and certainly Frampton does, that meeting the late Steve Marriott, the ex-Small Faces vocalist and guitarist with whom he formed the group Humble Pie, was one of his earliest brushes with good fortune. "We recorded five albums together before I left and went on to start a solo career," Frampton recalls. "Steve Marriott was a great teacher for me, as well as being the best singer with whom I have ever worked. God bless you, Steve!"

By the early-to-mid '70s, Frampton had formed the backing group, Frampton's Camel, recorded his first solo album, and had even been considered for membership in one of rock 'n' roll's biggest groups, The Rolling Stones. One of his earliest bands, The Preachers had been managed and produced by former Rolling Stones' bassist, Bill Wyman, and before he was 15, he had appeared with the group on the top-rated British music TV show *Ready Steady Go* alongside The Rolling Stones. A decade later, in 1975, Frampton was driving into Manhattan when he heard on a local radio station that he was one of the five guitarists on the short list to replace guitarist Mick Taylor in the Stones. "I almost crashed the car," Frampton recalls. Of course, it was Ron Wood who got the nod, but though he didn't know it at the time, he would have little cause for regret.

The following year, his double live album, FRAMPTON COMES ALIVE, recorded at San Francisco's Winterland, was released. It showcased a strong set of songs along with Frampton's facility with the voice box, which immediately caught the ear of the record-buying public, and produced a number of major hits, including *Show Me the Way*; *Baby, I Love Your Way*; and *Do You Feel Like We Do*. It went on to become the best-selling live album ever, having sold over 16 million copies with current sales still reportedly in the 100,000 copies a year range.

The late '70s were less than kind to Frampton as he survived a near-fatal car crash in the Bahamas and almost succumbed to the slings and arrows of outrageous fortune that accompanied his act- ing debut in the promisingly titled but ill-conceived film, *Sgt. Pepper's Lonely Hearts Club Band*, in which he played Billy Shears.

A 1991 reunion of Humble Pie was tragically cut short by the death of Steve Marriott in a house fire and, since that time, Frampton has continued to write, record — FRAMPTON COMES ALIVE II was released in 1995 — and tour, often as a journeyman member of the band with some of his old musical friends, including Ringo Starr and David Bowie.

We spoke to Peter Frampton one fall morning at the Gibson Guitar Cafe, just around the corner from the Nashville Arena, in downtown Nashville.

I first took an interest in the guitar around 1957 or '58 after watching some of the rock shows that we had then in England. It would probably have been Cliff Richard and The Shadows, Hank Marvin being the lead guitarist of The Shadows, which was sort of a Ventures-type band. I loved both The Shadows and The Ventures and I know both, but I am par- tial to The Shadows only because they are British. [Laughs]

I saw Hank Marvin playing a red Fender Strato- caster and wanted one of those immediately. I also saw Eddie Cochran playing a Gretsch guitar on TV, as well as people like Buddy Holly, who were all playing these American electric guitars. That was the first time I saw elec- tric guitars and got interested.

My first guitar, which my father bought for me, to shut me up I think, was a cheap old nasty steel string, what would be the equiva- lent in England of a Sears acoustic. We don't have Sears there, but I can tell you it was really nasty. If you could play good on that, I guess there was a future in you. Once I realized that I could electrify this acoustic guitar, I bought a pickup, stuck it on, and then plugged it through the family radio as my first amplifier.

My first decent electric was a Hofner. They were German. I guess Paul McCartney had the same problem because he had a Hofner bass, but they were great. What I had was a Hofner Club 60 which was virtually Hofner's version of a Gibson Les Paul. That's where my interest in Gibson guitars started, because I couldn't get or afford something like that. The rhythm guitarist from the original Searchers used to use a Hofner guitar. They had a great sound, were a little difficult to play, but, again, good training. There weren't a lot of American guitars around. In fact, in 1958 — I didn't own an electric at all at that point — when Hank Marvin had that red Stratocaster, I believe it was the first one in England. Cliff Richard had gone to the States and Hank probably said to him, 'Bring me back a Fender, would you?' That was highly regarded.

When the American guitars did arrive in London, they were displayed behind glass in the big music stores, like the Selmer Music Store in the Charing Cross Road area where all the music shops were. You couldn't touch them; they were beyond reach.

As most English guitarists around my age would say, they learned the complete repertoire of The Shadows, and I can still play most of it now. After that, The Beatles came out and we all had to start singing, because we were playing mostly instrumentals up to that point. And then it was just a case of trying to find as many different guitarists who would be influences. When I was about 14, as well as listening like everyone else to Eric Clapton, The Bluesbreakers, The Yardbirds, Jeff Beck, and people like that, who I still listen to, I decided that, even though everybody was going that way and even though the blues, which I love, was a beautiful, seductive style, I decided to go a little bit more to the jazz side. That's when I was in a semi-pro band that played a lot of jazz stuff as well as R&B, so I was given a long list of guitarists that the leader of the band thought it might be a good idea for me to catch up on — Wes Montgomery, Kenny Burrell and Grant Green, who both played with Jimmy Smith, and the very young George Benson, who was playing with the Jack MacDuff Trio when he was about 16.

Django Reinhardt also had a great influence on me early on because my father had brought that album into the house. I hated it to start with because it wasn't The Shadows, it was jazz. [Grimaces] But each time I'd go back and look at the record collection, I'd get it out and play a track from it and all of a sudden that music took over. It became very seductive to listen to. Don't get me wrong, I still can't play like Django, but he's one of those players who have been a terrific influence from the emotion he put into his playing — a sort of gypsy emotion that he had. So I just started listening to as many jazz guitarists as I could — I'd listen to them and try to take a part.

You are the sum of all the parts, aren't you? So, it's not like you consciously say I'm going to play just like that. Hopefully, what happens is you pick and learn from as many people as you can. I'm still doing so and from that comes your own style. I feel I have a pretty recognizable guitar style that is a mix of rock, jazz, and blues. One of the main bands I was with that helped formulate this sort of approach was Humble Pie. We got together to play good rock 'n' roll music, but Steve Marriott was very R&B influenced as well as rock 'n' roll influenced. Then I had my jazz influences. So you've got a rock track with an R&B voice and a jazz lyrical solo over the top, which was pretty unique for that time.

Part of the reason that Humble Pie was as successful as it was was the combination of Steve's intense vocal renditions — he was one of the best singers of all time — and the juxtaposition of the rock sound against the jazz — the down and dirty against sweet and lyrical. This was the way I wanted to go style-wise.

:| |•|•|

Prior to Humble Pie, when I was in a band call The Herd, I went up to London and I wanted to get a Gibson, but the only one I could afford at the time was a short scale, single cut away Melody Maker. It was very thin, but it had a Gibson pick up on it, probably a P-90. I can't remember. It was used immediately, the same day, on a session to create a real sort of overdriven sound. Then I bought a Les Paul. I would go back and forth between all my guitars — Fender, Guild — and then, more and more, I would play the Les Paul. Then I got an SG, and soon it was all Gibsons. That was just my sound; it was a full sound.

When I was touring with Humble Pie in about 1969-70, I was playing on a 61 SG, which I loved, and decided that I wanted to get a 335, cherry semi-acoustic. I swapped the SG for the 335. As it turns out, we were a little loud as a band for a semi-acoustic guitar and when I went to play that night, every time it was my turn for a solo, I'd turn up and it would be wooooo, wooooo — I was feeding back all over the place, so I was obviously a little disappointed about this. We were playing two sets at the Fillmore West, playing with The Grateful Dead, and this guy came up to me after the show and said, 'I see you were having a little problem there.' I said, 'You're not kidding.' I said I wanted to go back to a Les Paul, especially for this band, and he said, 'I'd like you to use my Les Paul tomorrow night.'

So he came to the coffee shop in the morning with the case. It was a three-pickup black Les Paul, like the one you see on the front cover of FRAMPTON COMES ALIVE. I started to sweat. It was beautiful. It had just been re-finished by Gibson, It had a '54 body with the older pickups on. It was a Black Beauty, and he had routed it for three pickups. That basically evolved into what they call 'the Frampton model.' I played it that night and I don't think my feet touched the ground; I was just levitating because it was such a unique guitar.

And that was it. Apart from a number that would need a clean rhythm, where I would use a Fender, it was 90 percent Les Paul and 10 percent Fender from then on. And I really couldn't play anything else. I couldn't even play another Gibson at that point. It was like that was the guitar; you just get locked in. It becomes second nature; an extension of your arm. Obviously, everyone sees it on the FRAMPTON COMES ALIVE cover and associates me with that guitar, but, unfortunately, it left us. In 1980, we went to South America. We were traveling with the equipment most times, but we had a day off so we put all the equipment on a Venezuelan cargo plane and it never really got where it was going, unfortunately. I lost a lot of guitars, but, in the realm of the fact that three people lost their lives in that plane, that was much less important. A guitar you can get again — but maybe not that one. There was something special about that one. At that point it was panic, because I really couldn't play anything else, or felt I couldn't. That was like my partner, my Lucille, if you like.

It was difficult after that. I went out after that tour and literally had no guitars. There were a couple, but most of them went. I had to sort of start again, and I think that out of that negative came a positive thing because then it got to the point where I felt that as long as it was a decent instrument, I could pick it up and play it and feel confident with it. Still, I always gravitate back to a Gibson of some sort. Even though I play a lot of different types of guitars, I have a soft spot for Gibsons.

I make some modifications to the three pickup Les Paul. They had some strange sort of wiring on a three pickup so you couldn't isolate various pickups so basically the third pickup, that most people hate because it gets in the way, doesn't bother me. It's just an added color that I like to blend in with the other two pickups. So really if you forget that third pickup is there, there's a switch to control the two outside pickups and they are on the same two volumes that they would normally be on. One of the tone controls is the master and the other becomes a volume control for the center pickup, so I bring it in or take it out. It's totally separate. The Stratocaster has a center pickup and this is basically a Humbucking version of what that would be. It's a much fuller sound than a single coil. It's a fatter Strat setup, I guess.

[The question of the legendary Frampton voice box technique made popular on FRAMPTON COMES ALIVE is broached.] Oh, I'm sorry. They didn't tell you? I can't talk about that otherwise I'd have to kill you. [Laughs] I'm joking. It's something I get asked a lot about, obviously. In England, at about the same time I was first learning to play guitar, we had only one radio station in England. There's a couple more now, but then it was Radio One and it would play the Top 10 but it would also play big band music . . . it would play everything. There wasn't what you would call a straight rock station. Not like when we came to America the first time and it was like, 'Wow!' There was so much radio. So there was this small radio station in Luxembourg that used to broadcast at night until two in the morning. We always used to listen to that, except that it used to fade in and fade out because it was so far away. Their call sign was Fabulous 208 — that was the number and they used to have this sound like a talk box [that they used in announcing the station call sign.] I would always hear this sound and go, 'Wow! What is that? That's so cool!' I never really thought about one day making my guitar sound like that. I heard the same sound on Stevie Wonder's album MUSIC OF MY MIND. He put the synthesizer through a talk box and did a lot of the backing vocals, or effect vocals, through it. I went, 'Wait a second! There it is again!'

I was doing a session — I played on George Harrison's ALL THINGS MUST PASS record — and for the country-type songs, Bob Dylan had recommended to George that he should bring over Pete Drake, God rest his soul. He was a great guy and a terrific player. He came over and set up right next to me because I was playing acoustic. There was a slow moment in the session and he said, 'Watch this!' and he got out this tiny wooden box and it had a pipe coming out of it. He put the pipe in his mouth and plugged the pedal steel into this little, wooden box and started playing this song, *I Am the Guitar* or *I Am A Guitar*. In the '60s, he had a country hit with that song and I've got it on cassette now. My jaw dropped and I thought of Fabulous 208 and MUSIC OF MY MIND and it all came together, and there he was. There was a big smile on his face because everyone stopped what they were doing and just came right round because it's such a simple gadget but it's so effective. So I said, 'Where do I get one?' He said, 'I made this one and you can't have it.' Or something to that effect.

When I moved to New York from London, I found one and

locked myself away and learned how to talk with the thing. I then introduced it into the song *Do You Feel Like I Do* and also used it for the first time on record on *Show Me the Way*. It was amazing how that seemed to be something that, to this day, people still comment on. They say two things usually: 'I've worn out three copies of FRAMPTON COMES ALIVE' and 'What is that thing?' On my last record I put: 'Guitars, Vocals and What Is That Thing?' I think I'm going to do a book and a Hot Licks video on how to do talk box so people stop asking me. But, no, I don't mind. But it's amazing. Usually, the simpler something is, the more effective it is.

It was interesting to do the Glass Spider tour with David Bowie in 1987 and also to play on the record in Switzerland. We went to school together and we were from the same place. He'd gone off and done his thing and I'd gone off and done my thing, but we'd meet up every now and again. He had the number one single in England in 1969 with *Space Oddity* and we [Humble Pie] had number two with *Natural Born Woman* and we toured England. We had Dave Edmunds on that as well. It was a great tour. I always thought that would be it. I would play on the same stage but never at the same time. I've always been a huge fan of David's. He was like a big brother to me. I'd always looked up to him. He had always been in the local band that I wished I could be in. So when I got the call he said, 'I've just heard your latest record. I love what you're playing guitar-wise. Come over and do that on my next record.' That was about November of '86, and, when I was there, he either put something in my drink or… [Laughs] I'm not sure what it was, but seriously, after a couple of glasses of wine, he got me to say yes to the tour. I was going to say yes anyway even without the wine. For me, it was just great going with David around the world to places where I hadn't had recent records so I couldn't go there on my own. It was a luxury to be able to go to these places on David's ticket, and, what's more, he wanted me to play my favorite David Bowie songs and play guitar solos for two and a half hours for about seven months — and he paid me. So, it was great. It was a bit like being back in Humble Pie because the band was very forceful and high energy and I got to stand out there and do the opening riff to *Rebel, Rebel*, which is killer, as simple as it is, and play on numbers that had been played solo-wise by Stevie Ray Vaughan, Robert Fripp, and Adrian Belew. I obviously played my interpretation of those songs, but to be put in the company of those peers was a very nice feeling.

:| |•|•|

I was seven when I got my first guitar and it became my silent partner in life. It became extremely important to me. At that age, I wasn't chosen all that much for the soccer team, but everybody always wanted me to bring my guitar to school and play the school concert. I was known as Pete, 'The Kid Guitar Player'. If I was happy, I'd go play it; if I was sad, I'd go play it. It was just something, unbeknownst to me at the time, that was almost therapy. I actually started writing instrumentals because of The Shadows. I started writing as soon as I could play three chords. It became extremely important. I'm in the luxurious position of having my hobby be what I do for a living. I've never worked a day in my life. It's hard work doing what you do, but I've never had to get a 9 to 5 job. There's many more hours in this job, but I never really called it a job. I work hard at it, but it's my hobby. Sometimes, I can't get enough of it and sometimes, I'll put it down for awhile. But it's just always there whenever I want it. I play every day. I'll take care of the house and what's going on, everybody goes to bed, then I go to my music room and turn it up....

John Hammond

John Paul Hammond III
Born November 13, 1943
New York, New York

: |John Hammond|·|·|

One of the sweet mysteries in the development of rock music over the years has been the strong affinity felt for blues music by successive generations of young, white musicians and singers with no obvious commonality with a music form rooted in both the despair and the celebration of the simple joys of life of an enslaved people from the deep South of the United States. Strange bedfellows indeed, but through their devotion to the music and their subsequent desire to master it in performance, blues entered the music mainstream and would become the bedrock upon which much of the popular music of the past four decades has been built. In America, artists like Paul Butterfield, Mike Bloomfield, Steve Miller, Charley Musselwhite, Harvey Mandel, Elvin Bishop, Nick Gravenites, Jim Schwall, and Corky Siegel, among others, were on the front-lines of popularizing the electrified, postwar urban blues that was being played in the Negro ghettos of the northern cities. And then there is John Hammond, son of legendary producer and A&R man, John Hammond Jr., who over 35 years and close to the same number of album releases continues to command a loyal following around the world with fans who share his passionate commitment to traditional blues music.

For the record, among his late father's many other major achievements in the world of jazz, folk, blues and rock music, was the production of Billie Holiday's first session in the '30s and, during his later tenure at Columbia Records, the signing of artists like Bob Dylan, Pete Seeger, Leonard Cohen, George Benson, Bruce Springsteen, and Stevie Ray Vaughan to the label.

So the younger Hammond — his late father was actually known as John Hammond Jr. — came to music naturally as he began to develop his chops on blues guitar and harmonica during college before becoming a regular on the New York coffee house scene in 1963. That same year, he recorded the first of many albums which have celebrated the blues in all its various styles and guises over the years. He won a Grammy for his 1984 album BLUES EXPLOSION and has been nominated on three other occasions for the same statue. He was honored with successive W.C. Handy Awards in 1994, 1995, and 1996 and, when the Bravo television network in the United States and Sony Home Video sought out a host for their production, *The Search for Robert Johnson*, Hammond was their natural choice.

Hammond, who still keeps up a rigorous touring schedule, has shared the stage with most of the blues legends over the years, including Muddy Waters, Willie Dixon, John Lee Hooker, B.B. King, and Howlin' Wolf. He has also influenced, toured, and recorded with some of the most important artists in American music, including Bonnie Raitt, J. J. Cale, members of The Band, Duane Allman, Stevie Ray Vaughan, and Dr. John.

We spoke to John Hammond in the loft of his apartment in Jersey City, New Jersey, and, as you will soon see, his enthusiasm for the topic of the blues and his favorite guitars knows no bounds.

I first heard the blues in my early childhood, I guess. My dad was a record producer and worked for Columbia and other labels and he took me to see Big Bill Broonzy when I was about nine or ten years old. Big Bill Broonzy is one of the greatest country/blues players ever, who made many records and traveled to Europe. He was one of those blues ambassadors, a really delightful man and a really great player and singer and a really nice person. My dad knew him and introduced him to me though it didn't really sink in until much later. I remember he [Big Bill Broonzy] had huge hands. I felt dwarfed. I felt like, 'Ooh, god, who is this guy,' but he played the guitar so beautifully, so delicately, at times.

When I was about 14, I used to tune into WLAC [Nashville] and deejays like John R. I'd listen to those shows every night. I sent away to Randy's Record Mart in Gallatin, Tennessee and got my first John Lee Hooker and Muddy Waters and Howlin' Wolf records, and a whole new world opened up for me. This was before I played an instrument. This was when I was just a fan.

I got my first guitar when I was 17 when I was in school in Ohio. It was a Gibson J100 with a big hole kicked in the top and I got it for 10 bucks. It was a great guitar. I got it from Carlotta Jones, who was in need of some money and needed to sell a lot of her stuff. I played that until I went out and got a Gibson J45 with an adjustable bridge. I got that in 1961, and on that Gibson I made my first album for

Vanguard Records in 1962. So between starting to play and record-ing my first record, there was only about a year and a half. Kind of hard to believe, but it's true. I'm in my mid-'50s now so nice career — nice start anyway.

I knew as soon as I began to play that this was what I wanted to do for the rest of my life. All my art school studies and college and stuff went right out the window. I began playing professionally when I was 19. I hitchhiked out to Los Angeles, stopped in Colorado along the way and played some gigs there. When I got to Los Angeles, I started a job at a gas station. One day this Porsche drives up and there's a Martin guitar in the back seat. This big guy gets out and tells me to fill it up. I said, 'Man, that's a beautiful Martin.' It was a D45, one of those expensive Martins. He said, 'Oh do you play?' I said, 'Yeah.' He said, 'Well play me a tune.' It was Hoyt Axton. He said, 'Man, you sound good. I'll get you a gig,' and he got me a gig at a club in Southgate called the Satyr Club. It was a paying gig and that's all she wrote. That was the beginning of many, many gigs.

:| |•|•|

*W*ith blues you can't help but be reverential if you love the music and you see the blues as being a traditional folk art. It's like some-thing that's handed on and handed down, but there's no two people alike. You're going to sound like yourself, even if you are trying to play it note for note like Robert Johnson, that's just the way that it is. Inspiration is inspiration and when you feel that incredible drive to do something from inspiration, there's no limits to it, no bounds.

Robert Johnson was the synthesis of all the blues artists from the middle 1920s through the middle '30s. He had listened to Charlie Patton and Son House and Lonnie Johnson and Blind Lemon Jefferson; he heard all the great ones and he came up with his own special style and sound. He was a phenomenal player and a great singer with a great voice. He was so intense and his songs were so vivid. The lyrics just had you right there.

There's definite links to all blues in terms of stylistic sound. The majority of Chicago blues is guys who moved up from the Delta area — not all — but a lot of guys moved up from Arkansas and Mississippi and Tennessee straight up Highway 61 to Chicago. There was more work there, less racism, and electric guitars came out in 1938 or so. Sure enough, bands and combos formed and a Chicago sound was born. It was based on the Delta sound, I guess. It just sort of progressed from there into drums and bass, harmonica, electric harmonica, and all that stuff, but it all came from the Delta sound and the Robert Johnson style. [Demonstrates]

I'm a traditional blues singer. Mostly, I record songs that I've heard over the years and just love and I've added my own two cents to play it my way. I'm a traditional blues singer, and therefore, when I go into record, I want it to be stuff that really sounds good, songs that hit me in a way that I think ought to be shared.

Back in the '50s, when I first got into the blues and became aware of the incredible depth of the music and how many stylists there were and how many good artists had gotten to record, I was exposed to the music of John Lee Hooker. There was an album on VeeJay called I'M JOHN LEE HOOKER. I heard this voice and it sounded like this man must have been nine feet tall. I imagined him as the kind of guy who ate three whole chickens at a sitting. The voice was that of a giant. In 1963, I was on the Newport Folk Festival on which John Lee also appeared. I'm waiting to see this guy, you know, this nine-foot giant, and this guy walks past me — he's about five foot five or so — and I heard him talking to somebody, and I realized *that's* John Lee Hooker, like a head shorter than me. I couldn't believe it. And he got up and just played acoustic guitar and opened his mouth and this incredible voice came out and the audience went nuts. He's a phenomenal guy. I got to play some gigs with him in clubs beginning that same year in 1963. I've known him now for over 30 years. I've worked on a lot of shows with him. I got the chance to record with him about five years ago, and once he recorded with me on an album, and it thrilled me to the core. To get to meet an idol of yours and to be able to share your thoughts with them, I feel so lucky.

Blues and early country music were so akin. They took from each other. The United States being a country of immigrants basically, there are little bits of culture from all over the world that make up blues and early country stuff. It's all connected and related. It's one of those wonderful phenomena to have a music spring up that's unique and yet there are little traces of other cultures in it too. It's just wonderful. Blues is popular all over the world as is country music. It's soulful, passionate stuff ... it translates, it just does.

:| |•|•|

I remember when I first got my Les Paul. I had a gig at The Fillmore East for Bill Graham. I had my band together. I was wearing a snakeskin suit, can you imagine? I had a suit made from a python skin backed with leather. It looked so cool, but, god, on the stage under the lights, I thought I was going to die, it was so hot. But I had to look cool and the guitar was so great. I've got a million stories and losses too. I've had guitars stolen from me that just broke my heart, and I had to go out and replace them. That's not easy to do when you get into a really nice instrument. It's tough to have to replace it and go looking for the one that has that sound. I've been very lucky and fortunate in my career. I've had nice things fall into my lap or come my way or I was fortunate enough to have enough bucks to buy what I needed and so, I'm just a lucky guy.

In 1965, I did my first tour of England. I went over there with my Gibson J45 guitar and I played for two months — I went by train. I was lucky enough to fall into meeting guys like John Mayall and Eric Clapton and Donovan and Graham Bond and Stevie Winwood, to name only a few. I was hanging out with Brian Jones; in fact, I stayed with him in his flat in Chelsea for a while. It was the right place at the right time and I got to meet these phenomenal players. It doesn't matter where you are from, if you are inspired by music, you transcend language, you transcend nationality, and you just become the music. That's what I found over in England. There was so much passion for blues and rock 'n' roll and country music. It doesn't matter where you're from, if you've got it, you've got it. Eric Clapton, to me, is one of the greatest musicians I have ever met. What a great player and what a great guy! The guy is admirable. I admire him so much. He comes from England, but, god, there are very few guys who can play blues like that. I've had those rare chances to be in the right place, at the right time.

I've also had a lot of great times recording. I think, perhaps, the most dynamic one that I ever had up to that point was in 1964. I had friends from Toronto whom I had met: Robbie Robertson, Levon Helm, Richard Manuel, Garth Hudson, Rick Danko, who later became The Band. I had become good friends with them up in Toronto, and when they were in New York playing some gigs, I asked them if they'd like to record with me on my next album and everybody said, 'Yeah, great!' We had one day to make an album. My friends Michael Bloomfield and Charley Musselwhite were in New York from Chicago and we got everybody together in the same place. Bob Dylan came up to watch the session and we had a great time and made an album [SO MANY ROADS] in a day. That was dynamic. It was a good record, too.

Because I'm solo artist, I'm very dependent on carrying the whole sound — the bass, the middle, and the treble. A Gibson guitar, to me anyway, has had the big bottom end on which you can ride on top. Without the big bottom, I'm lost. With the Gibson, not only is the neck just right — I don't know how to put it into words exactly — but there's something about the feel of a really great neck and having a guitar that instantly sounds like what you want it to sound like. Gibson is a tradition also. They've been making great guitars for a hundred years or more and it has always been a blues player's guitar. Their electric guitars have always been one of the major choices of blues artists, the Les Paul being a classic.

I bought my first Les Paul in 1963 and paid four hundred bucks for it, which was about normal at that time. That was a hot guitar, a gold top. I had seen a photograph of Muddy Waters playing a gold top Les Paul, so when I saw one in a store, I said, 'Ah, that's what I want!' and I got it. I played that guitar on so many records and so many gigs when I had my band together. That was my instrument. I've owned other electric guitars by Gibson. I've had a Byrdland and I still have my 1959 ES330. It's just beautiful. I'm fortunate enough now to be in possession of a Blues King, which I'm afraid to take out too often. I play a lot of clubs where things get knocked over. If I have an elegant concert to play or a recording date, that's when this guitar [Blues King] comes out and it makes me look good. The Blues King is probably the nicest electric acoustic guitar that I've ever seen. It has got full control right at your fingertips, literally, for volume, voice, tone, and all kinds of effects. The audience wouldn't even know you're doing it. It can plug into an amplifier and it can also plug in direct. It has got the dual switch in the back and it's got a fantastic action. I'm not a good spokesperson, I don't think, but I really do love this instrument. The first time I got to play this guitar in the studio was on the FOUND TRUE LOVE album and it could do anything. Acoustic, it sounds great. Plugged in, it sounds great. It's a wonderful instrument to play. It's important to have that feeling of confidence that your instrument is there for you.

I always take my guitars to a guy named Bob Jones in Brooklyn. He does the best work on guitars of anyone I've ever met. He does all of my repair work and this and that. I brought this guitar [Blues King] over to him to have it set up and he said, 'Oh man, this is beautiful!' but there was a little piece under the fingerboard that was incorrect, so he fixed it and it cost a couple of hundred bucks. I told my friend Merle Saunders [at Gibson] about the fact that I had some repair work done on it and he said, 'Oh man, you should have sent it back, we would have done it for free.' And I said, 'Well now it's really mine!' So this is my guitar and even though it was a gift from Gibson, I've got my stamp on it. [Laughs]

For solo artists, the guitar was always multi-purpose, because there was rhythm and lead and whatever, but in a band context, before the electric guitar, a lot of guitar players had steel body guitars with a resonator so that they could be heard over the other instruments. I think when the National Guitars came out, that was the first time the guitar could be heard over the band. Then, when the electric guitar came out, it eclipsed all of the steel guitars, and all of a sudden, you could be heard over the horn section. You just turn up the dial and you got it. Charlie Christian, Les Paul — there were so many early electric guitar wizards that changed the whole concept of band blues. The guitar really came to the foreground with them. You could do so much with it. Guys who I've admired playing electric guitar are guys like T Bone Walker, a phenomenal musician and a stylist who had obviously heard a lot of Charlie Christian. There was also Les Paul and Merle Travis, but the list is endless. There was a formative time when electric guitar first hit the scene and guys were just finding out how much could be done. Then you find a guy like Jimi Hendrix. He took the guitar up even another notch. What a virtuoso! That guy was phenomenal. I guess there's always another strata of guitar development.

I have a Gibson L1, the model they say that Robert Johnson played, or one like it anyway. This is made in Montana in the new factory up there. It's a beautiful instrument. I love it. The balance of it is just right and the neck action is fantastic.

[Pulls out guitar] This is a 1947 Country Western model. It's a J45 basically with a fancy neck and it's one of the nicest guitars I have ever owned or have ever played. I've probably had this from 1965 until now — 31 years, that's a long time. It belonged to Buck Graves — Josh Graves — who played with Flatt & Scruggs. I actually went up to him and asked him if this was once his guitar and he said, 'Yeah, that was my old kick around guitar.' I got a kick out of that. So, this is one of the beauties. It's all original except for this little truss rod plate which I got from my friend Matt Humanoff. It says "Johnny" on it in silver, so I thought that was cool.

I play everyday. I always have a guitar out. In my apartment, I have a stand with either a steel body guitar, an acoustic guitar, or a 12-string on it just to have around so I can have fun.

Guitars are really special and important to me. I'm very fussy and particular with what I like to have as my own and to be seen on stage with. I've always felt that I needed to have something I was completely satisfied with or I'd just feel lame. I've always tried to have an instrument that suited my style and esthetics. It had to look right. It had to be the right sound. I don't want to sound like a shill or anything, but Gibsons are my ideal of a beautiful instrument that has the right sound, the right look, and the right history. Robert Johnson played a Gibson, and if it's alright with Robert, it's alright with me.

Emmylou Harris

Emmylou Harris
Born April 2, 1947
Birmingham, Alabama

: | Emmylou Harris |·|·|

In the music world, the late '90s will be remembered, in part, for the enormous chart success enjoyed by female singer/songwriters, many of whom acknowledge earlier trail-blazers like Joni Mitchell, Bonnie Raitt, Rickie Lee Jones, and Emmylou Harris as inspirations in their work. Suggest this to Ms. Harris directly and the endlessly gracious lady deflects the suggestion. "I don't really consider myself an influence," she told Steve Hammer during a conversation following the release of her critically acclaimed WRECKING BALL album. "As far as a working woman on the road, yes. But a lot of us have been out there a long time, My God, Bonnie Raitt has been out there for years. Loretta Lynn — she's been out there. I know what you're saying. It seems like there's been this female population explosion. There are a lot of great women out there — Shawn Colvin, Nanci Griffith, and, of course, Tracy Chapman is making great records; The McGarrigles have always made great records. It does seem like there have been a lot of young'uns coming around. [Laughs]"

Back in the early '70s, Harris, who was the 1996 recipient of the Orville H. Gibson Lifetime Achievement Award at the Gibson Guitar Awards at the Hard Rock Cafe in Los Angeles and was a featured performer on the much-publicized Lilith Fair tour a few years later, was herself a youthful aspirant to a career in music as she frequented the Greenwich Village folk scene in New York, playing solo as well as sharing the stage with such folk music notables as Jerry Jeff Walker and David Bromberg. It was here that she was discovered in 1971 by Chris Hillman of The Byrds and subsequently introduced to the late Gram Parsons who bade her come to Los Angeles to work on his first solo album, GP. At the time of Parsons tragically premature death in 1973, they were linked personally and professionally, having toured the U.S. together with the group the Fallen Angels and recorded the album, GRIEVOUS ANGEL. Parsons' influence on Harris' musical vision from that point on, especially in her subsequent love affair with country music, cannot be understated.

In 1974, returning to Washington, D.C., she formed a country group with which she performed until 1975, the year of the release of her debut album for Reprise Records, PIECES OF THE SKY. She formed the highly acclaimed Hot Band during this period, which over the years has featured the cream of the crop of Nashville players including James Burton, Albert Lee, Glen D. Hardin, Buddy Miller, Sam Bush, Rodney Crowell, and Hank DeVito.

Since 1970, Harris has released close to 30 albums, picked up a half dozen Grammy Awards, and in 1980 was named the Country Music Association's Female Vocalist of the year. In 1992, she was inducted into the Grand Ol' Opry in Nashville and was presented with the Academy of Country Music's Minnie Pearl Humanitarian Award.

At the time of writing, Harris's live record, SPYBOY, was in the stores and she was anticipating the imminent release of the second edition of the award-winning TRIO album she had recorded with Linda Ronstadt and Dolly Parton.

We spoke to Emmylou Harris on a November morning in the living room of her home in Nashville, Tennessee about the role of her chosen instrument, the guitar, in her music.

I remember I was at a relative's house one Christmas — I was about sixteen — and my cousin had gotten a guitar for Christmas. I spent the whole day just sitting around plunking on it. I'd never been around a guitar before. I had been one of those children who had taken piano lessons unsuccessfully and I really didn't think I had any real musical talent. I had played clarinet and saxophone in high school, but I never really had an affinity for an instrument until I came across the guitar. There was an instant bonding. So, I asked for a guitar and my grandfather got me a $30 Kay guitar from a pawn shop in Birmingham, Alabama. I had to really want to play that guitar because it was quite painful to push the strings down. I still have the scars. When I was able to make a little money at different jobs, I bought my first Gibson, which was a J50. I was off and running after that.

We lived south of Washington, D.C. and could pick up the radio station from the American University which had a show that ran from 7:00 pm to midnight every night that featured folk music. I heard Ian & Sylvia, Son House, everything from black country/blues to modern singer/songwriters like Eric Anderson and, of course, Bob

Dylan, Judy Collins, Joan Baez. I heard a lot of music and I listened every night. I was in my room listening to the radio, doing homework, plunking around on the guitar. There really wasn't a lot of music or anything like that happening in my social circle; I taught myself to play the guitar and, anytime I heard something I liked, I would just get the record and try to figure out what was going on. I had two 'Introduction to Folk Music' books and whenever I did run across somebody who played the guitar, I would try to get them to teach me something. I was sort of in my own little bubble, isolated.

There was a certain intensity about the lyrics of folk music that appealed to me. When you're a teenager, you're very intense and full of idealism about life, and these songs tended to deal with tragedy. There were the old Child ballads, and then the modern songs dealt with social issues. I liked the immediacy of the lyrics and the melodies. Also, for the most part, they were pretty simple with only three chords so I could play them too. I found something that I connected with. Before that, most of the singing that I had done had been in church, in choirs, where the songs are pitched a bit high. I never really thought I had much of a voice because I wasn't comfortable up there in the higher atmospheres, but, with the folk songs, everything was down kind of lower and I could pitch it anywhere I wanted since I was accompanying myself. So it was a way to find my own voice and learn to sing and it was something I could do on my own. It didn't require anybody else around. I didn't really run with a big social circle in high school. I was a bit of a loner.

One of the people I had endless admiration for was Pete Seeger, and in the early days I wrote him a long letter. I got the feeling that he was just a great man, somebody who did what he loved and was passionate about it. I think it was just a way of reaching out in my isolation. Of course, that letter keeps coming up. Never write a letter unless you want the whole world to know about it. It was wonderful, though. He replied and he gave me some good advice. He basically told me not to worry about the fact that I had no experience and had not lived life and haven't suffered enough to sing music. He added, you'll suffer soon enough. [Laughs]. He said, 'Don't worry, life will come to you and catch up to you.'

When I started out professionally, I didn't really work the club circuit that much but I did play clubs in Virginia Beach actually. I was working as a waitress in the day and singing in the clubs at night. There were some pretty nice little clubs down there. There was a place called The Upstairs in Virginia Beach and a place called The Folk Ghetto in Norfolk and I played those two places on the weekend. I was trying to earn money to go to Boston University to continue studying drama because, at that point, I thought I still wanted to be an actress. But, the more I did music, the more I realized that music was my true calling, my true love and true passion, and perhaps my talent didn't really lie in acting.

When I decided to actually make my living at music and went up to New York, that's when I found that it was much more difficult. A lot of the clubs that I thought were still happening were closed down. The Gaslight wasn't there at that point and I ended up playing in basket houses for very little money and eventually had to go back to the only other thing I knew how to do, which was waitressing. There was the occasional time when The Bitter End would have somebody cancel, like a third opening act, and they knew they could call me on a moment's notice and have me come down and play. Gerdes Folk City also gave me some work. John and Mike Porco were wonderful in that way, so I was able to make a bit of a living. I really wasn't on the circuit and never was really able to make it as a folk singer. I think that at that point that whole scene, that I thought had been very vital, was kind of in decline. So I continued to work as a waitress and I got married and had a child at that point. I was pretty much out of the loop musically. The only thing that brought me back into it was the financial consideration, once I had moved back to Washington, D.C. to live with my parents after my marriage broke up. I was just trying to find a way to make a living and it was either waitressing or music and fortunately there was sort of a club scene happening in Washington, D.C. and I was able to work in different clubs there six or seven nights a week. That was where Gram Parsons heard me.

Before I met Gram Parsons, I had done some country but mainly tongue-in-cheek. I didn't think that I really had a talent for country and don't think I was really interested in doing country until I met Gram. He made me see the subtleties of it and the poetry in it. And singing with him really taught me how to sing. There was something about the restraint and the economy of the emotion that goes along with, first of all, singing harmony and, secondly, with singing harmony with country music. That is a real lesson in singing. It gave me a sense of style that I didn't have before because I had a voice, but I don't think I really knew what to do with it. I really believe that it was working with Gram that made me into a singer.

: | | • | •|

If I'm learning a song, I have to learn it on guitar. I'll write the lyrics down and then I find the key on the guitar, then I'll learn it on the guitar. How I play it is going to have something to do with how I end up singing it. While working with the band during the recording process, I will have worked up the song. I'll have found the key and I'll play it for them. What's been great about my musicians is that they have never made me feel like I'm just the rhythm guitar player — now let us take over and do the real work. In fact, they've always kind of honored what I've brought to the song as a guitar player, on the groove and the particular feel. A lot of the things I play might fall between the cracks as far as having a distinctive feel, and so the drummers, in particular, would play to what I was playing because it would have to do with how I was singing the song. If the rhythm section of the band takes that away from the singer, then all of a sudden whatever unique thing that the singer is trying to bring to the song is taken away. At least for me it's worked that way. And then there are songs that I have done which have a particular rhythm that I can't play particularly well and I just respond as a singer, at least in the recording process. Later on, on stage, I might find something that I can play.

Oddly enough, in this new band that I've got — it's just four pieces, including myself — I've been playing a lot more rhythm guitar that has a real kind of central position in the band. I've really enjoyed that. I find myself playing a lot more aggressively and playing right along with the drummer. That has been a real treat for me.

It's hard to describe my playing style. It's just something I developed and I don't exactly know what it is. I play holding a flat pick with my index finger and my thumb, and even when I finger pick, I do it that way. When I started originally, I used a thumb pick and finger picks, but I'm a person who loses things and I could never keep track of them. Everybody has got a flat pick on them, so, if you run out of picks, you just ask if anybody has a flat pick and you're all set to go. In fact, I find them everywhere. If I want to find a flat pick, I go down to the washing machine. That's usually where they all end up.

Depending on the song, I do like to play on the records because I find that, once again, I respond to the actual rhythm of my playing. But there are some situations where it gets in the way or we don't really need another acoustic guitar or maybe it's just better to cut the track with less instruments and leave a little more space. I would say that we always start by trying to put my guitar on it.

The WRECKING BALL album was different. I was working with a whole new team of people, including the producer and the musicians. There were a lot of unusual rhythms that I really responded to that were really exciting to sing to. I played quite a lot of guitar on that record.

One of the exciting things about acoustic guitars is that everybody ends up with their own particular style. It's like a fingerprint. Everybody comes up with something different.

I think I've always had an economy of playing because I didn't really play anything but rhythm. But I don't know if my playing has to do with my singing or my singing has to do with my playing because they're so connected. I'll work up a song and a lot of the phrasing will have to do with how I'm playing guitar — the feel that I get while playing the guitar. The guitar has always been very, very important to what I do as a singer.

I think there are some great rhythm guitar players. Don Everly is certainly one and then there's Keith Richards. People think of him as the great rock 'n' roll guitar player, but, when you think about it, it's just that great rock 'n' roll rhythm that he plays that does more for me than all the stuff going up and down the neck that a lot of other guitar players do. It's the groove that he gets on the acoustic guitar. That up-stroke… that's it; for me it's rock 'n' roll. I love Joni Mitchell's open tuning. I love the way she plays guitar. I do a lot of open tuning things. Tom Rush is another one — a lot of the folk guitar players like Joan Baez and Ian & Sylvia.

:| |•|•|

The J200s are just a great rhythm guitar, especially when you're limited to playing chords and rhythm. You want something that has a really full sound and just really feels good in your hand. There's probably nothing better than an A chord played on a Gibson J200. I really love the sound of it. It was 1976 before I actually discovered the J200. I'd had the J50, then I'd bought an SJN, but it wasn't until 1976 when I was living in LA and was friends with Fred Wallachy who runs Westwood Music. He called me and said he had a guitar that he wanted me to see. It was a Sunburst J200 that had belonged to Joe Walsh. I played it and bought it. That sort of started a love affair with the J200s. That guitar was actually stolen — though I eventually got it back — and I replaced it with the black J200 that became the one with the Rose. It became one of my side missions in life to find J200s because, in addition to liking the way they sounded, I looked on them as works of art, too, because I think they're quite beautiful in their design and structure. They're great, especially for country and rock 'n' roll. I have quite a few now.

I also have Martins; I love Martins. They're great for picking and they're great for bluegrass. They have a certain shimmer to them. In general, J200s are loud and they work great with electric instruments.

You can hear them over top of electric instruments and there's just a certain feel to those big chords. They sound big. When they're really good, they have a real evenness of tone. You really hear the low-end, the mids, and the highs. It all comes together in just one beautiful sound. You get used to the feel of the neck. Of course, the necks are different too. The neck on this guitar [J200] is very thin, and, as a matter of fact, Gibson have made a copy of this guitar for me. In measuring the neck, the neck is actually thicker on one side than the other. I got very used to that, so sometimes it's a little difficult for me when a guitar is not custom-made for me to get used to it not having that slight variation in the width or the diameter. And then you have the real thick neck J200s. I have an SJ200. It's a great sounding guitar and it's great to play, but you have to get used to it because it's a thicker neck. I tend to prefer the thinner necks, but this has such a great tone on it. This is the guitar that was used on all the songs that I play on WRECKING BALL.

The J200 I'm holding now belonged to Gram Parsons. I was able to buy the guitar a few years after his death. The person who had it came to me and she had it in a warehouse somewhere and I bought it sight unseen. I had seen it briefly when I knew Gram, but, at that point, he was not playing it. He was playing another guitar that he had bought, but he had shown it to me and he had shown me where it had had a run-in with an airplane baggage handler. You can see where it was fixed, right here, and another piece was put in. It was not a part of the tour that Gram and I did, but I knew about the guitar. I bought it not knowing whether it was going to be anything that was playable since it had been in a warehouse and was kind of in pieces. I think the bridge was off and there were various other problems, so I gave it to someone who put it back together and it turned out to be a fantastic guitar. It sounded great. It stayed in tune. It loves the road. It didn't matter how many times it got knocked around, it's one of those guitars that stays in tune no matter how high up you capo it, so it became my premier guitar, the number one guitar. I've had it out on the road for almost 10 years and I'm just in the process of thinking about retiring it because I think that it's starting to feel the weight of its years. It will still continue to be a great guitar and be played by me, but I think it might live in the music room because Gibson has been kind enough to make me a couple of new guitars that I'm quite happy with that I think are going to be able to take its place well enough for me to leave this home.

My newest J200 is the Montana Gold model which is great for playing a shuffle or a waltz. I took it to the Cowgirl Hall of Fame for the 'Patsy Montana' award, so I named it Patsy in honor of Miss Montana.

I also own a six-string guitar and a six-string bass because there were a couple of songs that I needed to work up on those particular instruments because of the sonics of it. I did a live album back in 1982 and I wanted to play a song called *Buckaroo*, which is an instrumental written by Don Rich and originally performed with Buck Owens. This was part of my vision of the record, so I bought a pink, paisley Fender Telecaster in honor of James Burton, who had been in my band early on. I taught myself to play *Buckaroo*. It was the only time I ever learned to play a lead, and I did manage to get a pretty good cut of it live and it went on the album. But, shortly after that, I decided that I don't have that facility in my brain to play lead parts. I'm a lead singer and a rhythm guitar player and I'm very happy with that, thank you very much.

It's really important to play your guitars regularly. I'm always working in a sense. You're always trying to think about the next project. When I come back off the road, I try to come in here and play the guitars and listen to music. I also keep a couple of guitars upstairs in my bedroom as well. You need to play your guitars. I had a guitar that was in a closet at a house where I was living in LA and I hadn't played it in a long time. I got it out one night to show it to somebody and there was a crack in the guitar. I thought, 'God, it's like abandoning or leaving your child in a closet, not knowing what was going on.' I don't want to collect instruments just because they're an investment. Any guitar that I've bought is a guitar that I love to play, that sounds good; it's not because it looks good. I know I said I like J200s because they look so beautiful, but some of them sound great and some of them don't. Some of them you have a bonding with and some of them you don't. It's because you like to play them and I think it's important to try to play all the guitars. Every guitar has a slightly different sound. Each guitar has it's own place where it kind of shines, just like people.

Guitars are not only an extension of yourself but also a tool. If you are a workman, then you need your tools. Part of your life is wrapped up in your work. I don't know what would happen if guitars disappeared from the face of the earth. I don't really play another instrument. I have a piano and I plunk around on that a little bit, but nothing has the affinity for me that the guitar does. We'd just have to invent them all over again.

Justin Hayward

THE MOODY BLUES

David Justin Hayward
Born October 14, 1946
Swindon, England

:|Justin Hayward|·|·|

The Moody Blues, who formed in Birmingham, England in the spring of 1964, immediately took their place on the front line of the British Invasion of the international pop charts in the mid-'60s with their irresistible cover of Bessie Banks' U.S. R&B hit, *Go Now*. This first incarnation of the group, which at the time was comprised of Denny Laine (later to become a member of Paul McCartney's Wings), Ray Thomas, Mike Pinder, Graeme Edge, and Clint Warwick, stayed together until October of 1966. The split, which may well be the shortest in rock history, lasted about a month before Thomas, Pinder, and Edge recruited John Lodge and Justin Hayward to the band as a second version of The Moody Blues was born.

Hayward's impact on the group's future musical direction was felt almost immediately as his *Nights In White Satin* composition from the group's concept album, DAYS OF FUTURE PASSED, recorded with the London Festival Orchestra, helped to bring the group their first U.S. gold record. *Nights In White Satin* was re-released in 1972 and peaked at Number 2 on the U.S. charts on its way to sales of more than a million copies.

Hayward, who is not often given credit for his outstanding lead guitar work and vocals within the group given the Moodys' tight orchestral arrangements, had already made a reputation for himself on the British music scene as a solo recording artist and as a member of various backing groups for Marty Wilde, one of England's top stars at the time, before joining The Moody Blues. Today, with a handful of solo albums to his credit as well as the album BLUE JAYS, recorded with band mate John Lodge during the group's close to four-year hiatus in the mid-to-late '70s, Hayward, along with the remaining original members of the group, Ray Thomas, John Lodge, and Graeme Edge, must surely look back in wonder that three decades have passed since *Nights In White Satin* heralded the group's re-emergence onto the rock scene. With 13 studio albums and a couple of live recordings to their credit, The Moody Blues continue to record and tour extensively today, playing to standing room only crowds of devoted fans, particularly in America.

We spoke to Justin Hayward on an autumn afternoon in the courtyard of his home at Kingston-on-Thames in England following a break in the action for the group after a lengthy summer tour. Hayward came armed with his beloved cherry red Gibson 335 and some guitar stories from those "days of future passed."

I loved music as a kid and sang as a child. Because I was so enthusiastic, my parents sent me to have piano lessons like a lot of kids — I was maybe five or six — but I couldn't handle the mathematics of it. And then I would see pictures in the paper of people with guitars and ukuleles. I just kind of knew that what I wanted was to stand there and sing. I wanted to stand, sing, and play, and there's not many things you can do that with. You don't want anything sticking in your mouth, so a ukulele seemed like the right instrument. After listening to the light program on BBC, I convinced my parents to buy me a uke and I learned to play that real easy.

There was a guy here in England that a lot of English boys will acknowledge as an influence on them in the '50s, a guy called George Formby. He did all those songs that were really easy to learn on uke, and when Skiffle came along, the uke was perfect for that as well. After that, my parents used to read a newspaper called the *News Chronicle*, and in it an advert ran for a guitar that you could buy by mail-order. It was about £2.10 and I pestered them and pestered them and they finally sent off for this guitar. I saved up for a pickup to put on it and I converted the radio, like all kids used to do, so you could plug a guitar into it, and then I was away.

Right at the beginning, in the early '50s, I suppose my greatest influence was Johnny Ray. I was born in 1946, so he was the first one I remember singing with that lonely kind of voice. In England, the beginnings of rock 'n' roll were just a sort of dim reflection of what Elvis and Bill Haley were playing, but my first rock 'n' roll hero was Buddy Holly in 1957. That was it. I knew exactly what it was that I wanted to do because there was Buddy Holly to be an example for us as well as artists like Eddie Cochran and The Everly Brothers.

The first professional job I had when I left school — I was very lucky really — came as the result of answering an ad in *Melody*

Maker. It said, 'Name singer wants backing guitarist.' I went up to a place in East London and Marty Wilde, a big rock singer in the early '60s, answered the door and it was like, 'Wow!' And it *was* like a 'Wow!' as well because I'm six foot two but Marty's six foot five, so I spent the next two and a half years knowing what it was like to be shorter. I got the job playing with Marty's backing group. It was a baptism of fire, but it was great.

When I started playing professionally with Marty Wilde, I had a Gibson 335 I'd bought when I was at school. I had saved up enough by playing a lot of gigs when I was at school to buy it. This 335 had a stop tail piece, a cherry one, and I had that one when I was with Marty, but I actually didn't use it because Marty was playing guitar himself. He had a beautiful old J200, a sunburst one, not a blonde one, and I was playing bass most of the time. When I played electric guitar, I was playing a Vox, one of those organy type sound things. Unusual sounds — a very wide, versatile sound — and only occasionally would I use the 335.

To this day, I've still got the 1958 catalog from Gibson when they first introduced the 335. That catalog was my bedtime reading. I loved the shape and the look of that guitar and the picture of the guy playing it in the catalog was a great pose. Chuck Berry was using a 355 or 345, I think, the same style of guitar, and it just looked great when I first saw him at Swindon, my home town. The sound he got from it was great, real clanky, a kind of dirty-old sound. And then, of course, a lot of bands like The Beatles, the Liverpool and Manchester groups, started using them as well. You put it together with a Vox amp and it's got a particular sound that's very, very versatile. It's a great rhythm guitar and switches easily to lead, so I always loved it.

The day before I joined the Moodys, I got a call from Mike Pinder to join his band. I was about 18 or 19 years old at the time and I'd really run out of money. This was just after playing with Marty, and I'd just sold my first 335, a '61, and it was like, 'Oh, no, I've got a job and I've just sold my guitar,' so I had to go out and buy a Telecaster. But I found another 335, a '63, in 1967 and I bought it.

It's a guitar that you either love or you don't. Some players just stay with it always. On our first tour of America with the Moodys in 1968, we supported Cream on their farewell tour, and Eric Clapton was using a 335 then, same as mine but without the tremolo, and I noticed that he would use it on the front pickup with a lot of the bass rolled off. I loved the sound that he got, a real kind of singing sound through those Marshall amps, and he was able to switch very easily. I'm the only guitar player in the Moodys — we never had a rhythm guitar player — so if I'd stop playing rhythm, the bottom would drop out of the sound. But, with the 335, you could always kind of cheat and keep it going, it had such a wide sound.

I found out a long time ago, again with the AC30 [amp] and particularly the normal input with the 335, if you turn it full up and maybe take some of the treble off, you could really get the combination to sing. This guitar [335] is so perfect for that kind of sustain. I know it sounds a bit 'Spinal Tap', but it really does sum it up. This guitar is able to vibrate, particularly with this kind of unusual tremolo arm — the arm only comes to [there] instead of right round [here] like it is on most guitars. It's easy to play down by the bridge and just lay your hand on the tremolo to correct the pitch just a little bit. Not to move it, just to correct it. So you can coax it in and keep a sustain going that vibrates through the whole guitar.

I got my sound initially with the Vox amp turned full up, and after that I discovered a little Marshall fuzz-box. I've never seen another one. They made it for a few years in the '60s, I imagine. I bought it right then, and it gave the perfect fuzz sound combined with the 335 guitar and an AC30. But then I've gone on since and gone past the AC30s. This guitar [335] sounds great to me with any kind of amp. Its got a special character and a color about it. If you get a good 335, its the best guitar you'll ever own. The awkward part is on the third string sometimes. It's a little bit dodgy intonation-wise on the third string, but you just have to feel that and correct it.

:| |•|•|

You know, a lot of people think that the first concert we did with the symphony was back in the '60s, but we didn't. We made an album with the London Festival Orchestra, but we never played with them on stage. The first time we actually played live with an orchestra was in September of 1992 at Red Rocks in Colorado. I assumed at the beginning of that experience that I would have to be very quiet with my guitar playing and just do acoustic stuff. My first instinct was to start with an acoustic guitar to be like them, all kind of woody and precise. It does work but, once they get some volume going, they need to be able to hear the harmonies and how to make it harmonic and gel together and this suits that purpose. This guitar [335] would blend in perfectly. In fact, the orchestras always liked it when they heard this guitar. It had a width and a size about it that really could help them along harmonically. It put a nice glow around the harmonics and it helped them with their pitching and their tuning. It wasn't quite so woody as having all acoustic instruments with it so, slowly, over more than 200 orchestral concerts, I'd come back to doing most of the orchestral shows with this guitar and maybe just a stereo splitter, just to give it a bit of width between two amplifiers, a Mesa Boogie and a Fender.

We did the first album with the orchestra and then it was our own insecurity that made us say, 'Well, we've done that and I wonder if people just like the orchestra or whether they like the Moodys.' Our second album was just us and we never made another album with an orchestra after that. It was always to try and test it to just make sure that it was really us that they liked and not identifying with that big sound.

I have to say, I have seen a lot of other bands work with an orchestra but I've never seen anyone do it as well as the Moodys. That's because we've got the songs that just work for it.

In the beginning, we saw ourselves as really an 'art rock' band. We wanted to be reviewed in *The Guardian* cultural section, or whatever. That was our idea. We never thought in terms of what we were doing having a mass appeal, and I think it really surprised us that it did. It took us a few years to actually register that this music was going to be heard everywhere. It took a long while for us to get our act together in that way and to become aware of that and not always just think of it as a small cottage industry. But, in the '70s, there was a resurgence, particularly in 1972 when *Nights In White Satin* from DAYS OF FUTURE PASSED, our first album, got to number one five years after it was released. Suddenly, that orchestral thing became the vogue again in the '70s and the whole pretentious rock thing took off again and there we were.

These days, in the U.K., we can sell a concert tour out, but it's hard finding a promoter that's brave enough to put his money where his mouth is. I think we'll always be able to play in this country and we enjoy it every time we do but it's just that the market for us is in America.

:| |•|•|

I'm primarily a songwriter, and I don't think there are very many people who come to a concert to watch my left hand really, but I have a particular style that a lot of people enjoy and I think that has always seen me through. I've certainly been interviewed and have had interest shown by all the guitar magazines down through the years, no matter how old the boys and girls are who write for them, so somebody must like it.

I often think that this guitar [Gibson 335], particularly, sometimes plays me, instead of me playing it. I can relax totally with it. This guitar means the world to me and I can't imagine life without it. I don't want to tempt anybody to nick [steal] it — it's not worth nicking — it just has value to me, but that's all you'd have to do if you wanted to hurt me. But it's a friend and it's something... let's just say that my wife understands it. My wife has always understood my relationship with this guitar. You're never alone with a guitar. It's a whole orchestra as well. I'm only complete as a person when I'm actually holding these guitars and playing them. The best songs that I've ever written have been written on these guitars.

When you get a new guitar roadie or guitar tech, you always have this heart-to-heart about how you feel about your guitars, how you want them to treat them, whether they've got names. I promise you, it goes on, whether they're female or male. It's something you can only really explain between two guys who are looking after guitars. But it is an extension of you and I feel that with a guitar and, especially with this guitar and maybe a couple of others, I am complete as a person and private and I don't need anybody else or the outside world to come into it.

John Lee Hooker

John Lee Hooker
Born August 22, 1920
near Clarksdale, Mississippi

:|John Lee Hooker|·|·|

John Lee Hooker, who was inducted into the Rock and Roll Hall of Fame in 1991, celebrated his 50th year in the music business in 1998 — and what a half century it has been. For the man who came to be known as the "King Of Boogie" and has been a major influence on the development of rock and roll, the saga begins in the mid-1930s as Hooker, the son of a sharecropper and fire and brimstone preacher who was less than supportive of his son's interest in blues music, fled the family farm and ended up living with his guitar-playing stepfather, Will Moore. From Moore, Hooker developed the gritty guitar style that has long been his trademark, and following relocations to cities like Memphis and Cincinnati, he ended up in Detroit in the early '40s where he worked as a janitor at a Chrysler car plant by day and played the clubs at night with a blues band. In 1948, Hooker made his first recordings for the local Sensation label and had immediate success on the R&B chart with songs like *Boogie Chillen*, *Crawling King Snake,* and *I'm In the Mood*, which are now regarded as blues classics.

Over the years, Hooker has been an acknowledged influence and inspiration for some of the biggest names in rock music, including Eric Clapton, Jimi Hendrix, Ike Turner, Jeff Beck, Jimmy Page, Carlos Santana, The Rolling Stones, The Animals, John Mayall, John Hammond, ZZ Top, Van Morrison, and Bonnie Raitt, many of whom have collaborated with him on various record projects. In the '80s, Hooker's profile was significantly raised through his appearance in *The Blues Brothers* movie and in 1989, with the release of the critically-acclaimed and best-selling album, THE HEALER, on which he was joined by a host of musical friends, including Carlos Santana, Robert Cray, George Thorogood, Los Lobos, and Bonnie Raitt. Hooker's seminal blues style was back inspiring a new generation of rockers. His duet with Bonnie Raitt on the track *I'm In The Mood* earned them a Grammy Award, and the project itself was honored with four trophies at the W.C. Handy Blues Awards in Memphis in October of 1990. Remarkably, the '90s have proven to be one of the busiest decades for Hooker in his career.

Hooker makes no pretense of guitar virtuosity, but if it's the "real, true blues" you're looking for and an instrumental and vocal style that is unmistakable, then John Lee's your man. "I don't play a lot of fancy guitar," Hooker once told David Rotenstein of *The Daily News* in Atlanta. "I don't want to play it. The kind of guitar I want to play is mean, mean licks." For Hooker, whose guttural vocals and bare-to-the-bone guitar work often conspire to send shivers up and down the staunchest spine, the feel's the thing, whether he's playing live or in the studio. There's no messin' with the blues. "When you're recording, you've got to do a song in one or two takes," he states. "You've got to do it while you're up for it, while you're fresh and have got the energy. You can wear yourself down going over and over and over it . . . take two, take five, take ten. Then you've got no voice and you've got no energy. You've got to run in there and hit it while you're hot."

We spoke to John Lee Hooker on an October afternoon afternoon in the kitchen of his home just outside San Francisco, reportedly one of five homes that he owns in northern California.

The first time I learned to play guitar was from my stepfather, Will Moore, in Clarksdale, Mississippi, on a little Stella guitar. He played a Stella and I messed around watching him, and when he got a new one, he gave me his old one. I worked on it everyday, and the style that I play now is the style that he played. He played a style that they don't play now. I wasn't old enough to go into places that he went into, but I learned from him at home.

After I learned pretty good, I left the state and came out on my own. I was maybe 15 years old, something like that, and I just took my guitar and boogied; I left. I come on to Memphis and worked in a theater for a little while on Beale Street. Then I came to Cincinnati and stayed there on Fifth Street living with a lady called 'Mom.' I worked at a little steel mill there called the Little Tank and Pump Company. I worked there for about a year or a year and a half, maybe more, and I left there and came to Detroit. I worked in a steel mill and at any little job I could get.

When I was in Detroit, there were more electric guitars around. Mississippi didn't have many electrics, mostly acoustics. Around Detroit and Chicago there were electric guitars. I didn't have them for a while until I ran into T Bone Walker and he gave me my first electric guitar. And I played around little clubs there until I got discovered. We'd sit there at night, drink wine, play guitars.

There was a guy by the name of Elmer Barbee, who had a little record store there and he'd record me on blanks. There were no cassettes in those days. He had a friend called Bernie Bessman, who had a big record store downtown. He was a distributor and he had a little label called Sensation Records and he signed me up because he liked what he heard, and my first recording was released on the Sensation label. That was *Boogie Chillen* and it got so big that they couldn't handle it, so they put it on Modern Records where it could go worldwide. Then there was *I'm In the Mood* and *Crawling King Snake*, which were also a big success.

:| |•|•|

*W*hen the Les Paul first came out, I bought one. I think it was in 1952, something like that, when they first come out. I bought that one and I played it on some of my records. I sold that one to a church and I shouldn't have done that. I wish I had it back now.

I like any Gibson guitar just about, but I lean towards the 335 more than the others. I really like the neck. It's got a nice neck. Carlos [Santana] gave me this one. He brought it to my house one day and stood outside and said, 'I've brought you a present.' I said, 'What?' And he said, 'Open the door.' And there it was. I play it all the time.

I started playing electric guitars in Detroit, but I used to play acoustics when I played coffee houses in New York when I lived there for a while. I worked with folk singers like Joan Baez and Odetta and Bob Dylan at places like Gerdes Folk City.

Though I learned guitar from my stepfather, I added my thing, like foot tapping and strumming, but it was still his thing. I changed it and brought it up to date and dressed it up, but the basic thing was his bottom. I just put my own personal touch to it.

I am sure nobody's got a style like me. Mine is unique, a really unique style. So many guitar players sound like each other, but mine is real dirty and slick and funky. Mine doesn't sound like nobody else but John Lee Hooker, so that makes mine outstanding. There's not a lot of fancy playing. I don't do a lot of fancy picking. I just straight play the blues and the boogie. A lot of people try to copy it, but you can tell it's not me. You can tell they got it from me, people like ZZ Top and a lot of other people. It's hard to explain, but it's something nobody's got but me.

You've got to have style; some people don't have a style. They've got other people's styles, but you need your own style to really go to. People have a tendency to copy players who have become famous like Jimi Hendrix. You've got to do your own thing. You can sound like somebody else, but everybody knows it's not the real thing. You're just a copy cat. If you do your own thing, you get famous for doing what you do best.

The blues is something you've got to have inside you. It's a talent. You can't find it in no books. You've got to come from your heart and soul with it. That's where it comes from. That's the only true, real blues. That's the only true, real music, the blues. Everything come from the blues, the roots. Everything else has just branched off from the blues.

As far as the younger generation, I'm glad that they caught on to my music and are learning about the real music, the blues. They often come by wanting to learn something and for me to tell them something about the blues. That's the world today, the young people and they're really into the blues and some of them are already playing them and I'm real happy they are. I'm not going to last always and I'm happy I'm going to leave something for them when I'm gone.

Steve Howe

YES, ASIA, GTR, ANDERSON BRUFORD WAKEMAN AND HOWE

Steve Howe
Born April 8, 1947
Holloway, North London, England

:|Steve Howe|·|·|

Steve Howe's passion for the guitar is boundless. His voyage of self discovery on his chosen instrument continues almost 40 years after he received his first guitar as a present from his parents for Christmas in 1959. He has since indulged his obsession with an ever-expanding collection of vintage guitars, a selection of which are gloriously displayed in a book he compiled with Tony Bacon in 1993 titled *The Steve Howe Guitar Collection*. Rather than regarding these instruments as museum pieces, Howe views each one as something of a companion-in-adventure in his frequent forays into uncharted musical waters. As he comments in the introduction to his book, "I'm constantly discovering fresh musical areas to investigate as instruments surface in the collection, providing new voices through which my music can speak."

Following stints with groups like The Syndicats, The In Crowd, Tomorrow, and Bodast in the '60s, Howe joined Yes in 1970, replacing departing guitarist Peter Banks. Beginning in 1971 with the release of their classic recording, THE YES ALBUM, Yes emerged as one of the most successful progressive rock outfits of the day. Through the '70s, and in the wake of the release of ground-breaking albums like FRAGILE, CLOSE TO THE EDGE, and TALES OF TOPOGRAPHIC OCEANS, the group toured extensively on both sides of the Atlantic. Despite the rigorous schedule, Howe managed to record and release a couple of solo albums, including BEGINNINGS and the STEVE HOWE ALBUM, during the '70s.

In the early '80s, with the future of Yes as a group in limbo, Howe became the founding member of Asia, the first "supergroup" of the decade, which hit the top of the charts internationally with the singles like *Heat Of the Moment* and *Only Time Will Tell*. In 1986, after Asia had disbanded, Howe joined ex-Genesis guitarist Steve Hackett in the short-lived group GTR, which saw its self-titled album reach number 11 on the U.S. album chart. The group Anderson Bruford Wakeman and Howe, which was formed in the summer of 1989, proved to be the precursor to a fully re-formed Yes in 1991. Howe's solo acoustic piece from the group's subsequent CD, UNION, earned the group a Grammy nomination the following year.

Howe has continued to explore various music forms — most significantly, "New Age," in collaboration with Swiss keyboardist Paul Sutin — throughout his solo recording career over the past two decades. In 1993, Howe set out on his first completely solo excursion, dubbed The Not Necessarily Acoustic tour, which featured many of the classic Yes tracks with which he had been associated, as well as the best of his solo material. In 1996, the year he collaborated with English jazz guitarist Martin Taylor on a recording project that showcased various vintage guitars from the Scott Chinery Collection, one of the most extensive and comprehensive collections in the world, he rejoined the classic Yes lineup while still continuing to pursue a wide range of solo projects, which, at the time of writing, included his latest solo album, QUANTUM GUITAR.

We spoke to Steve Howe at his home, located deep in the Devon countryside in the southwest of England. After observing the English tradition of afternoon tea in the kitchen served up by our gracious host, we retired to Howe's music room, which houses a large portion of his vintage guitar collection and, among other collectibles, a large picture of gypsy guitarist Django Reinhardt, who seemed to listen in with some interest from a wall behind us as we chatted about Howe's musical life and times and the role that the guitar has played in it.

*P*laying the guitar when I was young was sort of trendy, but I don't think that was the reason I started. Actually, I was quite attracted to a rather untrendy part of the guitar, dance-band playing, which was running parallel with my interest in rock music, where, of course, the guitar was twanging away. That was definitely a big inspiration, but I think I had a few of my own scores to settle. I wanted to play my own way, so I kind of refused to learn in the orthodox sense of lessons or manuals or tapes. I just learned by listening, and when I heard something I liked, I asked, how do I play that? And then I sat down and learned it. Often that meant that I broke through the barriers of learning because I really wanted to play a particular tune.

Around 1957, when I was 10, I wanted to play guitar, and after two years, I got a guitar. I just thought I could play straight away, like every bighead. So, for a couple of years, I really fumbled around in my bedroom, listening and imagining I was playing, and it just sort of took off from there. I just got together with people and I could play some of the tunes they could play and the next thing I was in bands doing Chuck Berry tunes. I knew all the Chuck Berry tunes, like *Down The Road A Piece,* that not a lot of people know, but it was the staple diet of a guitarist in a band at the time, and I did quite a lot of ground work with that stuff.

Albert Lee was the first major influence on my style, but that happened three or four years further on when I was out playing on a semi-professional or professional basis and I saw Albert play. He was the first guitarist that I actually saw in England, besides an early friend of mine called Yossel. He was the first guy I ever knew who had a Les Paul, and everybody was envious. When I first saw Albert Lee playing, it was with Chris Farlowe and The Thunderbirds and he had a two-pickup Les Paul, and then I saw him with a Super 400.

Django Reinhardt was a massive influence on me. The first time I encountered him was on a 10-inch record called DJANGO, with a guitar string on it. I bought it from some guy who lived across the street from me and he told me that this was the greatest guitarist in the world; look it says it on the back. So I bought it, put it on, and instantly knew that he was right. This guitarist was in another league altogether. In fact, on the Scott Chinery record, because of that Django record, Martin [Taylor], who's actually got his own group called A Tribute To Django, plays a Django repertoire piece called *The Sunshine Of Your Smile.* [Plays] It was a lovely piece— and *The Continental.* [Plays] Of course, he influenced me; every tune on that record stayed with me. And of course his *Nuages . . .* [Plays]. I just got hungry to see a video clip — it was only about two years ago — and I actually saw the video clip, but in that time I bought masses of the anthology and, of course, just picked up what I could from him.

I think you've just got to let people play at you and let the influence come round in its own time. Certainly I would have loved to have seen him play live. I was conscious of him as early as 1953, the same year as the Queen's Coronation ... I think Django passed away that year. I knew it said in the papers, "Django Reinhardt." So that name was there in the same category as Les Paul in my mind. Before I got a guitar, my parents had Les Paul & Mary Ford records, so that was always going around in my head. People would say [about the Les Paul sound], 'That's not a guitar! You can't do that on a guitar!' So there was always that idea that what I wanted to do on the guitar was maybe things people thought you couldn't do. At the time, we didn't even think you could play in the Chet Atkins style. In England, nobody had played in that style. [Plays] If you could play like that in 1953, you would have been considered quite something.

Though my early influences were the rock thing itself, my brother and sister steered me towards jazz and classical, and that's where I heard the great jazz guitarists. The first jazz player I really heard was Barney Kessel on one of the POLL WINNERS albums that he did with Shelly Manne and Ray Brown. As I got interested in jazz guitar, it seemed to make me want to play different things. Trends were changing and after quite a few years of Duane Eddy and The Shadows, which was our version of the instrumental groups like The Ventures, I think that there was a need for other influences for me. I had been in a blues group in the very early days and played quite a lot of blues material, so, as my career started to work, I didn't really want to play that style of music anymore. I wanted to play material of my own invention a bit more. Some of that early stuff is out on a CD called MOTH BALLS that covers 25 titles I recorded in the '60s, which is actually more than I knew from memory that I had ever recorded. There was actually more material than that, but we chose the 25 that we thought were worthy from a historical point of view.

One of the songs that The In Crowd, one of the early groups I was in, used to play was *Stop, Wait A Minute*, which came from the States. There was a guy at EMI Records here in England who used to give us released singles from the States that weren't out in England. We used to play that with such determination 'cause nobody knew what the hell we were playing. We were interested in having our own repertoire, so that meant, by the time 1967 came, we didn't play anyone else's music but our own. That was really healthy as far as I was concerned because, although I think guitar breaks and improvisation are the real key to music, I wanted to write music and establish a little bit more of a base on which to build a repertoire of my own. That's what I've continued doing.

I was in the group Tomorrow and, when 1967 came along, we went into EMI with producer Marc Wirtz and recorded an album. We were quite late in that psychedelic era to do what we were doing, but *My White Bicycle* had already come out, which was quite a powerful psychedelic record and had backward guitar. The whole thing was slowed down, actually, to make it very driving and labored. There was a lot of fun in learning during that period. In between that and Yes, which I joined in 1970, was a bit of a writing experiment with the band, but certainly when Yes came along, I really did want to have the opportunity to explore a little bit more, so when a guitar break came along, I didn't want to have to do it live. I'd do something live or do rhythm guitar live in the studio and then work on that guitar break later. That's part of the thing I'd enjoy doing.

Initially with Yes, it was really post-psychedelic music, getting mad with the music, getting kind of exploratory and using as many influences as possible. It didn't matter if the song had to be a specified length. It didn't matter if you had to stay in one style. The Beatles and The Byrds and all the groups that we admired had done so much or tampered with what they did — a few gimmicks, new recording techniques, a bit of production. After all, if you're going to play the electric guitar, you might as well learn about production 'cause it's pretty important to how your guitar sounds. Yes was a vehicle to not only learn more about stage work with great enthusiasm, particularly in America, because I was itching to get to the States but also, the recording things just meant that we had a little more time, though, compared to now, it was no time at all. We were checking in and out of studios all the time to make albums like THE YES ALBUM and FRAGILE. We didn't move into the studios and take over like bands today do. They sort of move in with their own furniture and take the place over for a year. [Laughs]

As far as being experimental, I guess it was to a certain extent, but they were the only ideas we had. In other words, if we hadn't had those, we wouldn't have had very much. I think we felt that we were taking some risks. We weren't confident in the sense of having a reason to be confident. We were confident because we were fair players and it was a good chemistry in the group to work with, but what happened beyond that was anybody's guess. By the time we recorded tracks like *Roundabout* from the FRAGILE album, I was able to explore things, and that's something I very much wanted to do. How I felt at the time was not so confident. It was a big risk because you didn't have the support of any acclaim. You were starting, like a lot of young bands do, with your own confidence. If somebody comes along and says, 'I like it!' then it's up to you how you deal with that, whether it undermines you or spurs you on to do better.

: | | • | • |

The guitar has always been a thing that has to feel right before it sounds right. If it doesn't feel real good, then you're not going to spend a lot of time with it. In a way, I felt that if I could get the right guitar, I thought this would take me somewhere else altogether, like when I got this guitar [blonde Gibson L5CESN] in Miami in the mid '70s cause I loved Wes Montgomery so much. I had the pleasure of seeing him live — I think I was 16 at the time — he was sitting there playing as close to me as I am to you now and he was brilliant. So you might buy a guitar with that idea in mind: it's a beautiful piece, mint condition guitar, and you sit there and want to play a bit of Wes [Plays] . . . but of course Wes isn't here.

So there was one idea that you were going to follow a bit of destiny, but, on the other hand, certain guitars give you the perspective on your work. They reward you, if they're great guitars. You feel great playing it and it sounds great, but all those things take a bit of work. At that time, I think I was shifting guitars. THE YES ALBUM was all done on the Gibson ES175D, the guitar I've played since 1964 exclusively. I kept playing this guitar, but I was moving on to the Switchmaster and the Super 400s, mainly big guitars. Certainly, when I did CLOSE TO THE EDGE, I played the Gibson Stereo [ES345TD]. That guitar was crucial to that period.

So each guitar had a reason for being there. It was a sort of opportunity, in my mind, for exploring different guitars, particularly Gibson guitars. There was also an originality about nobody knowing what guitar you were going to be seen with next. There had to be a really good reason for me to take a guitar on the road. All the guitars I've ever appeared with weren't there to pose with, they were there because, each in their own way, they were integral to the music.

If you want the colorful sound that different guitars can make, then you need to understand what guitars make what sound. That wasn't conscious in my mind. I could see the keyboard department of the band incorporating more and more keyboards, and suddenly the guitarist is incorporating more guitars, and I thought there was a need for the guitar not just to be one sound. I wasn't a guitarist who was just going to use one sound and rest on that, maybe because I was never quite sure what the sound was. Really, it comes from that guitar [Points to the Gibson ES175D], and that's the main sort of sound. It crops up on just about every record. It's on the recent Yes release, KEYS FOR ASCENSION. It's on the live material, because I played the old live material on it and on the tune, *That That Is*. It plays all the out solos and a lot of the detailed lead guitar work on it.

So, guitars are like vehicles. If you want to go in a four-wheel drive, go in a four-wheel drive. They take you somewhere and you need the right guitar for the right thing. I've played a great variety of guitars. I won't say I favor full bodies, but certainly I'm at home with some of these bigger guitars.

The ES175 is really a very key guitar for me. It's kind of contagious

and infectious. But dabbling with the guitar family became an obsession — instruments like mandolins, banjo guitars as well as instruments from other parts of the world like the koto and the sitar and
things. So I wanted to play anything with strings because I wanted to
incorporate that within my music. I didn't really see it as an outside
thing being brought in. It was like, 'Hey, that's also a part of me. I'll do
that somewhere.' It's only more recently that I've found textures in
the sound of various guitars where now I'll say I need this kind of 12-
string or that kind of 12-string. I'm certainly understanding better the
benefits of guitars with full bodies and pickups and, other times, without the body, so you've got more of that concentrated sound.

On the Scott Chinery record, there's a marvelous track where
Martin [Taylor] plays two Super 400s, a P Super 400 acoustic —
one of the Super 400s was a seven-string — and he does an introduction on a Lloyd Loar L5. This track, *All the Things You Are*, starts
with this L5 on its own, which is just the most amazing sound
you've ever heard, and then the P Super 400 picks up the rhythm,
then in come two Super 400 electrics. We had a lot of fun doing that
sort of thing, exploring, and I'm talking about my stuff, with Martin.
Martin has played quite a few different guitars in his time, and he's
never had so much fun. He really did enjoy it. But one of the hardest things was picking from such a vast collection of instruments.
We had to pick a usable amount for a CD. We thought that was
going to be about 35 guitars, and when we picked them, it got to
55, and before we walked out of the door, it was about 60. So we did
do a lot of exploring and, in particular in certain tracks, the Gibson
sounds. I do a track where I feature J200s, J100 Jumbos, as well as
the Southerner and the S Country Western in the style of The
Everly Brothers with a little bit of Buddy Holly thrown in.
[Demonstrates] To get that kind of feeling again was great fun, and
Scott [Chinery], thank goodness, gave us a lot of space to work in
creatively and support-wise, but at the same time he was there
enthusing and giving his final views on things. It was a really good
team project.

When I first got this Gibson ES175 guitar, I was really entranced
with it. It used to sit there and I used to stare at it. Staring at it, listening to records and looking at it, it soon became something else
to me completely, beyond a guitar, beyond an instrument or anything. It became a possession, something that you shared things
with. Of course, there's the work that I've done on that guitar. It's
never been re-fretted or altered in any particular way, which defies
certain rules. Once in a New York hotel, I was so afraid someone
was going to steal it that I put it in the bed with me, but there was

no physical contact. For me its the ultimate Gibson because of its versatility, its size, and its accessibility. It's practicability is unbelievable in the way you change the strings and keep it tidy. Its not a difficult guitar to live with. Its not heavy. And after watching people like Joe Pass and Jim Hall and Wes Montgomery and others play it, obviously I wanted it.

At the time, they had run out of these guitars in London and it was ordered for me. I went in to the music store one day and told them I wanted a 175 and they told me they didn't have any. They had sold the last one a week ago, or something. I waited a bit of time. It cost 200 guineas. Guineas, for those who don't know, were the pound plus a shilling. Neither guineas or shillings exist now, but anyway, that was the price, 200 guineas, and thank God my father could afford to give me the £60 deposit, so I just worked off the payments. How old was I then? 17! This was my first encounter with the commitments of life. This was a mortgage to me. I had to pay the installments because I had to keep it. When I first came out with that, people were shocked back then because I had been playing a small guitar called a Guyatone. It was a very, very small guitar, though I didn't think it was. It was Japanese, but nobody really knew where they were from. They were just there. I went to this [ES175], which appeared a very large guitar. To me this was the grounding I needed. This was the guitar I had worked for, sweated for, and labored for. If I got it in 1964 — I had only been playing five years — I was 17 at that time. I had just made my first record without it, which was actually Chuck Berry's *Maybelline* by The Syndicats and then I got this guitar and that was it. Now, I believed in my mind that I was heading somewhere. I had a guitar that I had to work at to keep, not just from a financial sense, but you couldn't play a guitar like this badly. That was in my mind. It had to be played well.

:| |•|•|

I suppose I've got certain criteria about my playing. The thing about confidence is that no way at that time was I truly confident about what I was doing. I wouldn't say I was bluffing, but I was worrying. [Laughs]. When people said, 'Oh, what are you playing there?' I'd say, 'Uh, I can't remember now!' I wasn't as stable in the '60s as I've become. You had to learn what people saying what they thought of your music was like. If you played something and somebody said, 'I don't like that' ... [Makes whistling sound and explosion noise to ape that of his ego crashing to the ground] ... it really hurt, but then you said it to him: 'Well, I don't like that bit either!' and then he felt like that. You had to learn this musician's reaction routine. I think a lot of people go to music because they can't deal with real life as it really is. It's a pretty hard thing to deal with, so you go to music as an outlet, as an expression, as a release, and then somehow you've got to get back in the mainstream again because when you're working with other people. It is just like a job. It's like, 'Get out of my office!' or 'Get out of my area when I'm playing!' So you have to learn a lot of things and there's nobody to teach you those things so you have to learn them quickly yourself.

I think some of the sessions I did with Marc Wirtz were truly groundwork stuff. I was in EMI Studio 2, full of people, orchestras tuning up and four guitarists all playing different things, just a whole lot of soupy music. The first time I was on my own, that was when I realized that you could take the time. You could get the guitar just like you wanted it, especially when there weren't 60 other people going, 'Oh it's the tea break now sir!' and 'I think the bass is out of tune!'

:| |•|•|

I almost ended up with a Les Paul one day because I was so upset that this [ES175] was so damaged that I didn't think I could play it again. So I went in, and while I was waiting for it, I was thinking, if it doesn't look right and it doesn't feel right, I'm going to get a Les Paul, but as you can see it was okay. The only thing I've ever done to it is change the pickup. This pickup for a lot of the early '70s was actually turned the other way around, and I think I did that because I didn't want to be as trebly as everybody else. Everybody was very trebly and I wanted to be sort of dull. It was a very weird thing to do because, when I did that, all I was ever doing was turning the treble on my Fender amp back up, so I decided to put the pickup back a few years later. Also, I used a very unusual plectrum, which I don't use anymore, called Specials, which are very thick and very heavy and actually dulled the sound even more.

[Holds up the 175] This [switch] was off the original machine head; it's a machine head button that fitted on there rather nice. These are very early speed knobs that I borrowed off another guitar or I bought them, but those are the real big ones that aren't actually from the right period. I put these machine heads on it. They're not actually the model they look like. They're actually the bigger Grovers, the Imperials with smaller buttons on. It's never been refretted. I never let anybody keep it over night. If anything's wrong with it, they've got to fix it while I'm there. I really got obsessed. I carry this guitar. It doesn't go with a case or anything. On my solo one-man show I like to take all the guitars that I can sleep easy with. So in fact for electric, I was using a Steinberger, which I think is a fantastic guitar. I like it very much because it sets me free in another sort of way.

This guitar [175] helped me, I suppose, to keep whatever originality I wanted to have because it's quite a different animal to play. The first question is, Doesn't it feed back? Why doesn't yours feed back? But I had always used a volume pedal, and I think that's why I always had control of the volume all the time. A bit like the steel players use it to bring things in and that's what I started doing. At a point, I started realizing that I could do something with it like Chet Atkins did with the arm and volume and tone. I still have one of those.

I'm a player and I can't bear a guitar, especially a great guitar, that's got impediments. Either it doesn't stay in tune or it has problems. Solve those problems! I think I've become more and more cautious about doing major changes. I've done some — I took a 55 Les Paul and put four Humbuckers in it. But I wanted to make a really special Les Paul out of that. That went pretty wacky. Of course, the purists don't like that, but I do because I'm a player more than a collector. It's more important for me to have guitars in great order. But when I look back sometimes, I think, like anybody, maybe I shouldn't have gone quite that far here or quite that far there. At the time, whatever was available I used to improve a guitar. You can't always go back and put it like it was before. That's why something like the L5 is so great; I do enjoy guitars that stay as original as possible.

With my collecting, I was the sort of person who could collect things in small ways and I think once I realized I wanted to collect guitars, then I thought, that's it with collecting, because if I'm going to go mad on the guitar thing, I'd better not collect anything else. The way that happened was by the '70s, before my first trip to America. I must have had a dozen guitars, things like a Levin Jumbo, a Vox bass, a Burns, this Gibson ES175, and the rarest Gibson I have, the FDH model, but I was itching to make a really important move and get to the States and really buy guitars every trip. That's what I ended up doing. Every trip was a guitar search, so in the early days, the early '70s, I went to the nooks and crannies of America, the nooks and crannies being the real hard places to find. I'd walk down Broadway in New York, looking in pawn shops, but a lot of the things I've got, I've got from people who deal and specialize in great guitars. Some of them I wouldn't have without them because I'd send somebody off and tell them that I'd like one of these and often they'd tell me, 'That's really rare. I don't know whether I can get one but I'll try.' A month later, they might have found it.

My collection is broad in another sense, and it goes back to the antique guitars. My earliest guitar dates circa 1780 and it's a five-course [a course being a closely-grouped string or strings] guitar from France. I got into the antique side because I just knew there was something else about guitars that people were missing, and you've only got to buy a book called American/European Musical Instruments by Baines — it's most likely out of stock or in the reprint mode — but that's the old bible of what a great guitar was. Of course, there was a Panormo and other great guitars. That's what put Gibson in a different perspective because he [Orville Gibson] was making guitars before the turn of the century, and on Scott [Chinery]'s record, I had the pleasure of playing a couple of his original Orville's. The design he had in those guitars was remarkable. The idea of being able to play vintage — vintage means '50s now to the guitar collector — was really something. If you've got to say antique, you've got to say antique.

I started collecting lyre guitars, which I particularly fancy as well, but having 30 or more pieces from the Gibson world makes me a 'Gibsonite' I guess because there was this old expression, to be a 'Gibsonite' or 'Gibsonette' or something. So, collecting was initially influenced by the 1961 Gibson catalog, I've got to own up, because in there you had the Johnny Smith, the Super 400, the L5 and so on, so when I wasn't listening to early pop records or Duane Eddy, my head would be in this catalog thinking, 'Where will I ever get a Gibson Tal Farlow?' Well, you know, I was lucky enough to do those things and I do appreciate that a lot. That's why I want to stream-line the collection so that what I've got speaks about why I wanted to collect guitars and, I think it does now more than ever now that I've pulled it in and focused on the real great guitars and other string family instruments — Gibson also makes great mandolins — that I've been lucky enough to get.

Tony Iommi

BLACK SABBATH

Frank Anthony Iommi
Born February 19, 1948
Birmingham, England

:|Tony Iommi|·|·|

"**I**t seems pretty clear to me that the day the young Iommi put his fingers to the riff that became *Paranoid* was the day the entire genre of 'Heavy Metal' music, in all its now diverse forms, was born," states guitarist Brian May of Queen as part of his introduction to the official Tony Iommi web site [www.tonyiommi.com]. "I was almost there! I too was in a group just beginning to create the sound that seemed to be in our heads screaming to be let out — rock music built around electric guitars, fully driven into distortion, was about to become the voice of a new generation in the West. Iommi made that first distillation and created a true monster."

James Hetfield of Metallica, in praise of Black Sabbath, takes that thought one step further: "Sabbath was everything that the '60s weren't. Their music was cool because it was completely anti-hippie. I hated the Beatles, Jethro Tull, Love, and all that other happy shit."

Black Sabbath had its beginnings in Birmingham, England with Iommi, bassist Geezer Butler, drummer Bill Ward, and vocalist Ozzy Osbourne and a jazz/blues group with the unlikely name of the Polka Tulk Blues Band. That outfit evolved to Earth and then to Black Sabbath following Iommi's return to the group following a short stint with Jethro Tull. (That's Iommi playing guitar with Tull during their appearance on The Rolling Stones' *Rock and Roll Circus* TV show.) The Black Sabbath name, which came at Iommi's suggestion, was inspired by a movie poster for a 1963 Boris Karloff film of the same name. "It was Iommi who came to rehearsal one day and said, 'Isn't it funny how people pay money to watch horror films. Why don't we start playing scary music?,'" singer Ozzy Osbourne recently recalled. "And when he came up with that Black Sabbath riff — that was the scariest riff I've ever heard in my life."

The group signed their first record deal in 1970, resulting in the band's eponymous debut album, followed by PARANOID, which put the group on the map on both sides of the Atlantic. Sabbath released an average of one album a year between 1970 and 1978 prior to Osbourne's departure in 1979. Ronnie James Dio was recruited as vocalist for Black Sabbath, 'Mark II' which recorded the landmark albums HEAVEN & HELL and MOB RULES. The years since have seen the group change line-up frequently with Iommi remaining the constant.

A reunion of three of the original members took place in the summer of 1997 as Iommi, Osbourne, Butler, and ex-Faith No More drummer Michael Bordin headlined the 21-date Ozzfest Tour of America. In December of 1997, original drummer Bill Ward rejoined the group for two Home At Last concerts in Birmingham.

Iommi, who at the time of writing was working with California-based writer/producer/musician Bob Marlette on his first solo album, had also just had two Tony Iommi 'signature' guitar products released on the market — a Laney amp (the GHT100TI) and a Gibson pickup, the first Signature Humbucker that Gibson has ever made that produces the same output and unique tone that Iommi, a left-handed guitarist, gets on his SG guitars. Iommi, who writes a regular column titled "Heaven & Hell" for *Guitar World* magazine, was presented with the "Best Guitar Riff Ever" award in 1995 at the Kerrang! Music Awards that placed *Paranoid* above Led Zeppelin's *Whole Lotta Love*, Deep Purple's *Smoke On the Water*, and Metallica's *Enter Sandman*.

With a stack of Tony Iommi 'signature' Laney amps as a backdrop and with a Tony Iommi 'signature' Gibson SG in hand, the personable Black Sabbath guitarist spoke to us late one autumn afternoon at the Laney Amplifier factory in Crawley Heath, just outside of Birmingham in England.

*B*elieve it or not, I started in music on an accordion, because my whole family played accordions. I had one when I was about nine years old. After playing that for a while, I wanted to play drums, but for my parents, that was out of the question because of the noise. I turned to the guitar not long after that.

But, there was a time when it looked like I'd have to give it up. I took off the ends of two fingers on my right hand when I got them trapped in a machine. I used to do electric welding and the metal had to be pressed. The person who pressed it didn't come into work that day, so I did it and I did it wrong, obviously, and it took the ends of my fingers off. I was about to leave my job that day, turn professional, and go to Germany with a band. Of course, that was totally finished. I couldn't do that. I was devastated. I went to various people trying to see what I could do, to see if anything could be put on the fingers, and they said, 'No, you'll just have to change your career and do something else.'

But I wouldn't accept that, so I went back home thinking about what I could do. I made some tips out of a Fairy liquid [dish-washing detergent] bottle and I melted it down, put it into a ball, got a hot soldering iron, and made it so it would fit the finger. I sat there for days just rubbing it down to make a tip. I glued leather on top of that so it would grip the strings and it worked. I wouldn't say that it defines the sound I get on guitar. It has added somewhat to the style, I suppose, because I actually had to create a different style of playing because there were certain chords I wouldn't be able to play and I had to think of other ways to play them.

Developing a guitar style after the accident was very difficult because you had to re-think the whole thing. There was nothing that you could do now that you could do before. For weeks or months, I had these two big bandages on, so I learned to play with my little finger more. I strengthened that finger up by just playing and, to this day, I still use the little finger for a lot of stuff. I also changed the style of chords and how I would play them.

From the very beginning, there was a band here in England called The Shadows who were an amazing influence on me and guitar players from my era because they were an instrumental band and one of the only good instrumental bands that we had from England. That kind of got me into playing guitar, and, after my accident, I got into Django Reinhardt and more jazz and blues-oriented stuff. At first, when I lost the tips of my fingers, I thought it was all over with, but then somebody that I worked with — the manager of the firm — came around and brought me a Django Reinhardt record. That sort of sparked me on. I said, he's done it, now I'm going to have a go.

Initially, I went through various bands with Bill Ward, the drummer with Sabbath. We were together in a couple of bands for about three or four years before Black Sabbath. I was at school with Ozzy. I didn't get on with Ozzy at school at all, which is no great secret, but later on, when Bill Ward and I were looking for a singer, we happened to see this advert, 'Ozzy Zig requires gig.' So we went around to this house and knocked on the door and who should answer but Ozzy. I said to Bill, 'Ah, forget it! I know this guy. It's never going to work.' So off we went back to my house and a couple of days later

Ozzy came around to my house looking for a drummer. Bill was there at the time and he spoke to him, but, in the end, Ozzy, Bill, bass player Geezer Butler, and I decided to get together, and for the most part we've got on ever since then really.

We started off playing blues. Everything was a 12-bar. We realized we had to do something of our own, and at the time, I worked with Jethro Tull for three or four weeks. I left Black Sabbath — or Earth as we were known then — and by being with Tull for that short time, I learned that to get on you've really got to work at it. You need to rehearse, be up early and get cracking at it. I learned a lot from Ian Anderson really.

It didn't work out for me being with them. It just wasn't right, so I came back to the band with a different attitude. 'We've got to do this if we want to get on and start rehearsing at nine or ten o'clock,' even though I had a job getting up as much as anybody else, but we did it. We got to rehearsals and really started working on it. The sound came from basically playing heavy blues, turned up. That's how it was.

We were interested in the sword and sorcery thing like anybody's interested in UFOs or something to do with the supernatural. It was only as an interest. It was an interest in as much as Geezer and I went to see a lot of horror films. We just loved to do that, but we never practiced it or anything, even though it got a bit hairy sometimes. Alex Saunders, the head chief witch of England, started attaching himself to us. There was another band at that time called Black Widow, and they used to do stuff on stage and we quite often got mixed up with them. I think the first album did it. As soon as the first album cover came out with an inverted cross on it and the woman on the front, it sort of labeled the band forever. That was it, we were doomed to be 'satanic' from that day on.

With the first three albums, we followed a very similar direction. We had the same approach on all three. On the fourth album, we started experimenting more with acoustic stuff and even had to bring in a string section and we recorded it in LA. We had always recorded in England before so it was a totally new approach.

With SABBATH BLOODY SABBATH, which was the next album, we tried to take the same approach. We had the same everything, apart from the studio, which was no longer big enough for us because they had bought a big Moog. We came back to England, went to an old castle in Wales, started writing again, and came up with SABBATH BLOODY SABBATH. The approach started changing. We used string sections on that as well, so it was more of an experimental stage for us. That lasted until NEVER SAY DIE, which was the last Sabbath album with Ozzy.

After that, we did HEAVEN AND HELL, which was a different thing for us because we brought in a different vocalist, Ronnie James Dio. It was a very exciting period for us really because we could go on stage and know that there were 20,000 kids there. You knew the show was a sell out. If you like, it got a bit boring because you'd know what was going to happen. We'd lost that spark and the excitement of it. When Ronnie came in, it was good because we really had to try and fight for something again.

Again, we went to L.A. and rented a house for a year. Eleven months had gone by and we hadn't done a thing — this was with Ozzy — and that's when it came to an end. It just couldn't go any further. We had to bring somebody else in. At the end of that year, we had virtually got the whole album written with Ronnie. That was HEAVEN AND HELL. MOB RULES came after that. Again, it was a new adventure for us and using keyboards opened it up a little bit for me because I always used to write the chord structures and then Ozzy would sing over them. I'd write the solo part and Ozzy would sing on that as well. When we had a keyboard player whose particular part is done for a solo, that's the solo.

I never heard the term 'heavy metal' while living in L.A. for as long as I did. When I came back to England after about five years, I heard this term 'heavy metal'. I did this interview for *Melody Maker* and the guy was going on about 'heavy metal', and I thought, what's that. I hadn't got a clue what that was because I've always referred to our music as 'heavy rock', so I was very unfamiliar with the term 'heavy metal'. He explained it and that's been it ever since, but I've never put ourselves out as a 'heavy metal' band. I suppose it sounds like we are. I didn't like the term 'heavy metal' on us because I thought we had a wider scope than that.

After Ronnie [James Dio] left, we auditioned singers, which was a real pain. We had some of the strangest people you've ever heard sending tapes in, people into witchcraft and god knows what else, again, thinking that we were all into that. Eventually, we came up with the idea of doing something with Ian Gillan. We met up in England in a pub, I might add, and, as things go, you get totally rat-arsed and you finish up at the end of the night and you've got a band together, which is exactly what happened. [Laughs] That was the next stage and we went into rehearsals with Ian, which was, again, real different. It was different for Ian as well because he didn't know quite how to take it. I enjoyed it with him and he remains one of my better friends. We weren't sure we were even going to call the band Black Sabbath at that time, but of course, as things happen with the record company, it was called Black Sabbath.

The original line-up finished in 1979. Dio came in then and that went on until 1982 or something and Gillan came in about 1983. After Gillan, I did an album, which was supposed to have been a solo album, which ended up as the Sabbath album, SEVENTH STAR. Glenn Hughes sang on that. From that point on, I had a couple of different other singers and we just made a number of albums really.

I'm writing now for a solo album. It's great working with other people for me because it's widening my scope of playing.

:| |•|•|

*W*hen I started off, I think my first guitar was a Watkins, then I had a Burns guitar, but I always wanted a Strat, so eventually I got one, left-handed, which was really difficult to find in this country. I loved the Strat for years until the first album when I went to use it and it broke. I happened to have a Gibson SG, which I'd just bought about a month before the first album as a spare guitar, but I'd never played it. In those days, you couldn't just get a new pickup, especially over here in England. It was terrible trying to get a new pickup. I took it to a guitar shop and they told me the guitar was finished and that I'd have to use another guitar. So, for the first album, I used the Strat for one track, *Wicked World,* and then it broke, so I was on to the SG and I never looked back. I always used the SG after that.

I like the SG because you can get to the top frets easily, especially for me after I chopped off the end of my fingers. It's a light guitar and I just like the shape of it — I always have liked the shape of it.

I'm the first guitar player to come out with 24 frets. I went to guitar companies and they said you can't build 24 frets, it won't be harmonically right. They also said that you can't use light gauge strings because the guitar won't stay in tune. So I started a guitar company here in England. I backed a mad professor and he came up with the guitar I wanted — a 24-fret guitar. We did all the experimenting and, later on, guitar companies started catching on to it and making 24-fret guitars and using light gauge strings like that, including Gibson.

This particular Gibson that I'm holding is a one-off, 24 fret Gibson SG that J.T. at Gibson made for me, and he also put a 'whammy bar' on it, which is the first one they've ever put on an SG. So it's great.

I always have my own pickups, which I've designed and tested through the years and found one that I really liked. Then we made them with a guy in Birmingham by the name of John Diggins who made guitars for me. He worked with me on the road for a while so he knew everything that I needed, which has been a great help even with Gibson. He's told them what sort of feel or what I need and they can make it. J.T. at Gibson is great and we've got quite a bit coming up in the future. We've renewed our relationship and we're coming up with some new plans.

I have worked with Laney Amplifiers for more than 28 years. Dave designed all of this stuff. I got in touch with Lyndon Laney and Dave and Lyndon came to Monmouth, where we were recording, to talk about building a new valve amp or tube amp. Dave is the one who's very clever with all of this stuff. We played a sound and we said we like this idea and that idea and Dave sort of put the thing together. They listened to my stage sound initially and said, okay, this is what we're looking for. Let's try and improve on that, which they did. They still keep coming up with new ideas.

I was looking for a great sounding amplifier that you could just turn on without millions of knobs and graphics and stuff and get a great sound. I thought there was a big hole in the market for something like that. They provided exactly what I wanted. There was a real quality of sound and also it stood the test of touring as well. Some of them you can go out there and they'll blow up. These have had a right hammering over the last year while we were out on tour all over the world in terrible weather conditions and everything. They really did take a pounding. They're also built for people in the crew so they can set up easier. Dave got together with my guitar tech and they've worked on the best way that these things can be linked up.

I personally didn't like transistor amps, and when Laney did change over to doing a lot of transistor amps, I was upset. I think Dave and Lyndon and everybody really wanted to go back to doing tube amps. The transistor was a bit hard for me. I didn't like that sound. I like that warmth of the valve and the response it gives. It's like the difference between tape and digital recordings. Digital is a harder sound. It the same between a valve and transistor.

The good thing about Laney is that they make their own speakers and everything at this factory. It's all under one roof, which is great because, when I want to try something out, they don't have to bring in stuff.

B.B. King

Riley B. King
Born September 16, 1925
Itta Bena, Mississippi

:|B.B. King|·|·|

Outside of Eric Clapton, who was obviously a disciple, B.B. King can do more with less notes, can wring more emotion from six guitar strings, than most players on the planet. Perhaps that comes as no surprise when you consider the course of his life, as writer David Ritz did in co-writing King's autobiography, *Blues All Around Me*. "The way B describes pain — feelings of being misunderstood by his children, sadness about the collapse of two marriages, hurt suffered from racial insensitivity — flow from him like spontaneous music," observed Ritz. "His stories seem to carry the same theme as his blues: 'Mistreatment,' says B, 'makes me sad.' But, in telling the tale, his rhythms turn grief to joy and his suffering sounds like a song."

Born in rural Mississippi, King was initially influenced by the gospel music that he heard in the Deep South, but in the '40s during a stint in the army, his love affair with the blues and the guitar blossomed. After the war, he headed for Memphis, and with the help of blues harp legend Sonny Boy Williamson, King became a regular on local radio station KDIA. It was a turning point in the career of B.B., the Beale Street Blues Boy, as he came to be known during that period. It was here that he met many of his own blues idols and where he ran into Ike Turner, who signed him to the Kent/Modern/RPM group of labels with which King would have the first of many hit R&B singles in 1952 with *Three O'Clock Jump*. By this time, he was on the road constantly throughout the year, a rigorous schedule he keeps to this day, though he is over 70 years old.

Over the years, King, who was inducted into the Rock and Roll Hall of Fame in 1987, has picked up a houseful of honors, including an honorary doctorate at Yale University, a Presidential Medal of the Arts, and seven Grammy Awards, as well as Lifetime Achievement awards from the Grammys, the Songwriters' Hall of Fame, and the Gibson guitar company. But perhaps more gratifying than all of those tributes is the ultimate knowledge that he helped blues cross over to the mainstream and in the end affected the course of the history of contemporary music.

"Without a doubt, B.B. King has influenced more rock and blues musicians than anyone else in history," guitarist/vocalist Bonnie Raitt wrote in tribute to King on the dust jacket of his autobiography. "There is simply no one else with more raw passion or eloquence.... He's also the kindest and most generous person to other musicians I know.... There are reasons why he's been loved and revered for so long — it's the dignity and heart he brings to his life as well as his music, and the fact that he's always true to why we loved him in the first place."

We spoke to B.B. King, in the company of his beloved 'Lucille', his 'signature' black Gibson Custom ES335 guitar, backstage at the Concert Hall in Cincinnati, Ohio, just prior to a concert on a particularly chilly late autumn evening.

*W*hen I was young, back in the country, we didn't have guitars around much at the time, so we would take the wire off a broom that you'd sweep the floors with. That wire's pretty good — it's what we call bailing wire — and you take one nail, nail it up on the back wall, and then you take another nail and put it down at the bottom. You could put something like a small brick underneath it, which would make it look and act like a bridge, and the nut would go at the top and, the more you tighten it, the better sound you get.

My first guitar was a little red Stella, about two feet long, which had the round hole in the center. A man, who lived not too far from the farm where I lived, had it and I got my boss to buy it for me. It was one of the loves of my life at that time.

I had several guitars, though. I had a Silvertone, which Sears-Roebuck made, and I also had an Epiphone during the period when I was about 15 until my 20s. Basically, it was a matter of any guitar I could get. The first Gibson was the Lucille model. The nickname 'Lucille' for that guitar came from the time I used to play at a place in Twist, Arkansas. It used to get quite cold in Twist, Arkansas, so they would take something like a big garbage pail, set it in the middle of the dance floor, half fill it with kerosene, and they would light it, and that's what we used for heat. People would dance, and usually they would dance around it and never disturb it. One night, two guys started to fighting and one knocked the other one over on this container. When they did, it was already burning, so it looked like a river of fire and everybody started running for the front door, including B.B. King. The reason for running for the front door was because they always nailed up the back to keep people from sneaking in. Anyway, when I got on the outside, I realized I had left my guitar and I went back into the building for it. When I did, the building started to collapse around me, burning real fast, so I almost lost my life trying to save my guitar. The next morning, we found out that these two guys, who were fighting, were fighting about a lady that worked in the little nightclub. I never did meet her, but I learned that her name was Lucille, so I named my guitar Lucille to remind me never to do a thing like that again.

In the church, my pastor played 'electric' guitar with some kind of a pickup on his acoustic that electrified it. When I left Mississippi and went to Memphis, I got a good job working at a place called the Newberry Equipment Co. We made tanks — not the shooting tanks, but the ones you put under the ground to hold fuel for service stations. That's when I got my first guitar and first amplifier. I had a Gibson amp and a little black Gibson guitar. That was the first 'Lucille'. I don't remember the number on it but it had the 'f' holes and I put a dual pickup on it. The neck on Gibson guitars has been, from then until today, so beautifully rounded that it just fit my hand so and that was one of the reasons I wanted the solid body, black one.

:| |•|•|

The sound, the amplified sound. See, I had played so long without electricity and had learned to sustain the sound pretty good. I used very heavy strings then because the drug store where I bought my strings in Indianolo didn't sell but one kind called Black Diamond and that was it. Some of them were like that wire I used to hang up on the side of the wall — big strings! I don't even know today what gauge they were, but my E string would be equal to my G string that I'm playing now. So, I was used to that. But once I got an electric guitar, I found that I didn't have to play as hard. I didn't have to hit the strings as hard to keep the sound going, and I guess I sort of learned to manipulate the sound a little bit — cheat if you will — and the guitar then seemed to sing to me and that's what I really wanted to do. Not to just pick, pick, pick …

[Demonstrates trademark trill sound] That sounded so much better to me. I don't know how to tell you this, because I had nothing really planned, but the guitar sounds so much better to me when I would play like that. I learned how to do that well enough not to break strings every time I do it. People think, 'Oh, my god, he's gonna break the strings!' but I can kind of hear. What you do is push it up three or four intervals and, the way I think of it in my head, I first hit, shall we say, the E to G, C to D, then push the D up to E, and then back to C again. This is the way I hear it in my head, so, whatever position I'm in, I can still hear the tonic, the third, fifth, and the tonic again, then I'll hit the ninth and push it up to the third again, then the fifth, then the tonic. Most people know me by this. [Demonstrates] That's my trademark and I do it without knowing I'm doing it sometimes. It seems to talk to me.

When I hear the guys playing the slide, like the country players playing the steel, it just goes all through me. That's what started me 'trilling' like that. I do it with all fingers. After hearing that sound in my head, I kept trying to reproduce it. Even today, I don't play exactly what I hear — pretty close, but I still hear something I don't play. I'd say sometimes, if I'd see it, I wouldn't know it. Now, when I pick up the guitar, I have to fight myself to keep from doing that [trilling]. It's such a habit now that it's hard to break. The action is right in the wrist. It's not like some seem to think [bends the string]. Some of the kids tell me they've figured out the technique pretty well but can't seem to master it. I guess it started with me because it was many years before I was able to live in a place that had electricity. In the early years, we had no electricity, so I only saw electric lights on the weekend when we went to town. Finally, when I was about 19, they started to run the lines out and then you didn't have outlets for the electricity around like you see today. We had one light hanging down and, in order to plug in any other accessories, you had to have an adapter where you put the bulb in that thing and put it up in there and you'd put your cords in that. That's the way we had electricity.

One of the reasons I play single string so much now is because, in my years working with bands, I was never able to sit in the rhythm section like other guys. Every time I'd sit in the rhythm section, guys would say, 'Go ahead, B.B., play, play!' So I guess I had a pretty good idea how to sort of pull the rhythm section and show off a bit myself, and I think that's how I got started into it. But I guess I'm what they call a lead guitarist. I can't play rhythm worth anything. If I'm playing behind somebody, I can push them pretty good. I can support them, but not me. I think in my case, though, without playing the chords, I learned to play a rhythmic 'chop' behind my own playing to give me a sense of where I am. [Demonstrates] Nobody can do that like Chet Atkins, though.

T-Bone Walker was a great influence on me, but before him I had people like Lonnie Johnson, whom I'm still crazy about. I carry records and have tapes on him today. Most of the kids are crazy about Robert Johnson, and, although Robert was a great guitarist, he didn't do it for me. It was Lonnie Johnson that did it, then Blind Lemon. But both of these played acoustic guitars, singing the blues.

But when I heard T-Bone Walker playing the electric guitar and that single string style he did — I still can't do it — man, I just went crazy for that. That seemed to me was the sweetest sound this side of heaven. I'd never heard nothing sound like that. Then when I did see him, he had one of the big full body Gibson guitars. The big one — it had three pickups on it — and he would play it lying on his chest. I can't even play it straight up. His sound was so precise. It seemed to me that he never missed anything. Every time he hit a note, you knew it was T-Bone.

So I think that helped me, though, to develop my own style because, not being able to play like any of the guys I idolized like T-Bone, Charlie Christian, Django [Reinhardt], Segovia, a great classical guitarist — and I could play like none of them, still can't — I guess my brain don't work with my hands.

Actually, there's another guitar player, other than T-Bone Walker, who I don't talk about as much but was equally influential on me, and that's Johnny Moore. There was the Moore Brothers. One played guitar with Nat Cole and that was Oscar Moore and the other one, Johnny, played with Charles Brown. They had the Johnny Moore Trio. Man, he would hit chords like major sevenths. Oh man, his playing would just drive me crazy. He had other ways of playing the same chords. I never could get them. I can play it behind other people on certain songs, but, you know, for most of the blues — real, deep blues — you've got to be very, very careful when using chords like that because they won't sound right. Some kids think I don't know any chords. I do know chords. I just can't accompany myself with them.

:| |•|•|

People often talk to me about the blues being sad or melancholy. I think there's two sides to the blues. For example, if I play ... [Demonstrates with guitar and vocal] ... "Got a sweet little angel, I love the way she spreads her wings. Sweet little angel, love the way she spreads her wings ... " See the guy is happy. "When she spreads her wings around me, I get joy and everything." He ain't blue at all. But then, on the other hand: "Nobody loves me but my mother, and she could be jivin' too ... " Now that's about as low as you can get with it.

Robbie Krieger

THE DOORS

Robby or Robbie Krieger
Born January 8, 1946
Los Angeles, California

:|Robbie Krieger|·|·|

The story is now well-known of how the Doors formed after a chance meeting on Venice Beach in California between Jim Morrison and Ray Manzarek, a classically-trained pianist who had come to prefer boogie to Beethoven. He listened to some of Morrison's spacey poetry amd lyrics and knew immediately that there was great potential for a musical collaboration between them. It was the summer of 1965, and The Doors began rehearsals prior to their move into some of the dingy clubs along Sunset Strip. They eventaully landed themselves a regular gig at Whiskey A Go-Go, where Manzarek, drummer John Densmore, and guitarist Robbie Krieger, who had played with Densmore previously in the group Psychedelic Rangers — and spells his name both as Robby and Robbie — developed a competent, even mesmerizing music presence on stage. But it was Morrison, the self-proclaimed Lizard King, possessed by the demons, spirits, and drug-induced specters of his own mind's creation, who increasingly became the focal point of the band.

The first Doors album was released in January 1967, and though the critics raved over Morrison's singing and stage presence, it was the song *Light My Fire*, which, in part, featured Krieger's memorable guitar solo, that would remain the musical moment that would largely define the Doors' place in rock music history. Over the next two years, as the other members of the group found the commercial touch with single releases like *Love Me Two Times* and *Hello, I Love You*, Morrison was becoming increasingly disillusioned with his status as rock star. The drugs and heavy drinking took their toll and his behavior became more and more unpredictable. He gained weight, grew a beard, and hid behind dark glasses in an effort to divest himself of his rock star image and escape the whirl of media attention. He eventually fled America for Paris with his wife, Pamela Coulson, dreaming of living the artist's life on the banks of the Seine writing books and poetry. Instead, his life came to an end under mysterious cricumstances — he was found dead by his wife in their bathtub of what has variously been reported as pneumonia or a heart attack. Pamela died three years later of a heroin overdose.

The story is one of which legends are made — and biographical films. It was the use of the Doors' epic piece *The End* in Francis Ford Coppola's film *Apocalypse Now* in 1979 that brought on the first surge of "Doorsmania." Danny Sugerman's controversial book on Morrison and the group, titled *No One Gets Out of Here Alive*, was published a year later and it became the catalyst for Oliver Stone's biographical film on the group in 1991 with Val Kilmer as Morrison and Meg Ryan as Pamela Coulson. Robbie Krieger was portrayed by actor Frank Whaley.

The Doors were inducted into the Rock and Roll Hall of Fame in 1993, and for Krieger, who has continued with an active solo career over the past two decades, starting with the 1977 album, ROBBIE KRIEGER AND FRIENDS, while pursuing a career as an artist that has seen his works exhibited throughout the U.S., it was a once-in-a-lifetime experience. "That was pretty cool," recalls Krieger. "We got to play with Eddie Vedder [of Pearl Jam] and not only that, we got to see The Cream get together and play for the first time in I don't know how many years. It was really cool just to be at the rehearsals and see all that happen."

We spoke to Robbie Krieger one evening in the backyard of his Hollywood Hills home in Los Angeles, California.

*W*e had a piano at our house when I was a kid and my mom played a little bit, but my dad had all these great 78 rpm records. A lot of them were Rhythm & Blues from the '40s, so I used to listen to those all the time and I really dug them. I knew there was something there because, on the radio, nobody was playing anything like that. Around 1956, when Elvis came out, he started singing some of the stuff I had heard on those 78s. I thought 'Yeah, this is cool!'

The first kind of guitar that I really dug was Spanish classical and flamenco. At first I just borrowed guitars. I went to school up at a place near San Francisco called Menlo, and some of the guys had guitars that I would borrow. Then, finally, I got my own guitar. It was a Mexican flamenco guitar; a really nice guitar.

John Densmore and I had a band called the Psychedelic Rangers with another friend of ours, Grant Johnson, who is a great keyboard player, and another guy, Bill Wolfe, who had taught me how to play guitar up at school. The Pyschedelic Rangers only made one record called *Paranoia*. The music was like the name, psychedelic. It was kind of bluesy, but it was also patterned after the group Arthur Lee and Love a little bit.

The fact is, I hadn't even played electric guitar until about six months before The Doors started. I had only played flamenco and folk music. I did a thing like Bob Dylan with a harmonica holder and folk guitar. I hadn't played electric yet until I saw Chuck Berry play one day at Santa Monica Civic. It was a great show. This was before Chuck got bored with it all. Boy, he was so great that I traded in my flamenco guitar for a Gibson SG.

In those days, I tried to be simple and not overplay any one thing. Even though I like that Chuck Berry show, I tried not to play Chuck Berry riffs, which is what everybody else was playing up until that time. I just wanted to be different. I wanted to play something that didn't sound like everybody else.

When we formed The Doors, we didn't really have any specific musical philosophy in mind. We just started playing. Jim Morrison always liked the slide, which nobody was really playing much yet, and I think that's why he wanted me to be in the band. We ended up using the slide quite a bit, but, other than that, we had this Vox organ that we got for free from Vox and that sort of became our sound out of necessity.

The fact that we didn't have a bass or a rhythm guitar player meant that I had to play all of those roles a little bit. The fact that I played with my fingers on my right hand allowed me to play a little bass with my thumb and rhythm and lead all at the same time. Ray Manzarek played the keyboard bass, which was kind of an odd sounding thing, but it was not as punchy or anywhere near as efficient as a real bass, so I ended up playing some bass-type stuff. For instance, on *The End*, I would tune down and just keep a drone going with my thumb.

I always played with my fingers, you know, finger picking, mainly because I had come from playing flamenco and I never had learned to use a pick. One day, I read an article by Wes Montgomery and he said if he had to do it all over again, he would learn to use a pick. That's when I learned to use a pick. It took a long time, but I'm glad that I did because there are a lot of things you can do with a pick that you can't with your fingers. After I learned to use the pick, I became obsessed with speed like everybody else. It's nice to be

180 | •| •| **Robbie Krieger** |:

able to do both. I mainly use fingers for slide now.

Too many kids today, who are learning to play guitar, learn the wrong way. They should be learning from the old blues guys and learn how to play with their fingers first and then learn the pick later. It's what you play more than how much you can play that counts.

To begin with, The Doors played not only at the Whisky, but we also played in New York for about a year, every night, at various clubs, and that's where we really became what we were. A lot of those songs really evolved on stage compared to what they started out to be. It was kind of neat because we had the time to improvise. Some of the songs got stretched out to more that three minute songs, like *Light My Fire* or *The End* or *The Music's Over*, and we could do whatever we wanted. Every night would be different, so it was really great for improvising. Most bands really didn't get the chance to do that as much as we did.

On the first album, it was exactly how we played live because we didn't have the money and the studio time to do anything else. I think maybe that's why the first album still stands up today because we had played those songs so many times, over and over, and by the time we recorded them, it was just a matter of turning on the tape machine and playing. And I think a lot of times that turns out to be the best kind of album. As we went on, we had more money and more studio time and more tricks to fool around with and it became more of a studio thing.

One of my favorite songs with The Doors was *Riders On The Storm* on the L.A. WOMAN album. One day we were just fooling around playing *Ghost Riders In The Sky* ... [plays a segment of song] ... and it sort of sounded to Jim like "Riders on the storm," so I guess that's where he got the idea for the words. And, musically, it had the same kind of ambience because of the sound of the guitar — the surf kind of guitar.

My favorite solo with The Doors is the one on *Music's Over*. I wished that I had done a better solo on *Light My Fire*. We only had two takes and that was one of my favorite solos to do live, but I never really thought that I got that one good, but every guitar player that comes up to me always says, 'Hey, I learned your solo on *Light My Fire*. It's really great.' So maybe it did turn out okay.

:| |•| •|

Ray Manzarek had a lot of old blues albums. He came from Chicago and used to see Muddy Waters and all the guys from

Chicago play blues. He had a John Lee Hooker album and I remember we used to take acid and listen to it. His song *Crawlin' King Snake* really got to all of us, I think. At first I thought, 'Well, he [Hooker] ain't much of a guitar player,' because he didn't play much, but, after hearing him on acid, I would say I really learned to appreciate him because he was so primal or primitive or something, not only in his singing, but his guitar playing as well. It really taught me the importance of simplicity and just playing whatever is important rather than playing a lot of notes. A lot of the gys who are really good technically often lack on the emotional end, but there are also some guys who can do it all, like Stanley Jordan. I think he's incredible. A lot of guys who had all the talent in the world, like Pat Martino for instance, he has said that he could play as good as he can play now when he was at the age of 11. That make s me so jealous. I think some people may have been into music in their past lives or something. It came harder for me. [Laughs]

Django Reinhardt was another one of my favorites because of the way he played and the emotion he had. Les Paul was great because he took that kind of playing and added all the electric stuff to it and all the tricks of the studio. It was great playing with Les Paul at his recent birthday party. I went and saw Les Paul at his club in New York one time and we had a good time there. He then came out to the west coast to do a show on his birthday at the House of Blues in L.A. and they had about ten of us guitar players come up and sit in with him. It was pretty cool. I think I was the only one who called a song that he knew — *Georgia*. He loved that and he really got into that one.

As far as my choice of guitars, I always liked the Gibson SGs. They were red for one thing, but the main thing was that they had this nice long neck with a lot of frets so you could get up really high and do stuff up there without having to bend your thumb around the neck. They were also fairly cheap. It was just an all around good guitar for the money. With The Doors, I always had SGs, but, three or four years after The Doors, I never used SGs again. I alway sused Gibson 335s and 355s. I used Fenders for a while but always came back to Gibsons.

This particular SG I'm holding was made by Gibson with the idea that they would put it out under my name. Unfortunately it hasn't happened yet but maybe it will one day. It's a really cool SG because it's got Tiger wood. Most SGs are just painted. It's also got this graphite neck which has really held up well. This was one of the first graphite necks they ever used. It's got gold hardware and stuff. They said it would be too expensive to put out, but I think it would sell no matter how much they charged for it.

I've always taken really good care of my guitars. I would never do like The Who and Jimi Hendrix used to do, burning your guitar and stuff. It's funny we should be talking about that. I was just speaking with Ravi Shankar yesterday and he was saying that in India the musicians really look to their sitars as sacred almost. He said he was really appalled at Monterey Pop when those guys burned their guitars.

My stage set up is kind of odd. I've been using the guitar synthesizer which Roland makes. I have a pedal board, which has all the regular kind of effects on it, and then I have a volume pedal for the synthesizer, which is like a pickup that mounts on the guitar and then it runs over to a synthesizer in the rack. Then I have Midi pedals with which I can change programs on the synthesizer at the same time as the effects on my guitar. I can mix the two sounds together with the volume pedals. It makes for some pretty odd sounds sometimes.

Since The Doors, and with my solo work, I became more interested in music for music's sake. I got infatuated with jazz/rock players like John McLaughlin. My idea was to try to combine jazz with rock but in a way that was different than those guys were doing. Larry Coryell and McLaughln were jazz guys who could play a million miles an hour and they tried to take that into rock 'n' roll, which was kind of cool. My idea was to take rock 'n' roll guys, like me, and move towards jazz with a rock feel and more of a rock 'n' roll sound to the guitar that I think a lot of the rock guys had more experience with. With The Doors anyway, half of the guitar thing was the sound of the guitar. We spent a lot of time on getting feedback and all those things just right, whereas your jazz guy would pretty much turn on his guitar and put it through a little Fender amp and that would be it. It's a great sound but it's the same for most of your jazz players. I wanted to take those ideas and try and incorporate jazz riffs into that kind of music.

I'm not sure I influenced many people guitar-wise. My style was kind of odd and I haven't heard a lot of people try to copy it. I do hear a lot of Doors influence on the radio, that's for sure. There are so many groups that do try to sound like The Doors, which is fine with me.

Brent Mason

Brent Mason
Grover Hill, Ohio

:|Brent Mason|·|·|

"There's thirteen hundred and fifty-two guitar pickers in Nashville and they can pick more notes than the number of ants on a Tennessee ant hill." That's how many extraordinary players you'll find in Music City U.S.A. and the extent of their picking proficiency, according to John Sebastian in the song *Nashville Cats* he recorded with the group The Lovin' Spoonful back in the '60s. The song was meant as a tribute to the backroom boys and girls in the music industry who ply their trade as session musicians out of the glare of the spotlight, heard but not seen, on the thousands of records that are released every year.

Sebastian's hypothetical figure of 1352 regarding the number of guitar pickers extant in Nashville is certainly open to question on either the plus or minus side, but few people would argue if you placed one particular guitar player, by the name of Brent Mason, in the low numbers at the top of that list.

Now that name may not ring a bell, but be assured that if you've heard records by country stars Alan Jackson, The Mavericks, George Strait, Brooks & Dunn, and Trisha Yearwood, among others, you've heard Mason's work. Despite the anonymity of pickers like Mason, some fans of the guitar and of the people who play them can often sniff out the ace from the joker on any recording, like devotee Butch Snyder, who posted the following message to the 'imusic' Brent Mason Bulletin Board on the Net. "I started out playing jazz and rock," Snyder wrote. "I migrated to country-style playing via Albert Lee, Jerry Donahue, and a few others. I noticed a while back that on virtually every country song being played on the radio, the electric guitarist sounds the same. Now I know why. If you had a guy playing in the studio who could play like that wouldn't you use him anywhere possible? I kind of got a little disgruntled with today's country style. It seemed to sound to much like '70s rock. Along comes Brent Mason and he single-handedly put the much-needed 'twang-punch-bite' back where it belongs. He has rejuvenated my interest in country super-picking."

Though Mason, who has also had some success as a songwriter, has built his considerable reputation in the country field, the recent release of his solo album for Mercury Records, titled HOT WIRED, gave him the welcome opportunity to showcase other sides of his musical personality. As Mason recently told a writer at the 'imusic' web site [imusic.com/showcase/country/brentmason.html] "... I grew up playing all kinds of things. I listened to as many pop, rock and jazz players as country guys. I do a lot of R&B-sounding things or pop or rock-type things on records, but people don't know it's me, because they associate me with my Fender Telecaster and the kinds of sounds and licks that I use on country records. But you get booked up, and you don't get a whole lot of chances to just get out there and blow it out. HOT WIRED gave me a chance to play in some other styles that have always been a part of who I am as a musician, to stretch out a bit, and to kind of pay tribute to some of my heroes, like George Benson, Larry Carlton, Pat Marino, Hank Garland and Jerry Reed."

We spoke to Brent Mason at his studio and in the backyard of his home in Franklin, Tennessee, a short jaunt down the road from Nashville, where, besides sharing some of his recording experiences with us, he demonstrated his virtuosity on a vintage, post-war non-cutaway Gibson ES300 and his much-used ES335.

*W*hen I was growing up, my folks played country music, so we had Merle Haggard and Ernest Tubb and Chet Atkins records around the house. My dad was a big Chet Atkins fan and he'd play a lot of his albums. That's what initially got me interested in the guitar. Of course, I play with a thumb pick, and so did my dad. He listened to Merle Travis. When I was about five years old, I said, 'Is that guy doing two things at once on guitar? Is that one guitar doing that?' And dad said, 'Yeah, he's doing the thumb-finger style.'

I listened to Jerry Reed a lot as a kid, but I played a lot of Chet's stuff too. They [Chet Atkins, Merle Travis, and Jerry Reed] all hung out together, so they stole a lot of stuff from each other. Travis played with the thumb back and forth, which I did a little bit. Reed was doing syncopated things, which I got into, but he got his stuff from Chet and elaborated on it. As I said, I listened to

Chet and Jerry a lot and I later recorded a song in their style of guitar playing. It's called *First Rule Of Thumb* with the bass lines and the melody on top. As I got to be 17 or 18, I listened to people like Jeff Beck and started broadening out from the country thing. James Burton, too — he was a sort of hybrid of players that influenced me.

My great uncle Kermit Mason, he and my dad — and sometimes me — we'd sit around the kitchen playing. He'd do the Merle Travis thumb picking style. That was way back when I was a kid. When my uncle passed away a few years ago, he left my dad this Gibson ES300 guitar. Dad gave it to me to use on a recording session. When I got it out of the case, it still had the price inside the guitar case. It was 625 bucks and that's from 1947. It's a great guitar. I used it on a few western-swing kind of sessions as well as on an album by saxophone player Kirk Whelan, who plays with Whitney Houston. He came and did an R&B/country-flavored thing. I also used it on a cut by The Mavericks. Raul Malo did a little jazz song and I did a little comp thing with his vocal. I used it on that. It's got the fat sound, but I've got lighter gauge strings on it, so it's a little wiry and you can get the twangy stuff, too, for jazz chords.

The first guitar I got was an Epiphone acoustic — a steel string guitar — and I had that for a good long time and I would work out those Chet Atkins and Jerry Reed finger styles. I'd work all that stuff out on the guitar and kind of dissect it by moving the arm of the record player back and forth and dig grooves in the record trying to learn the licks the hard way. But even before that, there was an old hand-made guitar we had around the house, and I would take it and use a table knife and play slide and blues. We also had blues albums and artists like Ray Charles and I'd play slide with that. My mom and dad played and my younger brother plays, so I had it in me.

There was no conscious effort on my part to take up the guitar professionally. I didn't really think about that. I'd just wake up and have a guitar next to my bed and pick it up. I'd go without eating dinner sometimes and play the guitar. Mom would say, 'Hey, aren't you going to put the guitar down for just five minutes?' and do this or that chore. Playing guitar was the thing I was the best at during my teens, so I knew that was what I was going to shoot for.

I was in Ohio at the time in a little town called Van Wert — actually it was Grover Hill, just outside of Van Wert. It was just a little bump town. There were some good musicians who came out of there. Lima, Ohio was like a little Bakersfield. There were guys playing that west coast style of music. When I was 16, my mom and dad brought me down here to Nashville and I met Chet Atkins and talked to him a little bit and he encouraged me. I had to go back home and finish school, though.

Before I came back again, I got married and worked in a factory. I had also been doing the club circuits on the weekends and maybe four nights a week just wearing myself out trying to get up and do this factory work and then go to the clubs. I finally got laid off there and I said, 'Let's go to Nashville! We've got to be there to get something happening.' Timing is everything. I initially worked the Stagecoach Lounge on Murfreesboro Road. It was a little honky tonk joint — a knife and gun club. I did that for about six years. When I first got here, a guitar player here in town by the name of Greg Galbraith, who worked with Bill Anderson, told me that there was a club that needed a guitar player and a singer. I told him to call them and we went down there and got the job and ended up there for about six years.

It was actually quite a hot spot for musicians. Musicians would roll into town from all over, and guys like George Benson would come in, believe it or not. Actually it was Chet Atkins who brought George down. He brought a lot of guys down, including Mark Knopfler when he was in town. We had a good, hot band. Some of the guys were ex-road-band players. We had a guy from Jerry Reed's group. Don Kelly was the band leader and he did some Texas blues. We mixed it up and did some cover tunes. It was a hot spot for a while, but I wasn't really getting anywhere. I was just scraping by because you don't get rich playing clubs. You have a lot of fun and keep your chops up.

Doing the STAY TUNED album with Chet [Atkins] was great. As I said, Chet came down to the club with George Benson that one night and he called me the next day and asked me if I wanted to play on this album, which was a compilation of great guitar players like Larry Carlton, George Benson, and Steve Lukather. That blew me away. I said I'd look at my book, and it looked like a snow storm, so I said, 'Yeah, just pick a day and I'll write it in!' This was my big break, I thought, and it was actually. I played on a tune called *Leather And Lace* with Mark Knopfler. I went in and over-dubbed on the thing and we traded off a little bit. After that, I got calls like crazy. Everybody was calling me to work on albums. I certainly give Chet Atkins credit for giving me the big break.

Since then, I've played on a lot of records and I get noted for a lot of Alan Jackson country-type stuff. Those sessions stand out because he lets the players take long solos. He's kind of got that mentality like: 'Hey, take 24 bars on this thing!' Alan's got that sort of honky-tonk mentality like: 'Steel guitar for eight and guitar for eight and fiddle for eight more.' He did a song, *I'm In*

Love With You Baby, But I Don't Even Know Your Name. It sounded like an instrumental on the radio.

I enjoy doing different things. I worked on Aaron Neville's record. It's really fun doing that because you can walk in and you're going to play something different every day. And also The Mavericks. The Mavericks play on the records, but I play a lot of the guitar stuff on there. That's sort of a retro kind of thing, which is fun because I have to put on a different hat for that. I've got to think more like Scotty Moore or people like that. There's also a lot of redundancy in town, we all know that. The material on my album [HOT WIRED] is hopefully now more recognizable to people as the way I really play as opposed to playing on other people's records. It gives me more of an identity.

:| |•|•|

A lot of people want to be studio players, and I say, if you want to be a studio player, stay up to date on what's happening on the radio and the tones of guitars and what type of guitar is being played on a particular piece of music. You see a lot of Les Pauls in a band like Lynyrd Skynyrd. Or, ZZ Top — what kind of guitars do they play? You have to look at things like that, especially if you're a studio player, because you want to have that knowledge of what instrument co-relates with what kind of music.

I use a number of different guitars on sessions, but I use a Gibson ES 335 a lot for the front pickup for lead solos, like little screaming ballad solos or something. And I'll use the 335 as well for mellow playing on ballads. It depends on the song. I'll just grab the guitar that works for it. Sometimes they'll request a guitar. I played an ES 295 with the Bigsby on it on the first couple of albums by The Mavericks. I used that a lot seeing that it was kind of retro type stuff.

Another piece of advice I'd give to anyone interested in getting into this thing professionally is to go to college and learn how to read music and educate yourself in that area. A lot of people don't want to be bothered doing that. They say: 'No man, I just want to play rock 'n' roll. I don't want to learn all the mathematics of it.' If you're a studio player, you really need to do that. You also need to practice a lot and eventually you've got to get to a town where it's happening, like Nashville, New York, or L.A., where you can go and actually witness a session and see how they do it. They're sewed up towns and it's really hard to get in, but, if you're great, there's always room for new guys. There's always going to be a new generation of players, so don't lose hope and don't think you'll never get in because there's already too many players.

You've also got to develop your own style. Try not to emulate people too much. We all do that when we learn how to play, but at some point, try to develop your own style. By borrowing licks from other people, sometimes you find your own style.

When you're a session guy, you're more of a chameleon musically. I may walk in and do the Alan Jackson stuff with its twangy style, then I'll walk in and play something that's more jazzy or bluesy or rock 'n' roll. You never know what kind of musical scenario you're walking into when you go into a session. It just goes from one type of music to the other. For me, taking all that stuff in, learning all those techniques way back, helped me out as a session player.

The way sessions go in Nashville, you walk in, you get a chord chart, and you wing it from there. Very seldom do you get a tape to take home and work on. We've just got to be creative and spontaneous, really. So a lot of times I'll grab a solo right on the run down. Sometimes they're the best, but we'll always have time to overdub a good one or set up some dates to work on solos. That's the way it goes here. There's really no pre-production at all. I think the most nervous I've ever been is sitting in a room of professional studio musicians whom I idolized when I was a kid. I was sitting in there with Larry London, the drummer, and I was a nervous wreck because I was just as much a fan of the players as I was the artist. I looked on the back of records and I'd see Larry London and David Hungate or something. When I sat in those studios with those guys, it was more like I was on trial. You felt like you'd better play your butt off on this thing because they are going to judge me from this. I was coming down on myself pretty hard. They were great guys. They wouldn't judge you on the first go round. They did want to hear you, though. It was like, 'Hey, here's this young guy. They say he's a hot picker. Let's see what he does.' I felt like I was on trial for a good long time doing sessions. But it went great. They were so nice. Larry London, who has since passed away, was very nice to me. I learned a lot from those guys. I played some sessions with Reggie Young, the guitar player. It was an experience.

It takes a while to really feel comfortable in a studio because you've got to be creative and spontaneous on the spot. If they say give me a great intro on this song, you've got to come up with it in five or ten minutes and you can't be shy; you've got to throw out the licks and hope they stick.

I don't play every day anymore, although, if I'm watching television or something, I'll have a guitar and tinkle around on it just to keep my chops going, just to keep my hands limber. I'm doing an album now, so I am writing more and playing more, but I don't practice as much as I used to when I was a kid. I wish I had that kind of mentality that I used to have.

In the studio you've got to be diverse. Sometimes if I'm doing calculated parts, I use the pick more than the fingers. But I think I interject my style a lot into the songs that are out these days.

Dave Matthews

DAVE MATTHEWS BAND

Dave Matthews
Born January 9, 1967
Johannesburg, South Africa

:|Dave Matthews|·|·|

Just when it seemed that rock music was becoming stodgy and predictable, along comes a character like Dave Matthews and his band to prove that there's still a little bit of elasticity left to the borders that define contemporary music as we enter a new millennium. Born in Johannesburg, South Africa but currently residing in Charlottesville, Virginia where the Dave Matthews Band has a small studio, Matthews has proven to be a veritable sponge when it comes to absorbing musical influences from the four corners of the globe. In considering his guitar style, it's obvious that percussion is his passion. Rhythm has become an integral part of his guitar style which defies description, and for the most part, duplication. He is self-taught on the instrument and he hears what he hears musically, transferring it to the fretboard in a display of chording and fingering calisthenics that you won't find in a Mel Bay instructional book. But, in the end, it works, as the rising fortunes of the Dave Matthews Band since 1991 will attest.

The band's sound proved infectious, and over the course of three major label CDs and constant touring, their fan base has grown to the point that DMB now find themselves at the top of the pop world. Their latest album at the time of writing, BEFORE THESE CROWDED STREETS, which included a guest appearance on background vocals by Alanis Morissette, debuted at Number One on *Billboard*'s Top 200 album chart and quickly sold close to two million copies on its first week of release in the U.S. Matthews, who sang on the track *Memory Hotel* on the Rolling Stones' album, NO SECURITY, had also teamed up with guitarist Tim Reynolds to release a double CD acoustic live set called LIVE AT LUTHER COLLEGE from a tour they had recently completed during a well-deserved break for DMB.

The suggestion was recently made to Matthews by Michael Vogel of *The Album Network* magazine in the United States that he was one of the most underrated guitar players making music today as he inquired whether Matthews felt that his playing ability has received the recognition and credit it deserves. "First of all, I don't touch electric guitars," was Matthews's reply. "It's just not my thing — I stick with acoustic guitars only. Secondly, I know I have a very unusual style of playing, where other more recognized and technically proficient players might look at me and wonder what the heck I'm doing. The purpose of my learning to play the way I do was more to accompany my singing. I figured out a style where I'm mentally playing the drums over a simple melody. I just try and put it all together and then not mess with it. For me, it's a real obvious way to play, but to others it is simply technically wrong."

We spoke to Dave Matthews, with his Gibson Chet Atkins SST solid-body electric acoustic guitar in hand, backstage at The Starwood in Nashville the afternoon of the Dave Matthews Band's concert that evening.

I think I was into music from before the time I can really remember anything — or at least that's what mommy says. I've always listened to music, but I grew up in a family where everyone listened to music all the time. There was lots of stuff going on, but I was sort of the one who ran with it. My mom played piano — not professionally — and my sister played piano and I played piano for a while — badly. I got my first guitar when I was eight or nine. I never really practiced too much. It became a little more of an obsession, I guess, in high school. But I never jammed. I never learned to play with other people. I was never in a band until the band I'm in now. I think I had a little high school thing, but that was more for drinking beer than it was for playing the guitar. I never really learned songs either. I had a little book of Beatles' songs and I learned a couple of those. I loved The Beatles. I learned some Cat Stevens songs, but really never did much of that either. I just would sit and play a lot. I have a really wrong technique of playing the guitar.

I grew up in New York. My family moved to South Africa when I was two, and we went back when I was 13 after my dad passed away. My family is from South Africa originally. I have grandparents and aunts and uncles and cousins over there. We moved back here after I finished high school, and then we moved to Virginia where my family had lived before. I sort of wandered aimlessly around the world for about five years with a base in Virginia. The band started in 1990 and I started writing and finishing songs in 1989.

I saw Stevie Ray Vaughan play once on TV — I didn't actually go and see him. There were all these different notes and all these different grooves. I was in high school and I was just young and I was just like, 'Wow!' he just has this groove going on. His right hand is just dancing and then he would add notes in over here. That was a big inspiration for me and that was how that kind of a drumming thing came out of it. I learn more from the guitar just watching. I have moments of inspiration. I'll see Robert Fripp playing and I'll say, 'Whoa, he's spreading his fingers out all weird!' and not know that it's because he tuned his guitar all funky, and then go home and try and find things that'll work when you spread your fingers out.

I think my profound lack of knowledge about scales and stuff also helps me find things. I have nothing to fall back on. There's no knowledge there. I just have to search and search until something goes: 'Hey, that sounds good!'

I think simple is really important. Maybe I think that because I can't move very fast. Simple is good because simple is easy. There's a song called *The Soul*, which Jane likes, where we add half a bar — Jane is my little sister. It's a funny thing because so many guitar players that I know who are smoking guitar players — I can't do any of that stuff — find it really hard to do, but it's the most obvious thing. [Demonstrates] It's just that one little slide and people go, 'I can't do that! I can't do that!' That's really satisfying. It's one of the simplest most satisfying things to get some lightning bad-ass guitar player who's like… [Mimics bad-ass guitar player screwing up]

There's a song by Daniel Lanois called *The Maker*. It's just an awesome song. Something with that song just struck me — I don't know how he plays it — it's on the bass, this drone, and just as he starts singing, the chords change. I thought, 'God, this is a genius idea!' so I stole it. But I did it with two steps. I just had this drone and the whole melody comes out of the chords. And I stop singing, then it goes back to the same drone, and it just waits until I start singing again. I think it's satisfying for a listener to hear that too because, as soon as I open my mouth, a whole lot of stuff happens and makes me seem a lot better singer, too. Satisfaction!

I love Bob Marley. One of the reasons I like African music a lot, and a lot of Irish music, is because they use beautiful melodies — and classical music for that reason, too. There's not a lot of music that doesn't do that. I guess there's quite a bit of pop music nowadays that seems to be not as adventurous with melodies. There are a lot of standard melodies and people have one note that they use.

There's a reason for that, but it's not what I'm doing. If we're going to do a drone, it has to be for a very specific reason. A lot of great music isn't really based in melody. Dylan had a lot of melodies but he was almost like a preacher the way he sang. Dylan was an example of a person who had beautiful melodies, but he also sounded like he was talking a lot, so it works. For me, I like to fondle as many notes as I can.

My percussion style of guitar playing probably comes from the fact I played so much alone. It was just my voice and my guitar, so I had to have something behind that would be a drum kit and a chord bass. I do it less now than I used to. I strum more now with open notes and up more than I used to because I'm writing with the band. It sounds more like piano. I love piano. I grew up listening to a lot more piano than I did guitar music. I think that's more like a drum, too, because you're hitting things, whereas with guitar, in general, it's not as much that, except for people like Fripp, whom I really love, and Adrian Belew. They get into these really percussive, syncopated, weird rhythms that I like a lot.

There's a lot of space in our band. We don't use a lot of distortion or fat sounds, although we're getting into that a little more, but it leaves a lot of space open. I know John Popper said that, when he plays with our band, there's so much room. Everything is so chopped because the saxophone isn't like a big keyboard, but, in a way, it is because it can do patches like that. Violin is the same way. It can be percussive, but it can also be like a keyboard patch and take up a lot of space too. Then they take the role of keyboards sometimes, but they also take the role of percussion. We're all pretty obsessed with percussion. It wasn't really a conscious thing for any of us, it was more that we just liked each other's playing regardless of the instrument. I love when Carter [Beauford] plays on the sax. It was the way he played, it wasn't necessarily that he was playing a saxophone. I was a fan of saxophone because it's an instrument that so many people play beautifully, but it wasn't an instrument that I thought about a lot until I met LeRoi [Moore], which is about six years before the band got together. He was really the reason that there's saxophone in the band more than the fact we wanted a saxophone. Boyd [Tinsley] was the reason we have a violin player, not the violin. It was them first, and the same with Stefan [Lessard] on bass. We all just really clicked with the music that was inside of us rather than the instruments that we played.

Some of our music is improvised on stage, but we know where we are. A lot of times we'll go off on tangents and we don't know where it's going to go, so it's kind of exciting. In our heads, we know where we are. We're not lost, but we go in a lot of directions, and there's a hell of a lot of improvisation and change. We don't change the set as much as our friends like Phish. There's a lot of bands that we get put into a category with for whatever reason, but we don't change our sets as radically as a lot of those bands from night to night, though we do change the way we play the song. It might be slower. It might be faster. The melodies change. The way I sing the melodies or the way the solos come in. There are some parts that we repeat like in *Satellite*. Probably Carter is the one who improvises the most there. We change melodies a little bit, but there's not a lot of room for that in that song because it's a piece and it doesn't have a lot of directions it can go in. A song like *Jimmy Thing*, there's a lot of space where we can run around and go off in different directions. Every song is different for that reason, I guess. Some songs invite improvisation and the rest of them demand more specific stuff.

:| |•|•|

I had an Ovation guitar for the first couple of years that the band was together. I don't know why. They're great guitars, but they don't sound the way I really want them to, and, also, the way they feel is real different. I always loved Gibson necks. Once the wire leaves the guitar, that's really the department of my guitar tech and sound engineer. They put things together and build things and make amazing toys for me to sound better. My obsession is more with the strings and with the neck, and I really like Gibson necks. They're pretty wide and kind of deep, and my hand fits on them real comfortably.

I started playing a Chet Atkins model [SST] four years ago. Every once in a while I would try other ones but, for the band setting, it's the perfect guitar. The sound that comes out of it — although we doctor it a lot nowadays because we've got more money — it just cuts through with all the other instruments. It's got its own space, which is important. Ovations could never cut through all the different sounds that were happening. It would just sort of get lost and sit in the background, whereas these seem to take up a real solid place in the sound, so I stayed with them for the band.

I've always played acoustic guitars, though I had an electric once. I guess maybe later on it will change, but I have this automatic urge to play power chords, which is not really my department. I want to turn the distortion up and pretend that I'm a heavy metal guy, which I'm not, although I like it well enough, but I'm more comfortable with an acoustic. It's hollow and it's more like a drum.

These [SSTs] aren't hollow, but they pretend to be. When I'm playing alone, I always play acoustic when I sit at home, whatever weird acoustics I find in stores or steal from friends. I just prefer it, probably for the same reason as the wire thing — the cable thing. The instrument is all there. It's like a piano. It's all at your fingertips and you're directly responsible for the sound. There's not a lot of machinery going on. Ignorance is bliss. I leave all that stuff up to somebody else. That's why I like the acoustic so much.

My playing style has definitely evolved. Playing with these guys, even with the improvisational side of things, I've never played a guitar solo in my life, but every once in a while I'll make an attempt on stage, so that's changed. I still approach the guitar the same way that I used to — maybe my knowledge has grown a little bit — looking at each string separately and looking at them almost like drums. I don't want to be redundant, but it is almost like that. Then, I guess, I started splitting things up a little more like in a song like *Crash* where I have something going on — in the bass there's a melody going on — then there's a drone that just goes the whole time through it. That's changed. I've become more obsessed by drone since the band's been together.

The way I write or the way I play is fairly simple; I doodle for hours and then bump into something. Each song is really different from my last one. At least I try to make them change a lot. I guess with each song I write, my guitar playing grows a little bit because I'm trying not to repeat myself. Sort of an obsession to try and run away from everything I've done in the past, to listen to what's going on outside and other musical things that happen to us everyday, like walking or driving or windshield wipers or whatever they are. There's a lot of music going on.

Although I write with a piano sometimes, we've never done any of that stuff. I sit at home and write a lot with piano. I don't know whether it's called writing, but I doodle and I find things that I like. When we write together, often Stefan and Carter might come up with something and I'll add things. That's another change that has taken place with me. Where originally I was writing for myself so it would be a complete song without everyone else, now we write together. I might just play a part, so that if I choose to do the song acoustically, I have to sit down and figure out what everyone else is doing and cover more bases. Now there are more songs where I have just the one part that I play, and then what Stefan's doing and what LeRoi's doing or Boyd's doing is what changes the chords and stuff. There's more of that and I think we'll move in that direction.

Initially, I was writing all the songs. More and more, we [the band] are writing things together, so I guess the way I'm going to be playing is going to change a lot with that as well. I think it's an obvious evolution. The evolution with us is we understand each other more. We're playing together more than we did five years ago, so we'll be writing more together. And we know each other more. Those are the sort of things that happen.

:| |•|•|

I don't go anywhere without a guitar. I don't know if it's an extension of my body, but I guess in a way it is. It just depends on how you look at it. It is a tool, but it's my favorite tool, the one that I'm most familiar with. I guess in the same way if I was a painter, the brush and canvas would be my tool or would be an extension of me. It's kind of a similar thing I guess. I'm really comfortable with a guitar, though. It seems really obvious to me now. There's a sculptor I know who says that what he's making is already there, he just has to find it. He made a 45-foot whale out of this Redwood tree that fell down. He doesn't cut down the trees. He only uses wood that's been used once already. He's a really cool guy. He's a Maori from New Zealand, but he lives out in L.A. now. He said that the thing is already there and he just has to go in and find it. When he made this whale, he got down to the shape of the whale and the eye — there was a black knot in the wood right where the eye was. It was awesome. He's a trippy guy, but he's very cool.

I kind of like that idea, so I just stole it and said that the songs that I write on guitar are there already. It's all done, I just have to pull it out of the guitar. That way you don't feel as responsible, so if I write a really bad one, I can say it's his fault, not my fault. I guess in that case it's not a tool but I'm its tool, which is probably a more humble way of looking at it.

I think that melodies have always been there and music has always been there. We just have to find a new way to unroll it because it has been there before us. Birds find their melodies the same way. Melodies and scales of humans really develop the same way. When you look at it through science, there are scientific reasons why harmonies work and why melodies work and why scales are the way they are. It all makes sense, so it's much deeper than we are, in a way, or we're deeper than we think we are. I like to think that all the sounds and all the music is already in us, and when you open the door and find something new that maybe nobody's heard before.... I find that if I write a new song that's really different from everything I've done, if it's good, if it's strong, if it's something that I really love, it sounds familiar and sounds like I've heard it a thousand times. *Satellite* was a song like that. When I first wrote that, I was like, 'What is that? I know it's something. I've heard it.' When I played it for one of my friends who plays trumpet, he said the reason it sounds familiar is because it's right. You know you've got it right. So that's a way to look at it, too. I feel almost as though things are just waiting there, because all of the combinations of notes and all the twist and turns, they're already there in a way. It's just a case of pulling them out. The universe is infinite, so they're infinite and the possibilities are infinite, so the music is infinite and you just pull it out of there and see what happens.

Scotty Moore

ELVIS PRESLEY

Winfield Scott Moore III
Born December 27, 1931
Gadsden, Tennessee

:|Scotty Moore|·|·|

In the prologue to his book, *That's Alright, Elvis*, on which guitarist Scotty Moore collaborated with writer James Dickerson to tell the story of his early association with Elvis Presley as his first guitarist and *de facto* manager, there's the fascinating story of Rolling Stones' guitarist Keith Richards's first introduction to Elvis, and, more importantly, to the guitar playing of Scotty Moore.

Against the wishes of his parents, Richards was listening to Radio Luxembourg, a popular European-based pop station with a signal that was strong enough to reach Britain, through the static on his transistor radio late one night in his bedroom when the Elvis single, *Heartbreak Hotel*, came on. He recalls jumping out of bed and running around the room to position the radio to get a more static-free reception as the song played. He reckons that may well have been the moment that changed his life. "I had been playing guitar, but not knowing what to play — without any direction," Richards told Dickerson. "When I heard *Heartbreak Hotel*, I knew that was what I was going to do in life. It was plain as day. I no longer wanted to be a train driver or a Van Gogh or a rocket scientist. All I wanted to do in the world was to be able to play and sound like that. Those early records were incredible. Everyone else wanted to be Elvis. I wanted to be Scotty."

Scotty Moore, who dropped out of school in grade nine to pick cotton so he could buy his first guitar, a Gibson ES295, joined the Navy at the age of 16 and was off to see the world in uniform. The experience opened his eyes in more ways than one. Not only did it expand his geographical horizons but his musical ones as well. He was introduced to the music of a number of the master jazz guitarists like Tal Farlow and Django Reinhardt during that period and began developing his own style in impromptu jams with a number of pickup groups during his time in the service. On his discharge, he moved to Memphis to work in his brother's dry-cleaning business in the day and play in the group The Starlite Wranglers, with bass play-er Bill Black, at night. It was with this group that Moore and Black first came into contact with Sun Records and its owner, Sam Phillips.

In 1954, the group recorded the D.O.A. single *My Kind of Carryin' On* for the label, which on July 19, 1954, released the single *That's Alright, Mama* by a new act known as Elvis Presley with Scotty and Bill accompanying. In those early days, before Colonel Tom Parker, Moore acted as Presley's manager. Moore, drummer DJ Fontana and Black, who died of a brain tumor in 1965, continued to record with Presley until the late '50s when Elvis went into the Army for two years. Moore bought the Fernwood record label and, as producer, had a Top Five hit with Thomas Wayne's *Tragedy* in 1959 before briefly reuniting with Presley in the early '60s as Elvis began to switch his career focus to movies. There was the famed comeback TV special, in 1968, but it would be the last time that Moore worked with Elvis.

Moore put down the guitar at this point to pursue a number of other interests, including producing and engineering. In 1992, he recorded a number of limited edition albums with old friend Carl Perkins, who was battling throat cancer at the time.

In the late '90s, Moore, who had been away from the music main-stream for close to a quarter century by this time, was suddenly back in the media spotlight again with a book, the Scotty Moore ES295 guitar, reissued by Gibson, and the album ALL THE KING'S MEN, on which he reunites with old bandmate DJ Fontana to record with artists like Keith Richards and Ron Wood of the Rolling Stones, Jeff Beck, Steve Earle, The Band, The Mavericks, The BoDeans, Joe Ely, Tracy Nelson and Cheap Trick, among others, who were influenced by Elvis's music in one way or another.

Of those early sessions with Elvis, Moore recalls: "Back then, we had no idea what we were creating as far as music history. We were just having fun and hoping we'd get paid enough to pay our gas back to town."

We spoke to Scotty Moore in his home studio in Joeltown, Tennessee, just outside of Nashville.

I guess the first music I was hearing was Grand Ole Opry stuff. We lived out in the country and had a battery radio — you didn't use it any more than you had to so as to save the batteries. As time went on, I started hearing R & B and other types of music. Anything that had a guitar on it was fine; I loved it.

My dad and my three brothers all played, but they were a lot older than I was. When they left home, I was nine or ten years old. I felt left out. In the back of my mind, not realizing it, that's when I made the decision to play the guitar.

There was a country and western group I put together when I came out of the Navy in 1952, and we worked around Memphis. I knew that to get some decent paying jobs, I'd have to get a record out and get some airplay. That' how I met Sam Phillips and finally convinced him to put a record out for us. Counting all the mothers and wives, we probably sold a dozen or two, but we became good friends. Through meeting Sam [Phillips], later on, I met Elvis Presley.

Elvis's first audition at Sun Records was like a preliminary pre-audition — the audition to the audition. We just played around with different songs for a couple of hours and it seemed like he knew every song in the world. Bill Black lived just a couple doors down the street from me, and he came down and listened. After that I called Sam and said, 'The boy's got good rhythm; I think he might be someone worth working a little bit with.' The next night, we went into the studio and out of that came *That's Alright, Mama*, the first record.

That song came about in a break in the audition, which is what this really was. Elvis had a lot of nervous energy and he just got up and started flailing his guitar, dancing around, and started singing *That's Alright, Mama*. We just fell in with some type of rhythm vamp. I think the door was open to the control room and Sam came out — this was after we had tried a dozen or so songs — and he said, 'That sounds different; what are you doing?' We said, 'Just goofing around.' He said, 'Let's try it no mic and see what we can come up with!' And that was it.

Sam had made an acetate of one song and took it down to Dewey Phillips's Red Hot & Blue show for him to play. We really had to hump to get a B side. I think he had 5,000 or 6,000 on back order in Memphis alone and he didn't have one record pressed at the time.

There were a number of songs that were hard to play, for one reason or another, but it was just a matter of getting that groove that you knew should be there. *Hound Dog* is a good example. While recording, we tried that sucker fast, slow, turned it inside out, on the second solo you could tell I was a little aggravated. It was an anger solo for sure.

We met [drummer] DJ Fontana the first time we played the *Louisiana Hayride*. Every time we had a date down in that area, we'd go and pick up DJ or he'd meet us. He came through playing a lot of strip joints and stuff and he just worked great with Elvis. When Elvis would do his moves, he'd accent them. If he needed to push a little bit in a certain part of the song, he'd do it, or slow back down. He wasn't just locked in on any one beat. We decided we were going to get him full time, and I think he actually went on the payroll in December of 1955. He was the highest paid one of the bunch at that time.

Playing with Elvis, we just tried to play something that we thought would fit the songs. None of us had any music training — we all played by ear and just played things that seemed like they would fit and tried to stay out of his way. With the three of us, I tried to play some kind of rhythm and more or less stab some notes here and there.

Half the time, I never played it the same way twice. I might have got in an envelope here or there and you'd stay within that, but, note for note, every one might be different. A lot of them, I had to go back and re-learn after we recorded them in order to do them on stage. Trying to do some of them now is really hard.

I didn't realize it at the time, but, when you go back and look at things, it was obviously in my mind to keep things simple with my playing. You tried to complement the singer and tried to play something that would fit the lyric, if possible.

Sam Phillips was a pretty tough taskmaster. He knew something when he heard it, if it sounded good, but he wasn't into: 'You've got to put this note there!' He was looking for overall feel — that's what we all did. But he'd push you: 'Let's do one more!' And sometimes he'd say, 'That's it boys' And Elvis would say, 'Well let's do one more.'

Everybody keeps talking about the magic in the Sun studio. It's just a room — four walls and a bunch of acoustic tiles. It was the people who were in there over the years that made it magical. I never heard anybody say 'Abracadabra!' when I was there. What you hear is what you get, and you can't monkey with it later, which ain't bad. That was just three microphones, and Sam really had his hands full. He used an omni-directional mic on Elvis's voice, so he didn't even mic his guitar. The vocal mic would pick that up. Back then, even with bigger bands, it was done with mic placement rather than with mixing. You'd get a balance on everything and then go and move a particular mic six inches to change the tone or change the leakage for better or worse.

:| |•|•|

On the Elvis sessions, I played a Gibson ES-295, a little gold guitar that they came out with. When I came out of the Navy, I'd been using a bunch of Japanese guitars, which I bought over in Japan. The frets on them were made out of beer cans 'cause they'd last about three months and you'd have to go get another one. I bought a Fender Esquire and a small Fender amp, but Fender just didn't have the right feel for me. I was down at the music store one day and saw this ES-295, which was like a big hollow body of the Les Paul. Boy, that thing sparkled. 'I've got to have it,' I thought. I started with that guitar and used it on all the Sun sessions until the last session we did. Then I got a blonde Gibson L5 and, at that point, got Ray Butts to build the Echosonic amp, which would simulate the sound that Sam [Phillips] was using on records. In 1957, I went to a blonde Gibson Super 400.

My favorite guitar is a blonde Gibson L5 — it was one-of-a-kind, which happens with guitars for no apparent reason. They're using the same patterns, but there'll be one, in a different style, that jumps out like that.

I also play a modified Country Gentleman model that was given to me by Chet Atkins. I modified it some because I never could use the tremolo. I took that off and had a Johnny Smith tailpiece put on it, and Chet had these red and white markers put on it. I was curious why, but when I didn't play for 24 years and went back on stage in 1992 with a Super 400, when the lights hit me, I realized why he'd done this. I couldn't see anything and the combination of the red and white show up under whatever light combination you've got.

When people ask me about my favorite guitar players, or the best I've heard, that's a tough question because there are so many of them. You can just go out here in Nashville and turn over a rock and three or four will jump out at you. There are so many different, great styles out there. Of course, there's Chet Atkins, Mark Knopfler, Martin Taylor, and Reggie Young, who I grew up with in Memphis on the music side of things, but there are so many more.

The arthritis is getting to my hands a little bit these days but I still play about two or three times a week and, when the hands get to hurting, I put it down. I've got great respect for the guitar. I guess it's a form of self expression, but then it's a tool as well. But, to me, it's a respectful tool. I try to keep it clean, not just throw it off in a corner when I get through using it.

I had a studio in Nashville called Music City Recorders, because while Elvis was doing all those movies and wasn't touring, I went off and did some engineering. I had always been interested in that. It didn't look like there was going to be any future out there with him doing all the movies, so, after the 1968 special, which was the last thing I did with him, I decided to devote all my time to other interests. I did a little producing and, of course, the engineering and, later on, got into a commercial print shop, and the first thing I knew, 23 years had gone by. I got out of all that and retired and thought: 'What am I going to do now?' In 1992 I got together with Carl Perkins and we did an album together and that same year I went down and did the Elvis Week in Memphis. I guess you just realize that it's in your blood and that's it.

Dan Murphy

SOUL ASYLUM

Daniel Murphy
Born July 12, 1962
Duluth, Minnesota

: Dan Murphy |·|·|

They called it The Minneapolis Sound and, presided over by Prince — now The Artist Formerly Known As Prince — and ultimately the other artists in his music circle, including The Time and Time members Morris Day and producers Jimmy Jam and Terry Lewis (Janet Jackson), its "Uptown" funk and sexy lyrics had a major influence on much of the dance/pop music of the '80s. But the Twin Cities music scene was hardly one-dimensional. By the mid-'80s, Hüsker Dü, the punk/pop trio who would have an enormous influence on the alternative music scene in the years to come, had released their classic double album, ZEN ARCADE, while Paul Westerberg's group, The Replacements, was similarly melding pop and punk to great effect on their definitive third album for the local Twin/Tone label.

It was into this Midwest punk scene that local hell-raisers Dan Murphy, Dave Pirner, and Karl Mueller first emerged in the group Loud Fast Rules. With the addition of drummer Grant Young and a welcome name change to Soul Asylum, they released a number of records through Twin/Tone while endlessly touring the club circuit the length and breadth of America in vans that had seen more miles than the space shuttle. They signed a major label record deal in 1988 with A&M Records, a less than agreeable experience that left the band wearied but wiser when they were dropped from the roster following a management shake-up at the company.

But the touring and the earlier recordings, though of limited distribution, had created a significant fan base. Soul Asylum signed with Columbia Records in 1992 for which they recorded their breakthrough album GRAVE DANCERS UNION, which includes their first major hit single, *Runaway Train*. Following some major touring behind the album LET YOUR DIM LIGHT SHINE in 1997, Dan Murphy found the time to hit the road with The Jayhawks and to continue working with Golden Smog, a group of musicians from the U.S. Midwest, which includes Murphy, Wilco's Jeff Tweedy, and The Jayhawks' Gary

Louris and Marc Perlman, who have recorded a couple of albums, including the latest, DOWN BY THE OLD MAINSTREAM.

At the time of writing, Soul Asylum was touring in support of their ninth full-length album, CANDY FROM A STRANGER, which had been produced by Chris Kimsey, known for his work with The Rolling Stones (STICKY FINGERS, TATTOO YOU, SOME GIRLS) and Peter Frampton (FRAMPTON COMES ALIVE), among others.

We spoke to Dan Murphy on a mild October night in an alleyway outside of a Hollywood, California studio where a few of the neighbors were convinced, with the proffer of a few bucks as a goodwill gesture, to stay off their balconies while the interview was in progress and the camera was rolling. Who says money don't talk?

I grew up in Duluth, Minnesota and moved to Minneapolis when I was about 10 or 11 years old. I started playing guitar when I was in sixth grade, so I started pretty young. I must have been 11 or 12. I had an older stepbrother and he played guitar. He gave me three or four lessons and taught me how to play Rolling Stones songs and stuff like that. That was kind of my social life. I used to sit in my room and play along to records, go and see concerts, smoke pot, and do what every other kid in America did in the '70s. That was pretty much my interest; smoke pot and play along to bands I liked. I learned their songs and took it from there.

I went through a lot of phases. I think the first show I ever saw was The Guess Who and Poco opened for them. That was kind of cool. I was really into Aerosmith for a while. I spent hours wearing out those records. The Rolling Stones I always liked and I sat around and listened to the Rolling Stones play blues and stuff on records like BEGGAR'S BANQUET and LET IT BLEED. I even liked the shit that everyone else hated. I thought that some of the songs on BLACK AND BLUE, like *Memory Motel,* were great songs with real pretty guitar figures and stuff. The first big rock extravaganza I saw was Nazareth opening up for Aerosmith. I was just blown away. It was so fucking loud. I thought it was great. I knew right then, that's what I wanted to do. I wouldn't have to work; I could do this.

I also thought that Thin Lizzy was a great band, then I discovered new wave and punk rock and was really into The Clash — really simple stuff, like powerful guitar sounds. Mick Jones, I thought, was a great player. Karl [Mueller], who is our bass player in Soul Asylum, took a trip to London in 1979 and he came back with leather bondage pants and his hair spiked and safety pins and stuff, and I was like, 'Karl, I don't know!' We formed a band in that spirit called Loud Fast Rules with Dave Pirner, who's our singer/songwriter guy, as our original drummer. We were a three-piece band. We really sucked, but we had a lot of fun. It was a good time. Karl started playing bass, and, literally, a week later, the first time he had ever picked up a bass, we were doing shows — sort of. Soul Asylum is just the continuation of that. It's pretty much the same three guys, and thank God, we've gotten a little bit better or I wouldn't be here today.

The long days that we spent on the road are all kind of a blur now. It seems like growing-wise and music-wise, it all happens pretty slow for us. I think we've just learned to play better with each other. If someone writes a song, we kind of have a responsibility to come up with cool parts and not overplay it. Our band, guitar-wise, is kind of simple on principle. We're not real flashy. It's mostly supposed to be complementing songs and singing. Mostly, with our band, it's about the songs first and we try to throw in a guitar solo or a chop. But, at first, when we were first starting out, it was a lot busier and kind of obnoxious in that way and now it's a little more easy on the ears.

In working up our song arrangements, if Dave writes the song, you usually have a pretty rough sketch of just the music, and he usually will play it for a while without any singing at all, just chord changes. We'll get kind of used to that, and then we'll let it sit for a couple of days and everybody will have the chance to make a tape and we'll listen to it. We'll come in with ideas and changing parts around. The cool thing about Soul Asylum is that it's more or less a democracy when it comes to rehearsing and songwriting and stuff. Input is always good in this band. It's not like one person sits there and tells you what figures to play on the guitar, because that wouldn't be any fun.

The A&M Records period was kind of dark for us. It kind of sucked, you know. You spend all this time making records and you'd like to be able to go to the local mall in America and be able to find them at the record store. That's kind of the point. I think at A&M they had two bands that started with S-O-U — Soundgarden and Soul Asylum — and they had some meeting and they picked Soundgarden. We put a record out and they put a record out and there'd be a full page ad in *Spin* magazine for Soundgarden and I'd go, 'C'mon guys, we have one out, too!' It wasn't any fun. We were pretty young and naive and you finally get a record deal with A&M and it's like a big deal. You're a 23 or 24 year old guy and you're going, 'God, this what I always wanted to do!' and then they're not behind it at all. I don't think Herb Alpert knew who we were. I met him backstage at a show and I said, 'Hey, it's Dan from Soul Asylum!' He said, 'Great.' I don't think he even knew we were on their label. That's just kind of frustrating. It's a reality of the music business, though.

Our experience with Twin/Tone Records was a little different. They were charming in a way. That was great. There were no expectations of you. It was kind of learning as you go along. One of those records, MADE TO BE BROKEN, I thought, came out kind of good. It has got some redeeming qualities on it. I can still listen to that sometimes but, musically, it's pretty sloppy and loose, but a lot of people really like that.

We recorded the GRAVE DIGGERS UNION album with Columbia. I really didn't know what to expect. It was our first record with Columbia and I'd heard lots of horror stories about them. Musically, it was a pretty special time for us. We had taken some time off — we'd been on the road continually — and we decided we weren't having any fun anymore. We took a year off and we wrote some songs and we started doing demos and practicing. We just started playing completely acoustically, which we had never done before. A lot of that record was just written and performed on acoustic guitars before we went into the studio. It's got a real different vibe than the records before it. That one kind of stands up well, too. I think some of the songs in there are pretty endearing, in a way, and that makes them easy to listen to over and over again.

A lot of our songs, like *Runaway Train*, for instance, are written on acoustic guitars. I think the old adage holds true that if you can write a song on acoustic guitar and play it to yourself and sing it and it doesn't sound boring and it sounds like a composition, it's going to be a lot easier to go into the studio and record it because, if it stands on its own as a composition, you can tell with just voice and acoustic guitar.

I think I've learned more about different chordings and chordal intervals over the years. I play a little bit of slide guitar now. Basically, if I'm having fun playing music, I'm a lot better at it than if I'm not. I try to keep it loose — not be too serious about it, not be too picky. For us, it's got to feel right and it's got to be played proficiently. I'm not really into real fancy, noodly stuff. I'm kind of envious in a way of people that can do that real well, but that's not us.

Dave has always been a pretty good singer. He can sing in key, which sort of separates him from a lot of our contemporaries — guys that can carry tunes, you know. I think after a while you just kind of get tired of yelling and jumping up and down. I mean, it was fun, but when you grow up, you grow up and your tastes in music change. I don't sit around and listen to Kiss records anymore — sometimes I do, but not very often. You just kind of move on and you try to push yourself or your music. A lot of people think that it's selling out. We don't make our records successful, other people do. We just make records. We don't consciously go in and make them with the thought: 'Oh, this is going to sell millions!' We really have no input into that. We don't pick our singles. We just make records and other people decide how they will react to them.

When we recorded *Runaway Train,* it felt like a hit. Dave's not big on choruses and that one has a chorus. I thought it was a pretty special song, but I was surprised that it was as big as it was because a lot of people hated it. It's weird you know, you have a hit song and it just gets overplayed and overanalyzed and you go to a karaoke bar and they've got it on there and you hear people singing it. It kind of changes your life in a way. I don't know if it's for better or worse, but it changes it.

When Booker T. Jones played with us, that was really cool. He kind of came in with charts for the music and had some furniture polish and dusted off the keys on the Hammond organ and just sat down and it was great. He played on one or two things, and you just wanted to hear him on everything. We thought of saying, 'Why don't you play on the whole record?' It was pretty cool. We got to meet a lot of inspiring musicians, and worked with a few, since we started and that's what makes it fun.

LET YOUR DIM LIGHT SHINE is more or less an acoustic guitar record. It's more of a big, rock record, but it's got a lot of harmony. It was a lot more fun to record than some of our records. For whatever reasons, it feels like the pressure is kind of off and we can just enjoy ourselves — and we kept the record company at bay. We just kind of did it on our own. I don't like a lot of outside influence, people coming by and scratching their chins. I would just as soon have it be the band, because that's the way we've always operated.

:| |•|•|

I remember the first guitar I ever bought — actually, I found it at a friend's attic. It was this house-paint green and black thing. That got old after playing it for four or five months, and I went to this guitar shop and bought a mid-'60s Gibson SG. Back then, they were about

$200. I used it for a while. I had been a bus boy at this Japanese restaurant and I saved up my money and went and bought a '76 Les Paul Sunburst, and, ever since, I've been playing mostly Gibsons. They make real good guitars. People talk about guitars all the time, but there's something special about the one you like and you kind of get attached to it, and the ones you write songs on, you remember. They just kind of get sentimental or something. There's a value you can't put on them.

I don't make any modifications to my guitars. It seems like every guitar is completely different. They sound different; they play differently. Usually, if I'm in a shop, I'll pick one up and I know within 10 minutes whether I'm going to like it or not. I used to do that DiMarzio pickup thing, and all that, in the big '80s, but, most of the time I've been with Soul Asylum, I've played Gold Tops with mini-Humbuckers. I kind of like them the way they are.

I try to play every day. Sometimes on the road, if we have a day off, the last thing in the world I want to do is pick up a guitar. I always find that, with writing on the road, you write the same song over and over again. It's like the Bob Seger song, *Turn The Page*. It's hard to not be influenced by your surroundings, and I think there have been enough road songs written. We usually come back from a tour with a bunch of those and we end up throwing them away.

I use some alternative tunings. That Keith Richards tuning, I use quite well. Nick Drake — I'm not sure if anyone is familiar with him. He's a finger-picking singer/songwriter. I think he killed himself about 1980. We did a tribute song on a record of his and I kind of invented this tuning — sort of like a C thing. I don't know whether it's what he used or not. I've been using capos a lot. I'm starting to mess around with that. Different voicings are important because you start getting tired of hearing the same E chord. They grow old after a while.

I have a really nice Gibson J50 from the same year I was born, 1962. On the video for *Runaway Train*, I have an old J45 that's all beat up — it's cracked. Someone had finger picks or something because its all gouged out, but it's got a really nice tone. I've got some with smaller bodies,'50s and '60s Sunburst ones. One time, I was in New York and we were making HANG TIME and there was the coolest guitar I've ever seen. It was from the 1939 World's Fair. It was a Gibson and had this pearl head stock that had the sphere and pylon, which was the symbol from the World's Fair. I wanted to buy it, but it was like $1200, and, at the time, that was half my record advance and I couldn't do it, but I'd love to find one of those again. I remember just going in and saying, 'God!' It was the kind of guitar you could hang on your wall and never even have to play.

For recording techniques, we have a tendency, when we play live, to always kind of go for that fuzzy guitar sound. On record, we try to make them a lot cleaner. It seems that they take up a better space. I'm over that grunge guitar. We use a lot of little amps. I like the sound of a big Marshall and stuff, but I've got some funky old Ampeg Reverb Rockets and Fender Tweed's and even Silvertone guitar amps. Sometimes, you crank those up and put an SM 57 Shure mic on them, and they sound great. They don't take up quite as much space in the mix, so you can leave room for your singer and stuff like that. But it's all kind of learning as you go. We try to use different guitars and different amps on every record so they've got a little different texture.

I think the ultimate compliment to me as a guitar player would be to say my playing was simple but tasty or effective. It's really taken from a songwriter's perspective. If Dave comes in with a song that I think is really special, I want to come up with a guitar part that is sympathetic to it rather than call a bunch of attention to my own playing. It can be really fun. It seems that the worst thing about music is if you sit around and think about it too much. By doing that, you kind of ruin it, so I kind of just try and free up my mind and go in there in a good mood and try to play.

Les Paul

LES PAUL & MARY FORD

Lester William Polfuss
Born June 9, 1915
Waukesha, Wisconsin

: |Les Paul|·|·|

I t's hard to imagine the modern recording industry without the influence of Les Paul. Not only has his impact been felt as a guitarist and recording artist, given the memorable body of work that he produced with singing partner and, as of 1949, his wife Mary Ford during their 12-year stint with Capitol Records beginning in the late '40s, but he also almost single-handedly revolutionized the sound of contemporary music and the recording process itself, from his earliest experiments with the solid-body electric guitar to his invention of the multi-track tape recorder.

Known variously in his teens as 'Rhubarb Red' or 'The Wizard of Waukesha', by 1938, having changed his name to Les Paul, he and his trio had become regulars on the Fred Waring radio show. When war broke out the following year, Paul, who had established a reputation as one of the top swing guitarists of the era, went to work in the armed forces radio service. In 1945, an old friend, Bing Crosby, was the catalyst for his signing to Decca Records, where he spent two years before making the switch to Capitol Records. It was here that Les Paul & Mary Ford, making use of Paul's various multi-track recording innovations, recorded some of the biggest hit records of the day, including *Mockin' Bird Hill*, *The World Is Waiting For The Sunrise*, *Just One More Chance*, *Tiger Rag*, *Bye Bye Blues*, *Vaya Con Dios* and the classic *How High The Moon*, which caught the ear of more than one aspiring rock musician in the early '50s. On the dust jacket of Mary Alice Shaughnessy's fascinating biography on Paul titled *Les Paul: An American Original*, Paul McCartney reveals that "We [The Beatles] used to start our gigs with the opening riffs from *How High The Moon*. Everybody was trying to be a Les Paul clone in those days."

Les Paul & Mary Ford retired in the '60s, but it would not be the last we heard from Paul. In the mid-'70s, he recorded the Grammy-winning CHESTER AND LESTER album with Chet Atkins and saw his name immortalized in the Gibson solid-body electric guitar that would come to define the sound of some of the most successful rock artists in the world. The original prototype of the Gibson Les Paul was known as 'The Log' and was the butt of almost universal ridicule. Even Gibson once referred to the solid body prototype as "nothing but a broomstick with a pickup on it." Needless to say, Paul, who won the Grammy's Trustees Award in 1983 and was inducted into the Rock and Roll Hall of Fame in 1988, has had the last laugh.

Throughout this book you'll find a number of tributes to Paul from various guitar players featured here who are either devotees of the Gibson guitar which bears his name, or are cognizant of his contributions to the field of recording over the years. Their words speak volumes of the high esteem in which the man, who has often been called 'The Thomas Edison of Rock 'n' Roll', is held amongst his peers in the world of contemporary music.

Since 1984, Paul has spent his Monday nights playing the Manhattan club Fat Tuesday's. "To keep your mind from getting old, the best thing to do is what you did when you were young, which is to go to a beer joint and play, one-to-one, for someone you can reach out and touch," he once philosophized, according to biographer Shaughnessy. We spoke to Les Paul at Fat Tuesday's in New York on an October Monday afternoon prior to his evening performance.

I first got interested in the guitar in about 1925. There was a harmonica player digging a ditch out in front of my house and, on his lunch hour, he would play. I listened to him from my porch and I said, 'I don't know what that is, but I'd sure love to have that.' So I stared him out of his harmonica. My mother said, 'You should have something to go with it,' and so I started playing the piano, but you've got your back turned to the people. She says, 'I doubt if you're going to find a piano everywhere you go.' It didn't seem logical; I agreed with her. Mom says, 'Try something else!' I tried the saxophone, and she says, 'Now you've got two things in your mouth. That doesn't seem to work right.' It finally ended up with my mother steering me to guitar.

So I sent away to Sears Roebuck. I got the guitar, and when I was unpacking it in the dining room, my mother came running in when one of the strings got hooked in the cardboard and the note twanged out. My mother says, 'That's beautiful; you play great already!' I said, 'Mom, I'm just taking it out of the case!' That's when I first realized that the guitar had this ability to sound good, no matter whether it was your first note or not. You could just pick a note and it's sweet and nice. I thought, at the time, that if that was a violin, my mother would kill me. If it was a clarinet, my mother would kill me. But a guitar, no matter what you do, it's very forgiving, loving instrument.

So, with that guitar and my harmonica, I went to a place called Bateman's Barbecue Stand, and it was out there that I had rigged up my mother's radio and telephone, and I sang into the telephone. The guitar was unamplified and I was singing with the harmonica into the telephone and the car hops would come to me with requests. This one fellow, who was in a rumble seat in the back seat of his car, he says, 'Red, we can hear the harmonica and we can hear your singing coming through your mom's radio, but we can't hear the guitar loud enough. Well, I thought, if I got my dad's radio, what I could do then is amplify the guitar. I figured, well, I'll take a needle, jab it into the top of the guitar, and turn it on. Everybody said, 'That's better!' So there was a needle in the top of the guitar, and, instead of playing a record, I'm playing my guitar through my dad's radio and singing and playing the harmonica through my mom's radio.

Everything was going fine, but there was just one thing bothering me. The guitar was howling and feeding back. It's fighting me. It's angry. So I said, 'What am I going to do with that?' I chucked some towels, socks and shorts in the hole and I muffled it; I just deadened the sound down. It helped a little. Then I poured plaster of Paris into my Sears Roebuck round hole guitar. That was better. Finally some kids came over to the house and I said, 'We've got to steal a piece of railroad track.' We got that piece of steel, and it was as long as the neck here. I strung a string on that piece of steel rail-road track, then I just took the diaphragm off the earphone of the telephone and placed it under the string. I ran into my mother and I said, 'I've got it. It's a piece of railroad track and it's the most beautiful sound I've ever heard.' Mom says, 'The day you see Gene Autry on a horse with a piece of railroad track ... ' I said, 'Stop it!'

My mother shot me down again, and I said to myself, 'What am I going to do?' What do you do if steel is right, but who's going to go around with a piece of steel and play it. So I went to wood and built a guitar from a four-by-four piece of wood. The first was fine, but it was anything but a lovable, likable guitar. I finally ended up using a four-by-four log. When I did, this is what happened. I went into a club and played the four-by-four. I played the *Sheik Of Araby* and hardly anybody liked it. I kind of got the drift. People hear with their eyes. I said, 'Maybe if I put wings on this four-by-four and made it look like a guitar.' I went back to the club and played it the following Saturday night and there was a great reaction. So if you walk in with something that doesn't look like a guitar, they see it, and to them it doesn't sound like a guitar. They don't react, so I said, 'It has got to be a beautiful piece of solid wood and then you'll have the sustain and you'll have the goodness and the advantages of a piece of steel.'

The prototype I requested Gibson guitars make for me was a flat top. The president of Gibson then, Mr. Maurice Berlin, said to me, 'What colors would you like on this guitar?' And I said quickly — and not even thinking about color — 'Gold.' He said, 'Why? Gold is a terrible color. It turns green. It's a real bad color.' But I said, 'Well, I love gold.' The president says, 'If he wants gold, give him gold!' The next one was black because I said you can see your hands moving. It's great when the light is on it. Black is going to be as rich as gold. So that's how those two guitars were born. Mr. Berlin asked a another great question. 'Do you like an arch top?' I said, 'I love it.' He says, 'Well, I'm a collector of violins and I very much like the curvature of the violin. Would you consider an arch top?' I said, 'That would be the greatest thing.' He says, 'No one else can do it. We have the tools to do it. If we arch that, we will have a beautiful guitar/violin look.' That's who thought of it and that's how that was born. The guitar was complete — and the rest is history.

I guess we can say now that the original one was made backwards, for it was made with a mahogany top and a maple back. That was incorrect. Then it was changed to a maple top. The cheaper guitar was the most expensive and the most expensive guitar was the cheaper one when they were backwards. Maybe a thousand went out the wrong way before we turned them around. That's kind of cute because they both sounded good anyway, and I'm not so sure that there's that much difference between the maple and the mahogany.

: | •|•|

My playing style, again, had to do with my mom when she said, 'Lester, you've got to be different in your playing. Your playing has to be so that I can recognize you from anybody else on the guitar.' I guess that my mother should have been an entertainer, or at least an advisor for the people, because she sure knew music and showmanship. As far as the sound is concerned, there was always this in the back of my mind that I would like something other than the acoustical sound of a guitar. We already have that. The difficulty with the acoustical sound was that, every time you picked up another guitar, you got a different sound. When you deal with the electric guitar — and you can vary the sound — the point was to get a sound, this big, round, shiny, full moon sound — the whole pie. You now have that rich beautiful sound. The sound is not a back pickup, it's not a front pickup, it's the whole thing. When you get that sound, you just say that this is better than any acoustic guitar — any amplified, acoustic guitar. This is its own world.

It had to be back in 1938 that Fred Waring said, 'What are you doing?' I was working on Fred Waring's radio show five days a week, coast-to-coast. The first show, I'd play an acoustic guitar. The second show, I'd play an electric guitar. So Fred said, 'What are you doing?' I said, 'Well, checking out which is the best sound.' I drew more mail than Fred Waring who was telling me to stop playing the electric. This is in 1938, and they're telling me, not my fans. People in the orchestra were all giving me the feedback and some said, 'Les, you should play electric! Les, you shouldn't!' And the mail poured in. And those were the people writing me or telling me — like Johnny Smith, like Tony Mottola, like great guitar players in that era were telling me I should, I shouldn't. It should be this way, it should be that way. These people, and the average layman, were telling me what to do, and Fred Waring and Jimmy Atkins, Ernie Newton, and myself went over between shows to 53rd and Broadway and we rehearsed with Fred Waring. We went up to the 11th floor and we listened to the first show, the acoustic, and the second show with the electric, and Fred says, 'We're going to vote on it!' I said, 'Okay,' and we voted. Unanimously, four of us voted electric, and Fred asks, 'Why?' I said, 'No you tell me why, Fred! Why did you vote electric?' He says, 'Because you can play as loud as a drummer or a saxophone player. You can change the tone. You can get to the people and you can't do that with an acoustic guitar.' I said, 'You summed it up very well Fred, and I'm going to stick to the electric.'

I've been electric ever since. And thank God, because it's not only accepted by me and my fans but by a great number of musicians today that play Les Paul guitars and the solid body. I'm very happy about it. So they discovered the same thing. You can do things with an electric that you cannot do with an acoustic instrument.

:| |•|•|

When I left home and went to WLS in Chicago, I got my first big treat to be on the WLS National Barn Dance and see the how the musicians down there operated. How things were evolving. You would see one microphone 20 feet away in this big auditorium and what they had going was that the person had to balance himself. Let's say you were in the studio and you had one microphone. What happened is your guitar was way down here and your voice was way up here. You're working at that microphone and you sing and play your harmonica that's going right into it. The guitar is underneath, so the guitar was not heard as loud and it got lost always going under them and away.

Martin came along with an excellent guitar that you could sing and play with under it and come out with a very rich sound. It was a favorable sound with one microphone and you could sing and play with it and you were whole. That didn't apply to some of the other guitars that were around. With Gibson, we had to find a guitar that would project and go across the room. It was almost an unexplainable sound that was created with the L5 electric. I might add that it was in 1928 that I got in my car and went up to Gibson and bought my first guitar, which was a 1927 L5. I still have it. Those guitars projected so that with an orchestra or whatever it was, you could get that rich sound. It wasn't too low, it wasn't too high, and to this day, if you listen to records of Count Basie — a good example would be Freddie Green when he played his rhythm — that rhythm was the key instrument in the whole band. You turn the volume way down and what do you hear? It wasn't the bass and it wasn't the drums, it was the guitar. The guitar proved to be the most valuable instrument in the whole band.

There were a couple of guys, including myself, who played an L5 on the *Barn Dance*. It didn't complement the singer as much as a round hole Martin, so Gibson came out with one like that. It was a Nick Lucas Jumbo, and I had to use those guitars to get that same type of sound when you sing and play. That's what the *National Barn Dance* gave me, and then, of course, I learned showmanship. How to sell what you've got. Like my mother would say, 'Sell it, Lester!'

Acoustic guitar all through the '30s was limping, first of all because it wasn't accepted and there was a lot of controversy about it. The union in Chicago, in New York, and I presume in L.A. — I hadn't gotten there yet — refused to accept the electric guitar being listed as a separate instrument. You just put 'guitar' down and it covered all of it. It was in the '30s that you used an acoustic for rhythm, never electric, because electric would sound awful — god awful — but it sounded great for the lead. It wasn't until later years that things like the Nat Cole Trio came along, and the Les Paul Trio, where we used electric for rhythm as well as soloing. Gradually, the electric guitar began to stand on its own, then the music changed. The music like they play today doesn't have rhythm like an L5 type of rhythm sound. They're not going, 'oompa-oompa' or 'chunk-chunk-chunk-chunk.' They're not doing that. Today, they're saying many things in many types of rhythm and it's entirely different and there's no demand at all for that sound — or very little.

High and low impedance, that's something that, again, goes back to the telephone in the late '20s when I was doing the hysterectomy on my mother's phone and I got that thing apart and she can't get any rings. Two rings and one short don't exist in my house because I've got the phone apart. But with the telephone, I admired what the people were doing at Western Electric and Bell Labs. I knew nothing about Bell Labs, but I did know that the phone company surely had their act together and I says, 'What are they doing?' I would ask people like the chief engineer at WTMJ in Milwaukee. I would go out there on Sundays and study electronics. One of the earliest things I discovered was that low impedance was so much better than high impedance. You can run long lengths of cable and you don't have the problems with low that you have with high. High impedance kind of puts you in a box where everything you do is kind of against you, whereas low impedance is much more stable. It's user-friendly to the people. With high impedance, you're apt to get hum, you get fluorescent light noise, you get a loss of highs. You just get a lot of variances that you don't particularly want. With low impedance, the telephone company figured that, it's so below all these noises, that you can run longer lines and it's much easier to work with. It takes longer for me to explain it than for me to find it. The '20s said to me, 'Go low impedance!' and so I was low impedance, low impedance, low impedance, just because it was done by the telephone company.

In order to get fine response — as good a response as your ear cries to hear — you have to sacrifice something, and so people like Fender and others, they would go one way, and they went the way of going for the full response. The other way was to take the pick up and make it as close as we could to full response, but also give the guy humbucking, which takes the noise out, and you would get something for nothing. The good part about it is that it does humbuck it out, but the bad part of it is that there is a phase problem. In that case, it's which one do you want? And you can't ask that; you get both. What I did was to piggy-back the pickups and put one under the other. When you put one under the other, you get a much cleaner, nicer sound, but you only get half the level, and the young generation today — and this goes back into the '60s — said, 'What we want is some really grungy, fuzz-tone distortion. We want to overdrive the input, and if we put the pickups side by side, we pick up more level and we can turn that volume up and we can cremate that first stage in the amplifier.' That's what they wanted.

My recording Les Paul guitars went by the wayside. Even though I use them today and like them better, that doesn't mean that what the kids want isn't right. The whole industry has gone to humbucking. If they want the clearer sound, then you go to a single coil pickup.

:| |•|•|

There was probably many a person out there fooling with electric guitar, prior to me or at the same time as I was doing it. I never claimed that I'm the guy that invented the electric guitar. I'm sure people were sticking phonograph needles or some magnetic coil under the strings since there was water. I only feel that I kind of did a solo on this thing all by myself and never thought much about the fact that I was one of the pioneers. I just never thought of it. I just said, this is what I crave to have happen, and my mother either shot me down or endorsed it. If she says, 'Lester, that's better!' I went on my way. I think the proudest thing is that I stuck to my guns even in the hardest times.

I don't even think the people at Gibson know that — and those who do know probably don't say much about it — when I called Gibson in 1955 or 1956, Fender came over to me and asked if I would join them. CBS owned them and Mr Campbell came to my home with my manager and laid out a deal. My manager said, 'It's a great deal,' and I said, 'There's only one thing wrong, I don't think I'm ready to put Les Paul on a Fender guitar.' I said, 'There's something not really right.' So I called Mr Berlin at Gibson, which was Chicago Musical Instrument at the time, and he said, 'Les, we sold off all the electrics and we're closing it down. The electric guitar is extinct.' Now, can you imagine someone laying this on me in 1956? 'Can I come back and see you?' I said, 'You do realize that Jimmy Page and Jeff Beck and Eric Clapton, all these people are running up and down 48th Street trying to buy a Les Paul guitar and they're paying five, six, all the way up to ten thousand dollars, for a guitar. There's a great demand out for those guitars and Gibson's going to do away with them?!' That was during my divorce, and when the divorce was over, I was ready to sign with Fender, but in the end I said, 'No, I think I'll go back and talk to Mr Berlin.' I went back there and he says, 'You're very convincing Les, will you back it up?' I said, 'I'll buy every one you don't sell, that's what I'll do!' and he says, 'You've got a deal!'

When they produced the first ones, they made four. Two, they kept, and two, they gave to me, and I don't think at any time was I more proud to help Gibson sell off that equipment. Unbelievably, we turned that thing around to go up and up and up and I just say that's the way the good Lord wanted it to be. I didn't do it. Gibson had their thoughts. That's when I told the Gibson people that maybe the wisest thing they could do is have the president of the company and his wife — and I told that to the president — go into a music store and wait on the people behind the counter and learn just what the real story is. The president said, 'I'd never do that,' but I think he should have. I think all presidents should do that. Henry [Juszkiewicz] are you listening? Actually, Henry is doing a wonderful job with Gibson. He turned it around from belly up all the way to the top, and I have nothing but praise for the man.

:| |•|•|

The sound that I get out of a guitar is probably one of the most important things in my career — getting a sound that is very distinctive. When I play the club [Fat Tuesday's] down here, people will come to me and say, 'We didn't know if it was you or not but we heard you coming down the street.' Or, 'We heard you coming down the stairs.' And he'd say to his wife, or she'd say to him, 'Do you think Les Paul is here?' And he'd say, 'I hear him; that's Les Paul!'

You have to have that identification, and if you don't have it... It's like Benny Goodman. Benny Goodman has a distinct sound, Artie Shaw as well. They are both playing the same clarinet. It's not the guitar, it's the player. I could pick up someone else's guitar and, in two seconds, I'd sound like Les Paul. Part of it is that, inside of you, you crave that sound, and if you've got some knobs to play with, in no time at all you're going to go that direction. It's built in you. Art Tatum, when he sat down and played the piano, had a touch. Everybody sat at the same piano, but they all sounded different. It's in their make-up.

My mother used to say, 'Beat your foot, do this, do that, look 'em in the eye when you talk!' All of the things that you would tell a politician today, my mother was telling me back then. She told me that I had to have my own sound. I came to her one day, and I had made *Whispering* for her. Many years later, we made another record of *Whispering*. When I went to Waukesha to see my mother — she was 89 years old — she said, 'Lester, you wouldn't get mad at me if I showed you something would you?' I said, 'No!' And here's my fan and she went to get the new record I made of *Whispering*. I said,

'Mom, I know what you're going to do.' And she said, 'Let me do it!'
And she did, and she said, 'Why? Why did you change your sound?'
I said, 'I don't know. I just probably lost it. I don't know why that
happened.' I had been retired for 10 years from playing the guitar
and went back and didn't go for that same sound. So driving in the
car today, we're at the George Washington Bridge and what are we
talking about? Sound! We're saying, 'Gotta get that sound!' I just did
the Coors' commercial and I've got that Les Paul sound. That's the
key to the whole thing. How do you get it? It's in your head and no
matter what guitar I picked up, I'd reach for that sound. It's what
pick you use, how you pick it; everything is involved, plus the fact
that you turn those knobs until you're kind of content.

Joe Perry

AEROSMITH, JOE PERRY PROJECT

Anthony Joseph Perry
Born September 10, 1950
Lawrence, Massachusetts

Joe Perry

There's a certain irony in the fact that Aerosmith, arguably America's foremost rock 'n' roll band and purveyors of the ultimate hot lick, should have had its beginnings in an ice cream parlor. But that, as legend has it, is how guitarist Joe Perry and singer Steve Tyler originally made contact in a place called The Anchorage in Sunapee, New Hampshire where Perry was spending his days serving up shakes and cones and playing in a group called The Jam Band by night. Tyler, who was a drummer at that point, shared Perry's rock 'n' roll ambitions, and by 1970, with Tyler taking on vocal duties and with the addition of rhythm guitarist Brad Whitford, bass player Tom Hamilton, and drummer Joey Kramer, Aerosmith was born. "We weren't too ambitious when we started out," Tyler has said. "We just wanted to be the biggest thing that ever walked the planet, the greatest rock band that ever was."

By 1972, the group had signed to Columbia Records, for whom they recorded their eponymous debut album in 1973. Over the next few years, the group built a strong fan base the old-fashioned way — by touring their butts off across the length and breadth of America. TOYS IN THE ATTIC, released in 1975, became the band's breakthrough album in the wake of tracks like *Sweet Emotion* and *Walk This Way*, which spotlighted Perry's facility with the hooky guitar riff. Having survived their appearance in the movie *Sgt. Pepper's Lonely Hearts Club Band*, which had proven to be a major setback for the careers of other participating artists, including Peter Frampton and The Bee Gees, musical and personality differences between Perry and Tyler led to Perry's departure in 1979 to pursue a solo career with his own group, the Joe Perry Project, with which he would record three albums: LET THE MUSIC DO THE TALKING; I'VE GOT THE ROCK 'N' ROLLS AGAIN; and ONCE A ROCKER, ALWAYS A ROCKER.

Perry and Brad Whitford, who had also left Aerosmith in 1980, rejoined the group in 1984 for an excursion they dubbed the Back in the Saddle Tour. If this was planned as a jump start to bigger and better things, it stalled badly early in the tour as Tyler collapsed on stage. The group's much-publicized problems with drug and alcohol addiction was obviously beginning to take its toll, but, by the mid-'80s, both Tyler and Perry had committed themselves to a rehabilitation program. In 1986, it was a rejuvenated Perry and Tyler that appeared on the single and in the video for the Run D.M.C. cover of the Aerosmith track *Walk This Way*. The single hit the top of the charts and turned out to be the precursor of a major comeback for Aerosmith.

Through the late '80s and '90s, albums like PERMANENT VACATION, PUMP, GET A GRIP, and the chart-topping ARMAGEDDON soundtrack album, which was driven by four Aerosmith tracks, would lift the bad boys of American rock to heights that they could only have dreamed of back in those formative years in Sunapee in the late '60s.

We spoke to Joe Perry on an October morning at the Sony Studios in New York City.

*W*hen I was younger — in my mid-teens — I tried instruments other than the guitar, like piano. I think I even tried clarinet for a couple of minutes, but nothing felt like a guitar so it just kind of stayed with me.

My first guitar was a Silvertone that my parents bought me. It was $11.00 or something, with a little 45 RPM record — a record's a round piece of plastic with grooves in it for those of you who don't know or have forgotten [Laughs] — that taught you how to tune. You'd put it on the record player and it would give you the little notes and you could kind of get the thing in tune.

As far as early influences, I just remember hearing Roy Orbison the first time and hearing those guitar chords ringing out. That's probably my first guitar memory. In those days I was influenced by the radio, everything from Ike & Tina Turner to Elvis. I'll sit down and listen to some of my favorite records that influenced me in those days when I first started, and that's always inspiring, because it brings me back to what the basics are.

I like all the blues guys, but when I want to really get the hair on the back of my neck to stand up, I listen to Robert Johnson. He can make the guitar sound like nobody else.

In those early days, I just kind of eased into all of this. I dropped out of school and went to work in a factory. I was playing on the weekends all the time, and it was just the thing that kept me going. It was something I did with my friends and played in a band, and I liked that, and like most musicians from that era that I know of, you always fantasized about doing what the Beatles did and going through all that. But I never sat there and said, 'Well, I'm going to be a rock musician and a rock star.' It was one of those things where all I wanted to do was have a gig next week and put food on the table. Other than that, it was all gravy.

I play what feels good, you know. I never thought of it as developing a style or anything like that. I like to play rock and roll songs. I just try to get by the vocals, because that's just something to take up time between solos. Most of my solos are pretty much improvised. My biggest problem is when I do demos and try to reproduce those solos. That's about the only time I have to sit down and learn something. Usually the demo is a one shot — you're going along and you blow — and then I have to go back and try to re-create that. Inevitably, I end up flying them in afterwards — taking them off the demo and putting them on the finished tracks.

:| |•|•|

Like I said, I had a Silvertone guitar, then I had some unknown Italian acoustic guitar that my parents provided me with. Then I got a Guild with F holes and semi-hollow body, then I went to see Jeff Beck play, in about 1968, with The Jeff Beck Group. At that time, I was working in a factory, in the foundry, and I can remember, after seeing him play, the next day I was sitting there thinking, 'Man, I just got to get a Les Paul.' So that next weekend I went out and found one. They were re-issuing Gold Tops then and I got one of those. That was it.

When I first started getting back into Gibsons again in the late '80s, I just thought it would be really cool to get one [Les Paul] from the Custom Shop that was kind of a BlackBurst. It's really hard to improve on perfection. The physics that Les Paul and Gibson reached, what more can you do to it, except change the color maybe. That's the original prototype. They put some mother of pearl on there, and I picked out a nice piece of wood at the Custom Shop, and it's a burst on both sides, which is unusual. There's maple on the back. About a year later, we got so many comments on the way it looked that Gibson came to me and said they'd like to do a production on it. I was flattered. They wanted to know what I wanted changed on it, but there really wasn't much I could change. The neck was a little fatter, a little closer to a '59, and the other thing is we try to use the lightest piece of wood we can get, because that's one of the things I noticed about the '59s; if you pick up a really good one, it's light. They sound best. We experimented with cutting out some sound holes to make it a little lighter and it has worked because, all of the ones I've picked up, all feel pretty consistent. Other than that, any changes are pretty cosmetic, though the pickups are a little hotter than some I've played.

That Les Paul Gold Top, one of my old friends just sent that to me, and he said, 'I think you'll like this one. I got a good deal on it and it's totally beat up. There isn't one place on it that hasn't been dented, but it sounds great.' I have a '59 back there. It's actually a '60, but we think it's a '59 body. This one here is a Les Paul with the Trans Performance computer in it. It tunes itself and just about plays itself. You can program different tunings and things like that. It's kind of fun to play with. The Gibson Firebird that I have is one of the few things I have left over from the early days that didn't get sold off by my ex-wife, so I'm kind of proud to have it. It sounds great.

I always consider myself a song player, not so much a guitarist's guitarist, that kind of thing. It's all about the songs to me. That's where it's at. The point is to try and be tasty and to try and play the right thing for the right spot. That's what I try and do; get the things to fit just right. Riffing for riffs' sake is not what I like to do. There's other guys that do it a lot better.

In some of the songs out there, I definitely hear my influence. My style is kind of blues-based and rock 'n' roll standard stuff. When I hear some of the things that Slash writes, I can hear some of that come through. I'm just passing on what I've ripped off from somebody else, so I can't take too much credit for it.

Tom Petty

TOM PETTY AND THE HEARTBREAKERS

Tom Petty
Born October 20, 1950
Gainesville, Florida

: | Tom Petty |·|·|

Most rock artists can usually point to that defining moment in their youth when they knew that their destiny was to pursue music as a career. For Tom Petty, his inspiration came from the 'King' himself — and in person — as he met Elvis Presley in 1961 on the Florida set of his movie, *Follow That Dream*. "And that was the end of doing anything other than music with my life," Petty once told *Rolling Stone* magazine as he recalled that momentous encounter. "I didn't want anything to fall back on because I was not going to fall back."

During his school years, Petty would play in a number of local groups before settling in with the band Mudcrutch, which eventually moved to Los Angeles and signed a record deal with Shelter Records in 1974. It was less than a fulfilling experience as the group's debut album was ultimately shelved following the poor showing of an initial single. Undaunted, Petty and two former Mudcrutch members, guitarist Mike Campbell and keyboard player Benmont Tench, along with bassist Ron Blair and drummer Stan Lynch from back home in Gainesville, convened to cut some tracks for a project that would become Tom Petty and the Heartbreakers.

Ironically, when the group released their debut album in 1976, it was in the U.K., where the influence of American acts like The Ramones were giving rise to the punk scene there, that Tom Petty and the Heartbreakers first found major acclaim with a sound that some would dub 'Power Pop.' It wasn't until 1977 that the single *Breakdown* marked the group's first Top 40 entry into the American charts. The band's rise was swift and sure from that point on in the wake of albums like DAMN THE TORPEDOES, HARD PROMISES, and LONG AFTER DARK, which saw bass player Howie Epstein replace Ron Blair in the band. The 1985 SOUTHERN ACCENTS album brought the group their first MTV Video Music Award for the track *Don't Come Around Here No More*.

In 1986 and 1987, Petty and the band toured the world with Bob

Dylan, who had co-written the track *Jammin' Me* on the group's 1987 CD, LET ME UP (I'VE HAD ENOUGH). The following year, Petty and Dylan, along with Jeff Lynne, George Harrison, and the late Roy Orbison, formed the Traveling Wilburys, who had enormous success with their self-titled debut and the sophomore set, VOLUME 3.

In 1989, Petty's debut solo album, FULL MOON FEVER, co-produced by Jeff Lynne and Heartbreaker guitarist Mike Campbell, stayed in the Top 10 of the *Billboard* Top 200 Album chart for 34 weeks. Back with the Heartbreakers, the chart success continued with THE GREAT WIDE OPEN (1991) and GREATEST HITS (1993), featuring the single *Mary Jane's Last Dance*, which brought Petty the Best Male Video Award at the 1994 MTV Video Music Awards as well as the prestigious Video Vanguard trophy for the whole body of his work in the video field. The double Grammy award-winning WILDFLOWERS (1994) was followed by the most successful concert tour in the band's career. 1995 saw the release of PLAYBACK, the best-selling 6-CD retrospective on the group's career, which also featured a companion long-form video. 1996 saw the release of the CD (SONGS AND MUSIC FROM THE MOTION PICTURE) SHE'S THE ONE, which featured ten songs from the film for which Petty wrote the instrumental score.

The late '90s has seen Petty receive a handful of tributes and awards for his songwriting, including the Golden Note Award from ASCAP, UCLA's George and Ira Gershwin Award For Lifetime Musical Achievement, and his own star on Hollywood's Walk of Fame.

We spoke to Tom Petty at his manager's office in the Melrose area of Los Angeles on a late fall afternoon.

I had an uncle working on a film set in Ocala, Florida and Elvis came down there. My aunt took me and my cousins down to the set, and we thought that looked like a good job. So that was kind of how it started. I'd always been interested in the guitar, going all the way back to westerns and to cowboys. Cowboys played guitars, so I always thought it was a pretty cool instrument.

I bought a Gibson Dove when I was 17 years old, and I've written almost everything I've ever written on that guitar, and I really treasure it. It works just as good as it ever did. Gibson used to have — and I guess they still do — a lifetime guarantee, so I thought it was a pretty good deal. I've always treasured it so much that I never take it on the road because I'm afraid it would get broken or somebody would steal it. I'm real proud to still have it because it's a fine instrument.

The first music I got into was, of course, rock 'n' roll. Rock 'n' roll was the thing for young people, when I was young — still is, I would imagine — but there was lot of country music around in the South where I grew up. At the time, I saw country as the music of my parents' generation, but I still watched all those shows because they played guitars. Years later, I realized that I truly did love that music as well. That was country in the mid-'60s, not what they call it now.

I liked a lot of Buck Owens stuff and a lot of George Jones and those great classic duets he was doing with Tammy Wynette. I loved all that. I don't really like country music past that era. At some point, it seemed to really go wrong to me. It became just bad rock music. It looked to me like these were guys who couldn't cut it playing rock and they kind of angled it this way. Maybe that's too bold a statement, but I really think it got a little confused. I was recently working with Johnny Cash, and he told me that he thought that country music now was for people who hated country. [Laughs] Beautiful! I don't know. I hate to condemn an entire genre of music because I'm sure there are people out there that are still really good.

But, as I said, rock was always the thing for us. There was an incredible freedom and an incredible power to the music. It was sexy. All my life, I've tried to put it into words, and I don't think I ever have. I don't know how to put that into words. It's like describing sex. It's just really good. So, yeah, I was bitten pretty hard at the age of 11 and everything went out the window — like sports. I never had an interest in anything again but guitars. Even now, at the age of 46, I'm trying to find something else that I'm interested in. Really! If I have spare time, I go looking for guitars. Kinda sad, isn't it? [Laughs]

I listened to records for a long time before I tried to play anything, or even imagined that I could play anything. And I really soaked up a lot of Elvis from those Sun records. Elvis has never really been rated highly as a guitar player, but, on those Sun records, his acoustic guitar is a lot of the record, like on *That's All Right Mama*. The Beatles, and specifically John Lennon, were a big influence, too — whoever was playing rhythmically. I loved all that.

Don Felder of The Eagles and I were boys together. Don was always the best guitar player in town and, as a matter of fact, I'm sure that the first live music that I ever saw was probably around 1962 or '63. It was a surf group called The Continentals and Don was the guitarist. I remember him showing me his electric guitar. It looked like a rocket and it was just so heavy. For a time — I think I was 14 and he was probably 16 or 17 — we worked in a music shop together. I bet he doesn't remember, but he actually taught me to play the piano as we hung around this music store.

I'm still pretty proud of being a good rhythm player. A lot of people really don't aspire to be good rhythm players. Around the '70s, that completely went away, but it's a handy thing to know. It's a handy thing to be able to drive the band. And it serves me well to this day because I can pretty much get the song over on my own. It's handy for the band because they just fill in around it. But I think probably that Elvis was the biggest influence on my guitar playing, in the beginning anyway.

: | | • | • |

*W*hen I'm working with The Heartbreakers, I just come in and I play them the song, and many times, before I'm through playing them the song, they're playing the song with me, and we take it from there. Around the time of the WILDFLOWERS album, I started to make demos, but I never really made demos, I just played it to them on the guitar.

About 80 percent of the time, I write songs on the guitar, then I use a piano the other 20 percent of the time. Sometimes, the piano's good because, if you're a guitar player, you tend to go to the same places, so maybe, if you've got an idea and you go over to the piano, you might hit something a little different.

We've never been really big on rehearsals, so the Heartbreakers have really done their best work in the studio when they don't really know what they're doing. Once they get too rehearsed, it seems to go away. So, usually, we'll set up in the studio and we'll record until the songs have run out. Then we'll take a break, come back with another handful of songs, and start again.

I still feel pretty rebellious, from time to time, although I don't really see it as a requirement. The requirement is to make good music — always was — and the rest just comes along. The worst you can do is be in your 40s and be trying to act like you're in your 20s. I find that very embarrassing. So we're fortunate that we still have a lot of young people that buy our records and come to our shows, but I think they do it probably because we don't try to condescend to them. We don't try to patronize them or act like we've been down that road — and we probably are still a little wilder than the average old man. [Laughs]

There's a lot of my old songs that I'm proud of. I'm proud that they still play them on radio. I never play them to be honest — it's the last thing that I would ever do is pull one out and put on — but, when I'm in the car and hear one — sometimes one that's 20 years old — I feel great about it: 'How great, they're playing that old thing! It holds up.'

But I still think of myself as a guy in a band. I've always worked in a group — in the same group — for a long, long time. I never would have been happy playing solo, although I've got a lot of attention for myself, but I'm not sure I really sought that out. I've always thought of myself as a guy in a group. Ever since I was 14 years old, I've made my living playing in a group. I started out playing dance halls and Moose clubs and anywhere you could play. And, if I think about how I see myself, I probably still see myself that way.

:| |•|•|

The first electric guitar I had was a bass — a Gibson EB2 bass — which I still have. From there I went on to a variety of Gibson basses. Being the least accomplished musician in the group, but having the best hairdo, I kept my job playing the bass. I think the first electric guitar I had was probably a Rickenbacker.

I used a Gibson Flying V when we first started The Heartbreakers, but when we toured with Bob Dylan, I used the Gibson 335 and an SG because Bob played a Fender and Mike [Campbell] was playing a Fender. Gibson has a little thicker sound. I've always had them around. I've always used the Gibson acoustics — the J200, The Dove, and The Everly Brothers' model. I still use all three of them, and I must have dozens of them stuck away for this or that.

The Gibson acoustic is not the same as a Martin. A Martin is a fine instrument as well. A Martin has a sort of a chime or bell sound to my ear, but the Gibson is a little more rugged and, perhaps, a little more rock sounding. I think The Beatles, who were my big influence — the Beatles and Stones — their acoustics were Gibsons. The Beatles had the J-160E, not the best sounding Gibson ever made, but it really worked on those records, and the Stones had the Hummingbird. I always thought they looked great.

There's not a great deal of difference between an electric and an acoustic; it's just a little bit of amplification. It's often just a little microphone here at the end of the neck. The rest is what you do with the amplification and the compression. I've always been amused by this 'unplugged' thing. They're definitely plugged in, from what I can see. You can do anything with it. We could hook up a wah-wah and a fuzz; it doesn't matter. I guess it's a different attack.

I use a lot of different tunings; anything I can get away with. I use the drop D tuning a lot, where you drop your low E down to D; that's a handy one. And open A, open G. Those are great discoveries, when you find them.

I hope my own personal guitar style has got better over the years. In the last four or five years, I've learned to be more of a lead guitarist. I've become a little more confident about soloing, and the band allows it a little more, so that's fun. I've gotten pretty good at finger picking. The guitar is a great thing because as long as I play one, I can still pick this thing up and suddenly realize, 'Oh, I didn't know you could do that! Didn't know about that. How did I miss that?' You can always discover more. And it's a cool instrument. You can take it with you without too much problem. It's not like the upright bass or harp. I've taught both of my kids to at least play a little on the guitar, because you never know when it may really come in handy.

My advice for anyone who takes up guitar is to just enjoy yourself and practice. It doesn't have to be such a serious thing that it consumes your life. I think when that happens, you really didn't have any choice anyway. But I do know a lot of people who play just to enjoy themselves and really get a lot out it. It's much better than, say, cable TV. It's an alternative. So my advice would be just to enjoy yourself, because that's what it's really about.

Mick Ralphs

MOTT THE HOOPLE, BAD COMPANY

Mick Ralphs
Born March 31, 1944
Hereford, England

:|Mick Ralphs|·|·|

When Bad Company arrived on the scene in late 1974, the music media was quick to herald the birth of a new 'Super Group.' Vocalist Paul Rodgers and drummer Simon Kirke had formerly been with Free, a band that made five albums and developed a strong fan base in Europe and America. Bassist Boz Burrell had played with King Crimson, among others, and guitarist Mick Ralphs had formed Mott The Hoople with Ian Hunter, a band that enjoyed much critical acclaim following the release of their landmark album, ALL THE YOUNG DUDES, produced by David Bowie. Add to that the fact that the group was the first act signed to Led Zeppelin's own label, Swan Song, and you could see that it wouldn't take much to send an eager-beaver rock journalist off the adjectival deep-end.

Ralphs had not been happy with the musical direction of Mott The Hoople, with whom he contributed guitar and vocals on five albums, or the fact that much of his material was not being recorded by the band because of Ian Hunter's dominance. In Mott, Ralphs had written *Rock And Roll Queen* and *Ready For Love*, a tune that almost became an anthem in the band's stage show. The latter song, which Ralphs had sung on the ALL THE YOUNG DUDES album, was added to Bad Company's repertoire when the band was formed.

The music that emerged from the band's first recording session left no doubt to their intentions musically. They found rock's common denominator — no frills, just an incessant, throbbing undercurrent embellished with strong vocal and guitar work. The band's sound found instant acceptance with the public. The first album, BAD CO., zipped up the charts, as did their first single, *Can't Get Enough*. The group's sophomore album, STRAIGHT SHOOTER, took squatter's rights in the Top 5 of the album charts for over a month, and in the summer of 1975, Bad Company sold out Madison Square Gardens in New York in the wake of another Top 10 single, *Feel Like*

Making Love. RUN WITH THE PACK, the group's third album, became their third million seller.

From 1977 to 1982, the original members of Bad Company released three more albums before calling it quits. In 1986, Ralphs and Simon Kirke resurrected the group with new members, but over the course of six albums through the late '80s and '90s, though there were some high points, including the releases DANGEROUS AGE, HOLY WATER, and HERE COMES TROUBLE, they weren't able to duplicate the early success of the band. In 1995, Ralphs released the solo album TAKE THIS!

We spoke to Mick Ralphs, with his Gibson Les Paul Jr. in hand, in the backyard of his home in the English countryside not far from Oxford. As a backdrop to our conversation, there was a gypsy caravan that was a present to Ralphs from guitarist David Gilmour [Pink Floyd], with whom he had recently toured.

The first thing that made me want to play guitar was a record called *Green Onions* by Booker T & the MGs. Up until then, most of the pop music of the day was pretty wimpy, I thought. No disrespect to any of them, but there were artists like Paul Revere and the Raiders and Bobby Vee — all that sugary, sweet, poppy stuff that I didn't really go for. I also wasn't really into The Ventures and The Shadows and all that kind of stuff like most people. I was probably too young, initially, for the early rock 'n' roll and R&B. I grew up in that era where it was all kind of really soft pop.

Then one day in the early '60s, I heard *Green Onions* by Booker T & the MGs [Plays lick from song]. I hadn't heard anything like it before. It was really rough but I thought, 'Wow! I like that.' I didn't really know who they were or anything about them but I pursued that kind of sound. I think I had a really cheap and horrible guitar at the time, because you couldn't get good American guitars in England then. In later years, the first decent guitar I got was the Fender Telecaster, and that's what, I found out later, Steve Cropper had used on that record. That was my start and then I got into soul and R&B and jazz, I suppose, and country and rock 'n' roll — anything that had that kind of guitar feel to it. Then, of course, you realized that the MGs were two white guys and two black guys. The feel of it and the overall vibe was enough to get me fired up.

As I said, initially, you couldn't get decent guitars in this country

[England]. I think in '64 or '65, the trade thing between the U.S. and England was modified so that you could then purchase fenders and Gibsons and get American albums, but prior to that you couldn't. Part of the reason all the lads from Liverpool had such a foot in the door with all that new music was the fact that they used to get stuff off the American seamen who'd come into port. Merchant seamen would need some money and they'd sell their B.B. King albums, their Miracles albums, and they'd have a Les Paul guitar they'd bought for $100 in the States but didn't need it. Then you've got these guys in Liverpool who are playing all this stuff on all these instruments you couldn't find. They were one step ahead right there. When the trade thing was lifted, you could buy Gibsons and Fenders, and suddenly everybody started listening to the American music. Then it was, 'Oh right, that's where they got it from!' The first Beatles album is nearly all covers — *Please Mr. Postman* and *You Really Got A Hold On Me* — and the same with The Rolling Stones. Their first album is nearly all covers, but that's okay. Good for them.

Working wth David Gilmour [ex-Pink Floyd guitarist] was great. He has very set ideas on what he wants, which is good. He's a perfectionist and very much into sound quality. Every gig we did was sound-checked, and for me it was a good lesson in a different way of playing. Obviously, his own style solo and with Pink Floyd is very distinctive. He uses effects a lot more than I do and he goes about his craft in a different way, but he's a very soulful player. He could just sit here and plug in and wail away, but I think in the context of what he's known as, he spends a lot of time getting the right equipment and getting the sound right. It was very good working with him because I was a good counterpoint for him. He liked my rough and ready style.

:| |·|·|

I guess the first guitar I had just before the Mott The Hoople period was a Gibson SG, which actually had Les Paul on the head. It's now quite a valuable guitar, though I didn't know it at the time. I used to trade guitars. I could never afford to buy more than one, so I'd have one and have to trade it in and have to pay so much a week to have another one.

I've used Gibsons a lot over the years, and, in Mott, I used a Les Paul Jr. for years after I saw Leslie West, the guitarist from Mountain, using one when I first went to the States in 1970. Here's this big guy using this tiny guitar, and it sounded great. I used one for years, and then used one in Bad Company when we formed that band in the

'70s. Since then, I've used mostly Les Pauls — the two pickup ones — and I've got a '59 original, which is worth an arm and a leg.

I liked the Jr., in particular. I liked the simplicity of it. To me, there's always two basic rock guitars: there's the Gibson and the Fender. But the Gibsons are made like a real instrument. They have a nice neck, which comes off at an angle. When they designed the solid guitar, from what I can gather, they were makers of real quality acoustic instruments, but people had started putting pickups on them. They wanted a guitar that looked like a real guitar and they just scaled it all down and made it solid. The shape from the back is like a big Gibson jazz guitar, but just scaled down, like a Florentine. You don't need the hollowness to make it sound good, so that's why it's made of mahogany. I like the craftsmanship and the way they're put together, and every Gibson I've ever had is different. The weight is different and the neck.

I went to the factory before they moved to Nashville. In the '50s and early '60s, they made fewer guitars because the demand wasn't there — the rock 'n' roll demand wasn't there — but the quality was there. This [Les Paul Jr.] is basically a cheap guitar, but it's beautiful.

When I first heard Leslie West, I liked the tone of the Les Paul — the power of the tone. I mean, Clapton used one in his first big outing with John Mayall. I loved that sound. When the Les Paul was designed, it was never designed to be played at high volumes, until somebody cranked it up one day and it sounded great. It's just got a sweet tone to it that's very distinctive. Now I've gone full circle; I've gone back to one of the Les Pauls that I used to used in the Mott days. It just sounds so great.

I was never conscious of developing a Mick Ralphs sound. I knew what I liked but I did find, as the time went by, that I could use pretty much any guitar through any amp and it would probably sound something like I wanted it to sound, so, in a way, I suppose that's a way of developing your own sound or style. But, obviously, you're more comfortable on certain guitars. If I was ever on the road and in a hotel bar and someone asked if I wanted to come and play and I'd say, 'Yeah, why not.' And they'd say, 'Well what do you wanna use.' And I'd say, 'Well anything; what have you got?' It doesn't bother me what it is.

I am terrible about fiddling with a guitar. I have a shed over there with loads of guitars, all in bits. I've got spares galore over there. It's a hobby, but I wouldn't touch these old ones. I do with the reissues — the Fenders and the Gibsons. I get them home and take them all to bits and put old parts on instead of the new parts and get the soldering iron in the back and get old pots and all these old nickel parts, because they're not nickel anymore. They're just like chrome. I like the old way they were made and the old parts they used. I understand why they changed it, but nickel looks better than chrome. So I've got a whole bunch of spares in drawers that have pickups — lots of Gibson pickups, of course — and pickup covers, bridges, knobs, and machine heads and volume controls and scratch blades. Never a dull moment. I've got more spares than Gibson has got.

I did actually change the pegs on this [Les Paul Jr.], I must admit. Sorry about that. But it is a hobby of mine. I do gut guitars. People come and have nightmares and say, 'What are you doing to that guitar?! It's all in bits!' But I get them all fixed up and back together, so it's alright. I don't mess with the really collectible ones. With Fenders especially, you can rip the necks off. They're all interchangeable. I must admit that, early on, I was quite nervous about tinkering with guitars, but then I started getting into it and I could afford to have more than one guitar. I would 'modi-hot-rod' them and change the pickup and so on. There's a whole bunch of parts you can get to basically build your own guitar, if you've got the time. You can buy the body you like, the neck you like; it's not that difficult really.

There was a historic Gold Top in my shed until I got hold of it. I've stripped all the paint off because there's a lovely wood underneath it. I'm just trying different pickups. I've gutted the back. Sorry, Gibson. I'll fix it, honestly. It's a shame they sprayed it gold and covered up such lovely wood.

I've been writing on this guitar [Les Paul Jr.] at the moment, but it's kind fo the flavor of the month. Obviously, you only need one guitar to play, but I find that working with a different guitar inspires me. Each new guitar is fun to play. It's rewarding, although I've got lots of other guitars. With my new guitar, I've been writing a lot of songs lately so it has helped to get me to that point. I've been using this on the demos I've been playing but I also write on piano quite a bit.

At the moment, I'm writing just to write. I've tended to write specifically for Bad Company, and there's certain parameters that you have to work within that fit that bill. It's good because, this time, I couldn't go out on this particular tour so it's enabled me to think in terms of other areas of writing. I did a solo album in the '80s on which there was an instrumental, a jazzy type thing, and a country song, and some rock stuff, so I'm just enjoying writing. I'm in the process of hopefully doing some writing with some other people in Nashville.

When I heard that Alison Krauss had covered our [Bad Company] song *Oh Atlanta*, I was chuffed to bits. I must admit, I had never heard of her. Last year, someone from our management said, 'Have you heard this CD? She's covered one of your songs.' *Oh Atlanta* was a song I had written in 1976. I put it on and it was quite different, but I thought it was great. She's very bluegrass — ethnic country, if you like. I met her in Nashville and she's a lovely girl. She had a big, big hit with it. I was really pleased. Do some more! She was hanging out with the guys [Bad Company] in Nashville doing some backups when they were recording there. I was hoping they would put *Oh Atlanta* out for the Olympics because she had re-recorded it with Vince Gill. He's hot!

As far as my relationship with guitars, I suppose there's a time when you do bond, or you have a certain kinship with an instrument, especially when you're on the road or in an intense work situation, you get attached to one particular guitar. I've got the old '59 Les Paul; that's always wonderful when I plug that in and use it for recording, though I don't take it on the road anymore. It's too valuable; people would steal it. If there was a choice where you had to have one, I'd probably go for the '59 because it's always been consistently good. I did actually use it on a couple of tours and it was wonderful. If I have a guitar on the road, even if it's a re-issue, I'll play it and play it until I get real tight with it. I must admit though, those guitars from the tour are sitting in the bar now. I get attached to them for the period I'm using them, I suppose. Because of my background, I've never kept anything long enough to get attached to it. When I started out, I had to buy stuff on hire-purchase or on credit so I thought, I'll kick that one and trade it in for another one. If I could go back and get those guitars, it would be great. I've got some guitars I wouldn't sell. One of them is a blonde '59 Gibson ES335. It's a cracker and I've had that for years and that's always nice to see when I pull it out of the box. Justin Hayward of the Moody Blues used to have one of those and I bought one of his guitars some years ago. He had a blonde 335. It was a stereo. I actually had that guitar and it was a matching one to my other one. I foolishly sold it. I did a trade with a guy called Gil Southworth who's a big dealer in the States. That's where Justin's guitar is. He'd probably like to get that back, wouldn't he? Call Gil Southworth!

I would hope that people think that I added something to the Les Paul guitar legend. I did go out of my way to try and create a distinctive sound based mostly on the influence from Steve Cropper, the simplicity and the basic raw sound so, yes, I suppose, I had a sound in my mind. If I've got my own style, that's great, I'm very flattered.

Slash

GUNS N' ROSES, SLASH'S SNAKEPIT, SLASH'S BLUES BALL

Saul Hudson
Born July 23, 1965
Stoke-On-Trent, England

Anyone who doubts that 'art' runs in the blood might want to check in with Saul Hudson (a.k.a. Slash) who's noted for his inspired guitar work as a member of Guns N' Roses, Slash's Snakepit, and Slash's Blues Ball. Not only is he one of rock's top guitar-slingers — and a reputed whiz on the BMX bike Motocross circuit in his younger days — but also a fine illustrator in the family tradition. (Check out the cover of Snakepit's IT'S FIVE O'CLOCK SOMEWHERE CD!) His father, Anthony, is an art director/graphic designer, with count-less album covers to his credit, including Joni Mitchell's COURT AND SPARK, and his mother, Ola, is a clothes designer, who has worked with some of the top stars in the music world, including The Pointer Sisters, Iggy Pop, the late Mick Ronson, and David Bowie, with whom she worked on the film, *The Man Who Fell to Earth*.

Slash — given the name by the father of one of his best friends in his junior high days because he always seemed to be in a hurry — was born in England, but, by the time he was a teenager, he was living up in Laurel Canyon, in Los Angeles, where Joni Mitchell, record mogul David Geffen, and singer/songwriter David Blue were neighbors. This early exposure to the inner workings of the music industry no doubt helped him when he finally turned professional. "I've been around peculiar kinds of people ever since I was little," he recently told writer Jeff Boerio. "So, it just goes with the territory; nothing phases me. And I learned a lot from other people's mistakes. I'm also really good friends with Ron Wood, who's known me since I was 12. I see what The Stones go through. I met the Aerosmith guys right after I'd gone through the whole phase of Aerosmith being the be-all and end-all band. Then getting to tour with them, and seeing what they had to go through, it helps."

When Slash's parents separated, he lived with his grandmother, a classical pianist, who gave him one of his first guitars. The instru-ment soon became his passion, and he played in a succession of bands before getting together with his old school pal, Steven Adler, in a group called Road Crew. This ensemble evolved into Guns N' Roses, which, by the mid-'80s, was developing a sizable following locally. They signed to Geffen Records in the spring of 1986 and released their debut album, APPETITE FOR DESTRUCTION, in the summer of 1987 as they hit the road for tours with The Cult and Aerosmith over a 14-month stretch. It paid off as APPETITE FOR DESTRUCTION finally hit the top of the album chart in America in August of 1988 on the strength of tracks like *Welcome To The Jungle, Sweet Child O' Mine*, and *Paradise City*, which serve to spotlight Slash's emotive guitar playing. The follow-up was the eight-cut mini-album, G N' R LIES, which produced the hit track, *Patience*, as the group continued their touring ways, courting disaster at every turn, as various band members, and in particular, rabble-rousing singer Axl Rose seemed determined to live up to the title of their debut album.

Controversy certainly had no effect on their album sales as, on September 17, 1991, the band's fans helped the band make history by gobbling up most of the 4.2 million copies of the group's albums, USE YOUR ILLUSION I and USE YOUR ILLUSION II, both issued on that day. It was the largest album shipment in rock history, and within weeks, the albums debuted at Number 1 and Number 2 on the U.S. album chart as well as in the U.K. During this period, Slash worked with new friend Michael Jackson on his DANGEROUS album, while tracks like *Live And Let Die, Don't Cry, November Rain,* and *You Could Be Mine* kept Guns N' Roses out on the road and in demand.

Following the release of their fifth album, SPAGHETTI INCIDENT, the band took, what has proven to be, an extended hiatus. In 1995, Slash put together the group Slash's Snakepit, which released the album IT'S FIVE O'CLOCK SOMEWHERE, and in the summer of 1996, he put together a band to play at a blues concert in Budapest, Hungary. The ensemble became Slash's Blues Ball, which toured the U.S. doing blues covers until the fall of 1997. At the time of this writing, Slash was reportedly in the process of re-forming Snakepit.

We spoke to Slash one afternoon, on the rooftop of the Summerfield Suites hotel in West Hollywood, with a smog-shrouded city of Los Angeles as a backdrop in the distance.

The first music I listened to, as far as England's concerned, was The Moody Blues and The Stones. That was the main music that my dad listened to. Then it went on to The Beatles, The Kinks, The Who, Cat Stevens, Joni Mitchell — the list goes on and on. My mom turned me on to the early blues stuff, and I remember when I first heard John Lee Hooker, my grandmother hated him. For my grandmother, coming from a black family at that time, to listen to stuff like that was sort of taboo in her family, so whenever my mom played John Lee Hooker or Muddy Waters, my grandmother would get fucking pissed off. But I think that was the beginning. Then there was Charlie Christian, and, I guess, somewhere around that time is when I got turned on to Eric Clapton, and, of course, Jimi Hendrix followed, and all the mainstays of rock 'n' roll guitar came after that.

You know, there's no verbal way for me of expressing what it was that I heard in that music [blues], I just heard it. But looking back on it now, there's a definite pattern of notes, like a soul thing, that has stuck with me over the years. I have always definitely known what I do like and what I don't like. I never really sat down like this and tried to figure out exactly what that is, but there's a definite pattern there.

The first time I got into guitar playing was through Steve Adler, who was the original drummer for Guns 'N Roses. He had some piece of shit guitar at his grandmother's house and a tiny, little piece of shit amp and a Kiss record. His grandmother would go to work, and we'd ditch school and he'd put this record on and plug this guitar in and bang on it, not knowing one note or chord or anything, and for some reason that turned me on. So we decided we were going to start a band. At that point, I didn't even know the difference between a guitar and a bass. I knew what it sounded like, but I had never technically gotten into the background of which instrument was which. So I figured if he's playing guitar, I've got to play the other one.

I went for guitar lessons for a couple of days without a guitar. The instructor said, 'You're going to have to invest in an instrument. What do you want to play, bass or guitar?' I asked, 'What's the difference exactly?' They both looked the same to me, except that one was bigger than the other. He goes, 'Well, guitars got six strings and bass has got four strings.' I said, 'I'll take the one with the six strings.'

And it turned out to sound pretty much where I was going anyway. I didn't really finish the lessons, but that's basically how I got started. I just started taking all the music that I really loved when I was growing up and just learned that.

I don't really have any technical proficiency on the guitar. [Laughs] I'm sort of lacking in that department. I play all the time just to keep my chops up, but, when it comes down to it, I hear what I want to hear, so whatever it takes to be able to produce that sound or those notes or that feel or whatever it is, I'll concentrate on it until I learn it. But from a technical point of view, I have no idea exactly what that is. I learn stuff from playing around town with different guitar players who have been around longer than me. You retain all that information and pick up what you can.

I have a lot of guitar heroes whom I grew up listening to and whom I've met since and they've taught me a lot. Keith Richards is one of those guys who's a natural rhythm player. I've hung out with him before, and he's what you would call a rock 'n' roller's rock 'n' roller. Hats off to Keith! Muddy Waters and B.B. King were two of the guitar players who were contemporary blues guys that I listened to and learned a lot of licks from. Doing the tribute record to Muddy was just one of those things where you go in and ask, 'What song are we doing? How's it go?' and then just go for what you know.

The first time I played with B. B. King was on his birthday when he first opened up the club on the Universal City Walk… No, actually it was the House of Blues. I just went to see him play and I had no intentions of being egomaniacal enough to ask if I could play. I'll ask to play with anybody, but I drew the line with B.B. King. As it turns out, someone told him that I was there, and, the next thing you know, he announced my name. I was up on a balcony with no guitar pick and a pack of cigarettes and a drink. I went rushing down there, and he kept me up on stage for four or five songs. It was an experience that led to two other gigs with him. It was really great, actually, and, to tell you the truth, I can't communicate how much I felt the compliment of being asked to get on the stage with somebody like that. I felt the same with Buddy Guy, who's another cat I played with, where he asked me up there and just let me loose; the same with Les Paul, Johnny Winter, and Mick Ronson, when he was still around. I've played with a lot of people over the last few years and it's always an honor.

I delve into different types of music and apply whatever my style is to a lot of different things that you wouldn't expect me to play. People usually relate me solely to Guns N' Roses and for that particular sound, but I've taken that sound and put it on other things where you wouldn't even know it was me for the most part. Some people say that they do, and that's sort of a compliment in itself. It's not necessarily that different than my regular style. I just incorporate different notes to fit the mood of the tune. I can't play fusion jazz, nor do I have an ear for it, but if you put me in context with say regular boogie stuff or slow blues or anything that's more or less emotional that has a melody, I usually can adapt.

Snakepit is more or less like early Guns N' Roses stuff. It's very straight, in your face, spontaneous hard rock; there's not too much difference between the two. The only real difference is the musicians in the band, but my approach to the guitar is more or less the same.

Depending on how complex the track is and whose song it is, I usually get it in the first couple of takes. If I'm improvising, an idea will come through, which I'll go back and try to recapture.

I was in a club the other night and the deejay there, I guess, happened to be a fan or something and he played a series of what I would consider extracurricular material that I played on. It was interesting because I had never listened back to it. I like playing with Iggy Pop, and Lenny Kravitz came out good. I'm real proud of the playing I did on the Michael Jackson song, *Give In To Me*, which nobody is really familiar with. They think *Black Or White* is the only track I ever played on with him. I had a great time playing with Paul Rodgers on the Jimi Hendrix and the Muddy Waters tributes. So, if you don't like it, you don't do it. I had a couple of bad experiences, but I don't dwell on it because you can't expect everything to go perfectly.

:| |•|•|

The first guitar I ever had was a copy of a Gibson Explorer and the next one I had was a copy of a Les Paul — an old Memphis copy. That one didn't last long either. And then I went through a whole slew of different guitars, searching for where I would eventually wind up back with — a Les Paul. It's the most versatile guitar for me. It has the most body and it looks cool. It has a nice round, thick tone to it — a rich tone. So if it ain't broke, don't fix it, as they say.

My signature Les Paul is really just a [Les Paul] Standard. The pickups are Seymour Duncan Alnico IIs. When I did the APPETITE FOR DESTRUCTION record, I used them and I've used these pickups ever since. Now I put them in everything. The rest of it, with the exception of the finish and the logo, is basically the same kind of guitar that I play when I'm playing live. The only thing is, I try not to fuck it up, because it looks so nice. The Les Paul is an entity unto itself. It's more or less a package: the neck, the body, the weight, the arrange-ment of the pots. If you like playing with a heavy guitar and you like the way that the Les Paul is arranged, if you play a Stratocaster, this can be a little awkward. I go to clubs and play somebody else's Strat, and I keep hitting the volume knob. You have to get used to it. You just get used to Les Paul necks, because they come as they are. I have to admit, I do like a less thick neck, like this, with a nice flat fretboard, as opposed to the one that has an arch to it. I really tech-nically don't pay much attention. If I pick it up and it feels good, that's it.

I try to play everyday even when I'm not working. As soon as I spend two or three days not playing, I start to feel like I'm slacking. Like with any muscle, it's something you've got to exercise, plus I just dig playing. I was in a club last night and walked in on this band. These guys must have been 60 years old from the Valley — some old blues band. Me and my friend Ted went in there and asked them if we could play. They went, 'Hey no man! You have no business get-ting up here.' I said, 'Just trust us. Let us up!' So we got up and played and jammed our asses off. If I keep doing that, I feel justified at the end of the night. It's like the only way to justify a heavy night of drinking. [Laughs]

Playing guitar is very much a hands-on thing for me. I spend most of my time either thinking about it or putting melodies and notes through my head, and, finally, when I do get a hold of a guitar, I incorporate those ideas onto a fretboard or I spend my time just having one close by so it's always next to me. It drove my wife crazy, I know that, but it's what I do.

Chad Taylor

LIVE!

Chad David Taylor
Born November 24, 1970
York, Pennsylvania

:|Chad Taylor|·|·|

*L*ive! crashed onto the alternative music scene in 1994 with the release of their sophomore album, THROWING COPPER, which, the band's lyricist/vocalist/guitarist Edward Kowalczyk told Jim Nelson of *The Album Network*, "was put together by our thoughts about rock 'n' roll and preconceptions of what it was like to be successful, and where we would be and what kind of feelings we'd have on-stage." Though that success would not come overnight for this quartet from Pennsylvania, neither at the front end of their career nor immediately following the release of THROWING COPPER, that all changed as the track *Lightning Crashes* from the CD began hitting the airwaves in early 1995. THROWING COPPER would go on to sell over six million copies and earn them the title of Top Rock Artist at the 1995 *Billboard* Music Awards at a time when many music industry pundits were starting to predict the imminent demise of the alternative music scene.

The genesis of Live! goes back to a kindergarten class at Jacob L. Devers Elementary School in 1975, which Ed Kowalczyk and Live! guitar player Chad Taylor attended at the same time. Through their school years, the two stayed in touch, and in the early '80s, after Taylor had formed a band with high-school mates and current Live! members Chad Gracey and Patrick Dahlheimer, Kowalczyk was recruited as their singer. Settling on the name Public Affection, they played their first gig locally in the late fall of 1987. The group changed its name to Live! — reportedly after Taylor had a dream in which he saw Matt Gracey, his guitar tech and right-hand man, wearing a hat with the word 'Live' on it — after they graduated from high school and began writing their own material and performing it, not only as the resident band at the Chameleon Club in Lancaster, Pennsylvania, but also at venues the length and breadth of the U.S.

In 1991, it was at the legendary CBGB club in New York that the group first caught the attention of the record industry, which resulted in their signing to Radioactive Records and the release of the four-track EP, FOUR SONGS, produced by ex-Talking Heads keyboardist Jerry Harrison. The group's debut album, MENTAL JEWELRY, with Harrison once again in the producer's chair, followed in 1992, as the band lived up to its name by continuing to tour heavily throughout America. The spring of 1994 saw the release of their breakthrough THROWING COPPER CD, which after 52 weeks on the *Billboard* Top 200 album chart in the U.S., finally hit Number 1 in May of 1995. That same year, the group set out on a highly successful world tour, which, with a break to record their third album, SECRET SAMADHI, co-produced with Jay Healy, continued through 1998. At the time of this writing, Live! were in the studio working on their fourth opus set for release in 1999.

We spoke to Chad Taylor of the group, an avowed avid collector of vintage guitars, on an October morning, in a vacant lot in the Soho district of New York City. Talk about your urban wasteland!

I always wanted to be a drummer, and, when I was ten years old, my dad bought me my first guitar, a Les Paul, and it sat in my basement for two years. I never really played it much. And then I saw a band at some sort of elementary or middle-school talent show and there was this guy playing guitar. All the girls loved him, and, instantly, I was a guitar fan. At the ripe age of 12, I decided that my hormones had kicked in.

Everyone in Live! was young — all 13 or 14 years old. So, of course, when we got together, it was strictly for fun and we played that way until the end of high school, pretty much just playing weekend dances, shows and that kind of stuff. Then it evolved into writing our own songs — our own material — and taking it further than that.

We played a whole lot of stuff, but it was based on what song was the easiest one to play. We weren't a very technical band — we still aren't really a very technical band — so we more or less relied on the elements of simplicity. One of my heroes is Neil Young and I really like Jimi Hendrix a lot. I like him more for his tone than I do for his playing. The same with Neil Young. Its more about tone than even playing.

When we did the first record, MENTAL JEWELRY, I don't think I was much of a guitar player then. I still don't think I'm much now, I've just learned to fool people better. It's kind of interesting looking back on that record because I can't even play the parts that were back on that record because I can't even play the parts that were on there. I was so busy; I played so much. And, at that time, you have to realize that I was 18 years old, so I wasn't quite accustomed to going out and drinking and playing. Then, as I got older, I realized that in order to have a couple of shots and have a beer when you're on stage, you have to slow all your parts down and make them a little easier to play, so I guess I evolved in that sense.

Most of the time my writing happens at home with just a small practice amp or an acoustic guitar, but always music first and always with a guitar. Ed [Kowalczyk] writes the same way as well. There's no real pre-set notion on how we actually write, although I would say Ed and I write the majority of the songs. Whether he's working on them by himself or working on the lyrics or melody or I bring in 50 percent, which might be the chord progressions or something to that effect, we definitely collaborate. But there's the band activity as well, which is more like a jam situation.

With *Lightning Flashes*, Ed and I had put the song together in its basic format. We tried to play it once with the band and it was just painstaking. We were on tour at the time and we went out to finish a six or seven week leg of a tour, took some time off, came back, and we just started playing the song at a rehearsal. The rest of the band couldn't remember playing the song, of course. We were right into it and all the parts were perfect. It was one of those rare instances where coming back to something worked.

Most of the time with us, if it doesn't come within the first five minutes or something, we usually just throw it out. That's really hard on Ed and me, but our band is a true democracy. When you spend as much time living together as we have, it can't really be any other way. Everybody's say has got to be equal, whether you're writing the songs or not. It's always been difficult, but we seem to be getting by.

To me, lead guitar is one of those really funny things. When I was growing up, I think the first guy I recognized as a lead player — the first time I thought, 'That's the lead guitar player and that's the rhythm player' — was Ace Frehley from Kiss. I decided instantly that I wanted to be like the lead guitar player. At that time, I started listening to The Stones and getting into more of what Keith Richards was doing. I'm not into real flashy leads. I'd rather play just one note that says it all 'cause I think that's harder to do anyway. At least, I think that's where I want to be.

Less is more in all music. There are some players who are involved with technique and they know scales and stuff like that. My background in music comes from a very limited knowledge. The guy who produced our current album, he told me to play a B flat and I had to sit there and look at the guitar and count it out and say, 'Well, here's B flat. Yeah, I got it; no problem.' But, it's not like I have a knowledge of the guitar as an instrument. As a matter of fact, I keep my knowledge very limited on purpose because it is just a big hunk of refined wood — an ax. You put a piece of metal on the end of it and you can chop wood. I think technology is one of those things that actually inhibits creative juices, so I think it's really important to just keep it simple.

:| |•|•|

My first guitar was a Les Paul, and I own several now. Actually, I probably own 20 or so. It's certainly evolved. I use different instruments for different songs, for different sounds, but there's a particular element to Live! that has absolutely evolved around the Les Paul. I use other Gibsons, too. I have a couple of L5s as well as some nice, old acoustic archtops and things like that. To me, I should be able to pick up any guitar and do what I want to do no matter how good it is or how bad it is. I just think that the Les Paul is one of those guitars, like the Fender Telecaster or the Stratocaster, that is one of the classics. I just tend to rely on those guitars.

I usually don't make any modifications to my guitars, but I have been known to add a capacitor just to change the tone a little bit. Other than that, I pretty much play the stock instrument.

I pretty much rely on my three favorite Les Pauls. I have a '54 Gold Top, a '56 Les Paul, and a '57 Triple Pickup with a Bigsby. Usually, they're the only three that I play in a live situation.

As far as unusual tunings go, there's D-A-D-F-A-D. I don't really know what that is. I guess that's a standard D tuning and that's about as radical as I get with alternative tunings. There's a couple of songs on SECRET SAMADHI in that tuning [for example, *Lakini's Juice*], but there are no alternative tunings on the previous two records, other than if it was a part that went in the background where I wanted to hit big open chords. Then, I would go to open tuning. If I open tune the guitar, I just can't play a chord and not sound like Keith Richards, so I stay away from that. I just keep it simple.

Glenn Tipton

JUDAS PRIEST

Glenn Tipton
Born October 25, 1948
Birmingham, England

: Glenn Tipton |·|·|

There are varied opinions on where the term 'heavy metal' originated as it pertains to music. The phrase actually first appeared in a
story by science fiction writer William Burroughs, titled "Nova
Express," in which one of the main characters, Uranian Willie, is
referred to as The Heavy Metal Kid. One of the first references to
'heavy metal' as it applied to rock music perhaps was made by the
late Lester Bangs, dean of rock critics. Then, of course, there was
Steppenwolf's reference to "heavy metal thunder" in the song *Born
To Be Wild*.

But no matter its origins, it has been a world of shag hair-dos,
black leather, chains, spikes, tattoos, and adolescent rebellion. At
its worst, critics have said, it promotes sexism, disdain for authority,
and sympathy for the devil. At its best, we humbly suggest, it's loud,
rude, and aggressive. Any old way you choose it, this musical *Sturm
und Drang* has always been just the thing to over stimulate the
Clearasil-spattered fantasies of teenage boys going through the trau-
ma of puberty and ideal for dissipating bouts of aggression in just
about anyone else.

There have been many sub-categories of 'metal' over the years,
but it's all basically of the same pedigree — bands that have built
their reputations on repetitive, hook-laden, metallic guitar riffs that
slice through thundering bass lines and the thudding persistence of
drums, set off by the banshee wail of a singer. In that regard, no
group has fit that profile as well as Judas Priest, who, at the close of
the '70s, *Rolling Stone* magazine opined, 'define the heavy metal
genre at the outset of the '80s ...'

Judas Priest, whose name derives from the Bob Dylan track, *The
Ballad Of Frankie Lee And Judas Priest* from his JOHN WESLEY HARDING
album, started out in the late '60s as a pop/rock cover band in their
native Birmingham, England. By 1974, with the addition of guitarist
Glenn Tipton to founding members K.K. Downing and Ian Hill, the

group heavied up significantly and had their first album, ROCKA ROLLA, released on the small Gun Records label. Fronted by the charismatic Rob Halford until 1992 and powered by the dual guitar attack of Downing and Tipton, the group achieved great mainstream success by the early '80s with albums like SCREAMING FOR VENGEANCE, which produced the group's first commercially-successful single, *Another Thing Coming*, and DEFENDERS OF THE FAITH.

The band's much-publicized law suit over the 1985 suicide attempts by two fans — one of which was successful — after they had listened to alleged satanic messages inscribed in the track *Better By You, Better Than Me*, came to court in 1990. In 1993, the court handed down a not-guilty verdict, but the long legal battle obviously had a disruptive effect on the group, and, during this period, original vocalist Rob Halford departed to pursue a solo career. In 1995, long-time Priest fan, Tim 'Ripper' Owens, who actually fronted an American-based Judas Priest cover band, replaced Halford. The following year, Tipton completed and released his solo album, BAPTIZM OF FIRE. In 1997, following a seven-year recording hiatus, the group released the CD JUGULATOR featuring the latest incarnation of Priest that included new members Scott Travis [replacing Dave Holland] and Owens, along with original members Hill, Downing, and Tipton. The group's latest album, at the time of writing, was '98 LIVE MELTDOWN, recorded during the group's world tour in 1998.

Knowing that Glenn Tipton of the group was something of a golfing enthusiast, we met him one September morning for a chat at the Waterstock Golf and Country Club, a short drive from London's Heathrow Airport, where we were bound that afternoon. Instead of a set of clubs, Tipton came armed with some prized Gibson guitars from his collection — a couple of road-tested SGs and a beautiful white 335.

My brother probably inspired me to begin playing because he was a guitar player. When he was out, I used to sneak into his room and play his guitar and think that he didn't know, but, of course, it was always seriously out of tune when he came back. [Laughs] That was the reason I took an interest in the guitar. Above all, though, I think Jimi Hendrix was my inspiration and still is today. I've changed and evolved through the years and I do consider myself a very '90s guitar player now. I've never rested on my laurels. I've always listened to the young kids as well, but Hendrix was a major inspiration. I know Hendrix wasn't noted for playing Gibsons, but there's no reason why you can't adapt your own style on any guitar.

My first guitar was a semi-acoustic Hofner, in actual fact, which I put a pickup on. It sounded horrendous and squealed and was never in tune. My next guitar was a Fender Stratocaster, which is the one I had stolen. It was an old salmon-pink one. The next guitar was a Gibson SG. That was the order of events. Since then, I've had a whole multitude of guitars of different shapes and sizes for experimentation.

I learned very quickly — you may say through impatience, really. In the early days, when I used to listen to other guitar players and try to emulate them or emulate their styles or certain licks they did, I never quite pulled it off. I never really played it like they did. And at first this used to frustrate me and I'd persevere until I got it as close as possible. But I quickly realized that you don't want to do that really. At some point, during the inspiration for that certain lick or that certain style, you should be quite happy that what you're doing is different. I think that realization was the single most important thing in developing my guitar playing style. I quickly learned that there is a real importance to creating your own character and accepting your own style and improving on that. If you sound like someone else, you're always going to sound like someone else. Its very, very important to get your own style. I think that's something that I have done — and I hope people who listen to my playing, would agree.

It's been great playing with K.K. [Downing]. It's healthy competition, and K.K. has got a different style from me, which is great. We've had an up and down relationship, in terms of temperament, through the band. We're best of friends really and have so much in common, but, musically, as always, you've got that healthy competitive spirit and there's a spark in there which inspires us both. It's great when we go into the studio because if I do a lead break, or part of a lead break, Ken [K.K.] is going to go away and say, 'I'm going to better that!' And I'll think, 'Yeah, that's good!' We work like that and it's almost like a step up. It's actually been great for both of us because it has improved our styles and our techniques by that healthy competition in a band. But having said that, there's no real competitive spirit. We're working to the same ends and our heart and soul is in Judas Priest and always will be.

:| |•|•|

These are guitars from hell really. [Holds up two well-used Gibson SGs] Dating back to the early days of Priest, I've never really been a person who collects guitars for the year or the value. To me guitars, if they play well and they sound good, are working tools that we take on the road. And, if they come out of that unscathed, if they're robust, they're good. These are two work-horses that have been to hell and back on Priest tours. They've sort of been 'mongrelized'. We played a gig at the Sheffield City Hall and I got a little bit carried away on stage one night and actually pulled the stacks and the amps down on it and it snapped the neck, but it has been put back together and I still use it. As I say, they have been mongrelized, but these two Gibson SGs are my sort of guitars. I don't sell guitars, I buy guitars and keep them 'til I either lose them or they get stolen or they die with me — and these two will probably die with me. They've been in bits and back together again. If you walk on stage with Judas Priest, anything can happen — and it does. You can see that they're battered, but they do a job.

I like guitars for specific things. I either use them in the studio or they go on-stage with me. And, if they go on-stage with me, they might not come back, but these are very tough and durable; they're great and they sound good. When you consider the technologies around today, these guitars still stand up to it.

I modify my guitars — mongrelize them. I've got a lot of old SGs — probably thirty — and I put bits together. I've had the neck snapped on these. I'll put a neck back on this one. I've actually designed my own guitars, but they've always been based on a neck from the SG, which I find is a very comfortable neck to play.

K.K. and I were approached to put guitars in the Rock and Roll Hall of Fame in Cleveland, and, I suppose, really, we had to pick the guitars that we had used most or that people associated most with us. In my early days, I will always remember a gig we did at The Top Rank in Newcastle during the early years of Priest and I had my guitar stolen during tour time there. I almost gave up because I had no more money. Newcastle's a long way to drive back to London with no money and no guitar. But The Top Rank gave me a check for a new guitar, and that was when I bought my first SG. I grew to love it very much, and from then on, in the early days particularly, I was associated with a black SG, which happened to be the one I bought.

I like the sound of the SG and the way it plays. I've always felt comfortable with the neck, the way it plays on a SG. Les Pauls are nice, but they're a little bit fatter and they're a little bit different to play. I use them for different things. The SGs are a good all-round guitar. Although I don't have the whammy bar on these, they've still got a great sound and they've got a great use in studio or for certain songs on stage.

Guitars to me are working tools. I don't have a lot of time for sentiment. If you ask me the year of a guitar — like some people will say it's a '57 or so and so — that's not me. But, recently, I was looking around for a Les Paul and I earmarked two or three to try — I really can't tell if I like a guitar unless I take it home and mess around with it. Just as I walked away from the store, I spotted this Gibson ES335 guitar on the wall. I asked the guy in the store to bring it along because it was perfect — it epitomizes guitars for me — to put on the wall in my studio. So he brought it along and we cranked it up and it just sounded like a dream. This is a guitar to hug.

There's two things in my life that I hug — three if you include the wife. One is an old Wurlitzer jukebox — I love it — and this guitar [ES335]. To me, this has got a better shape than any woman — or nearly any woman. It's an old blues guitar, but, in a sense, these guitars can be used for anything. When I compare it to the Les Paul, it's just got a nice tone and quality. When I plug this guitar in — these guitars are notorious for whistling and squealing — this one sings like a bird. I used it on my solo album. I think, of all the guitars I've got, this is my favorite and its great to hug. This is a good one.

:| |•|•|

It's a strange scene with regards to metal bands. The more aggressive bands have come from Birmingham or The Midlands [in England]. Why that is, I don't know. It's a very industrial area. It's a difficult area to get out of. In the early days, the fact that we were from Birmingham ... if we wanted people to come and review shows and that, they didn't really want to come past Watford, and we had to go down to London to get people to come and see the band. It's that fact that gives people the determination to get out of there really. I still live close to Birmingham. When I say get out of there, I mean to pursue your career. But there's definitely an inherent aggression and emotion from people of The Midlands. It's a quality which is unique and therefore different and I think that anything that is different, people love. I would say that's what makes people from Birmingham or The Midlands have that unique quality, which I think is an inspiration to other people.

And metal is not always a blues-based thing. I was brought up on the blues, if you like, and then progressive blues, Hendrix and so on. It's not that way anymore. I don't very often play blues anymore. I've tended to always try to move with the times and to adapt my style and update it every year. I suppose, really, the roots were there, but exactly what it is now that kids pick up on, I don't know. It could be anything really.

Travis Tritt

James Travis Tritt
Born February 9, 1963
Marietta, Georgia

: | Travis Tritt | · | · |

As one of the so-called Class of '89, a group of emerging artists that included Garth Brooks, Clint Black, and Alan Jackson who were destined to expand the audience for country music, Travis Tritt, like many of his contemporaries, is always quick to pledge his allegiance to his traditional country roots despite the rockin' good-time reputation he has earned for his music and stage show. "On the last album [THE RESTLESS KIND], I took a real hard left turn," Tritt explained to Wendy Newcomer of *Country Weekly* magazine in the spring of 1998. "I went back to the basic roots of country music and did as traditional a country album as I would ever feel comfortable doing. I guess, more than anything, I was out to prove something. I had seen so many articles describing me as the 'rebel rocker' or the 'romantic outlaw.' So many people seemed to focus on my rock and roll connections. I'm very proud of those connections and the fact that I've been able to do that kind of music over the years. But I really felt the need to show people that I was a country music artist first and foremost. Country music is what brought me to the party."

The party began for Tritt almost upon his graduation from high school in the early '80s as he met a Warner Bros. record company promotion man in Atlanta, who would be responsible for introducing him to the powers that be at the Nashville office. He was eventually signed to the label, and in 1989, his debut single, *Country Club*, from his first album of the same name, set the tone for his future career direction as it hit the Top 10 of the country charts. Since that time, Tritt, whose autobiography *Ten Feet Tall and Bulletproof* was published in 1994 to coincide with his CD of the same name, has sold more than 17 million albums. A licensed driver for SuperComp cars and past spokesperson for the National Hot Rod Association, Tritt won a Grammy in 1992 for his vocal collaboration with his good friend, Marty Stuart.

Typical of the camera-friendly ways of so-called 'New Country' artists, Tritt has appeared in a number of films, including the features *The Cowboy Way, Fire Down Below, Blues Brothers 2000*, and the TV movies *Rio Diablo* and *Outlaw Justice*. He has also contributed songs to a number of film soundtracks, including *My Cousin Vinny, Honeymoon in Vegas*, and *The Cowboy Way*. By the end of 1998, Tritt had 26 music videos to his credit, with 11 of them having reached Number 1 on the CMT: Country Music Television Top 12 Countdown. Actually, during the course of getting The Eagles back together for his video of their song *Take It Easy*, Tritt became the catalyst for the group's subsequent reunion, which included an album and tour they would dub, Hell Freezes Over.

"I like being able to say that I have a lot of fans who had never listened to country music before I came out," Tritt related during his *Country Weekly* interview. "That's probably the greatest compliment that I get paid. It's cool to know that you're not just preaching to the converted. I've been very fortunate to have an opportunity to work with other people like Patti LaBelle, David Lee Roth, and Buddy Guy. Because of that, I've been able to reach a lot of folks who probably would never turn on a country music radio station."

We spoke to Travis Tritt at the legendary Gruhn's Guitar Shop in Nashville, Tennessee on an October afternoon, which gave way to an evening of celebration at the Country Music Association (CMA) Awards show.

I've got pictures of my father and I sitting around when I was a little, bitty kid — my father played a Gibson guitar and I had a little toy plastic guitar when I was about two or three years old. There's a picture of me standing on a chair next to my dad and my dad playing that old Sunburst Gibson and me sitting there playing my little toy guitar. I guess it was from his influence first and then probably, later on, from avidly watching people on television like Glen Campbell and Johnny Cash and Mac Davis, all of whom had regular TV specials, and seeing those guys play guitars, that I got into music. It's just something that came naturally.

The only music that was in my house when I was a kid growing up was straight ahead country or gospel. There were a lot of old Hank Snow records around and a lot of Merle Haggard, George Jones, Lester Flatt and Earl Scruggs, Bill Monroe, Johnny Cash, Porter Wagoner and Dolly Parton. There were a lot of those albums lying around in my house and those albums were very influential. They were the only kind of music that we played. Buck Owens was a big influence, too — a lot of the country music that was popular in the '50s and '60s.

Still, I started out playing more of a folk style of guitar. I think people like James Taylor and John Denver, as far as acoustic guitar, were some of my biggest influences at an early age, and then, as I got to be 10 or 11 years old — I started playing when I was eight — it started going more towards a bluegrass style. I started going to a lot of bluegrass festivals throughout the Southeast with my uncle, and I was really influenced a lot by that. I definitely saw my rhythm style change from folk — more of a finger-picking style — to bluegrass. It was a gradual progression, and then, later on, as I started to listen to more blues and Southern rock, all of those influences played a part. It was kind of like building up my vocal influences, the same thing with guitar; it was a big smorgasbord of a lot of different styles and a lot of different people.

Playing guitar is something I'd never done on record until THE RESTLESS KIND. The way that I've always done albums in the past — the way that the band in the studio would learn the songs — is to go and sit in the middle of them in a big circle. I would sit and play the song down for them on acoustic guitar and sing it for them, and they would make charts based on that, and then we would go in and start turning the tape machines on. Even on past albums that I didn't play on, a lot of the guitar players that played acoustic guitar, like Billy Walker Jr. or Larry Byrom or some of these guys, would ask me things like, 'You played a little lick in the first chorus or in the first verse, could you show us what that lick is again?' I would show it to them and they would duplicate it again on the record. So a lot of the licks that have been played on my albums throughout my career were really mine. That's how they were written. I sat down and wrote them, probably on guitar. Most of my writing is on guitar and those were just the licks the way I heard them in my head as the song was written.

On THE RESTLESS KIND, we did the same thing but, when we got ready to turn the tape machines on, Don Was, who I co-produced the album with, told the engineer, 'I want you to set up a microphone for Travis to play guitar.' And I said, 'Don, I've never really done that before. Are you sure that's something you want?' And he said, 'Absolutely!' And I said, 'Why?' He told me that he would insist that I play on any of these tracks the same way that he would insist that Waylon Jennings play on any of the tracks because, he said, 'You have a definite feel and, while what you play might not be the conventional style that you might hear from a Nashville studio player, it definitely is in the pocket and it definitely has a direct relation to how the band plays the song.' It sort of becomes an adhesive — sort of like a glue — that brings the whole band in together. I started listening down to the tracks and realizing that he had a point. So, it was a great opportunity for me to get to play on record.

:| |·|·|

I have a Gibson J200 that basically I keep on the tour bus with me all the time. I keep it under my bed on my bus. Everybody needs to have a guitar with them on the road so that, when you get an inspiration, you can grab a guitar and do some writing. I have one that I write with when I'm on the bus and on the road. It's a great sounding guitar because of the big body and everything. It's got that big wonderful acoustic sound to it, and it's almost become a best friend.

I don't play every day. I try very hard to find time to sit down with a guitar, and that's one nice thing about having one close by. Even if there's only 10 or 15 minutes of down time, you can reach over and grab it. I heard Chet Atkins say one time that a true musician never feels comfortable without his instrument around or somewhere close by. You kind of feel like you're missing an arm or a leg or something and I think that's probably very true. There're a lot of times when I find myself really longing to just pick up a guitar and play. That may come in the middle of a tour when you're playing every night on stage, so it's a wonderful pastime. I've always enjoyed playing and I find myself constantly learning about guitar. I think that's one of the neat things about it. It's always fresh; there's always something new you can learn.

I've always been the kind of guy who likes a pretty loud stage volume, and because of that, acoustic hollow-body guitars like the Gibson J200 have a tendency to vibrate. The top vibrates and it starts a feedback, a low end 'woo-woo' kind of a rumble, and, although you can put little plates in the sound hole to stop that, being a hollow guitar, it still has that problem. I've never found a guitar until the SST that truly sounded acoustic no matter what volume you played it at and didn't have any of that feedback. The SST is a solid body guitar. It's very similar to a Fender Stratocaster or a Les Paul. The first SSTs were solid bodies. There're no sound holes, so it eliminated all of that vibration. You could play it at any volume you wanted to and never had to worry about feedback. Just recently, they've done some experimenting out on the road with a new SST that is a hollow body guitar. It's much lighter. I've been playing some of those on the stage, and I've found that the sound is fabulous and there is still no feedback. That is the great advantage to me. I still get a great acoustic sound without having to worry about the low-end rumble and the low-end feedback.

There have been so many people out there that have been influential to my playing style. From an acoustic guitar standpoint, obviously folks like Chet Atkins, Doc Watson, Merle Travis, and Tony Rice, and those guys at a bluegrass level. From an electric guitar standpoint, I've always been a fan of Gary Rossington, Duane Allman, and Dickey Betts. I really enjoy their style of playing. I've tried to incorporate little bits and pieces from each one of them through the years into my playing. There's a lot to be said for influences and those guys definitely were strong influences in my guitar playing.

When writing a song, I usually hear melody and lyrics and everything in my head at the same time, so it's just a matter of sitting down and working the chords out on a guitar and writing it that way. A lot of times I'll hear the licks right off the bat. When we were writing *Anymore*, I remember hearing distinctly what became a signature lick for that song. I can hit one note of that song in concert and everybody knows right off the bat what that song is.

When you start talking about conventional players in Nashville, most studio musicians play everything on the downbeat. When I play, I've always — because I played for so long in the bars and clubs as a solo act — tried to play rhythm and leads and runs and everything in between. There's a lot more stuff going on than just the up and down, one and three or two and four rhythm. When Don Was described my playing as unconventional, I think that basically was what he was talking about.

It was a long time before I got my first Gibson. I think the first real guitar that was a wooden guitar, not one of those old plastic models, was a Tempo. It was like a miniature guitar — small, with a short neck. Because the strings were so far off the frets, it was the hardest thing in the world to learn how to play. I've said ever since then to other people who have young children who want to learn how to play guitar, if you want to learn how to play guitar or you want your children to learn right, get them a decent instrument. Get them something good, because it's very tough and can be very frustrating to try and learn on something else. But that was my first guitar. I don't know what happened to that guitar; it's kind of disappeared over the years. I played that guitar for probably the first five years of learning how to play. My first real guitar was an Epiphone 12-string that I got for Christmas when I was 14 years old.

I didn't really get into electric guitars until the mid-'80s, and the only reason that I did at that time was because I was playing in little bars and clubs and usually over in the corner playing background music for people to eat dinner by, but at the end of the night, everybody was just drinking and you really want to get people's attention. I was wanting to do songs like *Johnny B. Goode* and that kind of thing. It's kind of hard to do them on acoustic guitar, so I really started getting into electric guitars at that point and really trying to let my hair down and rock a little bit toward the end of the evening. You just can't do that on an acoustic hollow body.

I still play a Chet SST 12-string on *More Than You'll Ever Know* on stage every night. I started out with that Epiphone 12-string because of the full sound, and, being a solo guy, you're trying to get as much sound as you possibly could out of the guitar and obviously the 12-string was the way to go for me, plus being influenced by people like John Denver, James Taylor, Gordon Lightfoot, and those kind of people. Twelve-string guitars were a mainstay for those guys. That was all part of what got me interested, and then, when I started playing concerts, the 12-string phase just kept working its way into a lot of my material. It was being played on a lot of my records, so to get that real full sound, I occasionally use that SST 12-string on stage. I've got a big white one now that I use for *More Than You'll Ever Know*, because the song starts out with just me and the guitar, and it's real full and gives a really sweet sound.

We've always been a guitar-based band. I've got four guys in my organization who are kind of utility men and can play several different instruments, one of them being guitar, so at one given point on stage, you may see four guys, including myself, playing guitars. I've always been interested in some of the records on which you hear different guitar parts — stacking guitar parts. I think I probably learned more about that kind of thing from Marty Stuart than anyone else. On the making of THE RESTLESS KIND, for example, we would go in and lay down the basic tracks, and then Marty and I would go back and stack maybe a high-strung guitar or a guitar with a capo up on the fourth or fifth fret, playing a little bit different positioning on the neck. We'd still stay in the same key and just stack different tones of different guitars on there. It really fills up the sound and it really makes it a very warm, strong tone, and I think that's vital to really making records that stand out on radio these days.

Bob Weir

THE GRATEFUL DEAD, KINGFISH, BOBBY AND THE MIDNITES, RATDOG

Robert Hall
Born October 6, 1947
San Francisco, California

:|Bob Weir|·|·|

"The name Haight-Ashbury alone conjures up images of psyche-delic drugs and meandering, pulsing rock music," observes Joel Selvin in his book *The Musical History Tour*, a guide to over 200 of the Bay Area's most memorable music sites. "The cultural revolu-tion fronted by the Jefferson Airplane, Grateful Dead, Quicksilver Messenger Service, Big Brother and the Holding Company and oth-ers was not relegated strictly to the musical. The old Irish working-class neighborhood has become synonymous around the globe with the sixties in San Francisco, a decade that left an indelible imprint on the area."

And, like that San Francisco scene of the '60s, those globe-trot-ting, psychedelic rockers known as the Grateful Dead — so-named after group co-founder, the late Jerry Garcia, saw the name in an Oxford Dictionary he was reading (?!) at a pot party — transcended the music as they ended up carrying the banner for a culture and an era that had begun to lose its relevancy by the mid-'70s. Be that as it may, the Dead recorded and toured constantly over the three decades they were active, and attracted, by the thousands, the most rabid fans that the rock or pop world had ever witnessed. They called themselves 'Deadheads', and many followed the band from concert to concert on their uncommonly lengthy tours. The group was inducted into the Rock and Roll Hall of Fame in 1994.

When Garcia died of an apparent heart attack in August 1995, Mayor Frank Jordan ordered the flags flown at half mast and a tie-dyed Dead flag hoisted over City Hall. On December 6, 1995, three decades after the Dead was born, the remaining group members officially laid the band to rest.

But that activist spirit of the '60s, which was so ingrained in the group's philosophy over the years and which manifested itself in projects like their Rain Forest Benefit Concert at Madison Square Gardens in New York in 1988, has continued with Grateful Dead founder and guitarist, Bob Weir. He remains an environmentalist, with a special interest in temperate and tropical reforestation, including coral reef preservation, while his humanitarian focus is on the rights of indigenous peoples, as well as children's education. Over the past few years, he has created a number of environmental children's books and audio cassettes with his sister, Wendy. He has also continued to tour and record with bass player and good friend Rob Wasserman, as a duo and as part of the band they call Ratdog.

We talked Dead history and guitars — and in particular, a treasured Gibson ES335 — with Bob Weir, one October afternoon in the living room of his home in San Rafael, California.

The son of some friends of my parents came over to visit and stayed with my family when I was 12 years old. He had a guitar that he let me play, and I guess I was hooked from that point on. That summer, I got together some money and bought a $17.00 Japanese guitar and started working on that. I had that for about a year and then upgraded. I saved my money and bought better guitars.

When I first met Jerry [Garcia], I was playing in a makeshift folk ensemble. We were called the Uncalled Four. That was kind of a common name back then, but we thought it was clever. One of my fellow bandmates and myself were wandering the back streets of Palo Alto on New Year's Eve of 1964, and we went by the back of a music store where Jerry used to teach. We heard banjo music coming from inside, so we knocked on the door and we found Jerry in there waiting for his students to arrive. We apprised him of the fact that it was New Year's Eve and, perhaps, he was out of luck. He agreed, and so we struck up a conversation. After a while, we broke into the front of the store and got a bunch of instruments out and played most of the night. We decided it was a lot of fun and we put together a jug band — a sort of a country/blues ensemble. That lasted for about a year, and then we electrified and became The Warlocks, who became the Grateful Dead.

Jerry had a leg up on me at that point as a lead guitar player. I think I was 15 or 16 and he was in his 20s. He had been playing a fair bit longer than I had, but it looked like a rhythm guitarist was going to be a good idea to have in the band, and so he played lead and I played rhythm. There wasn't much to go on back then. Rhythm guitar was pretty elementary, at least in rock 'n' roll. There was either the Chuck Berry rhythm or the R&B kind of stuff, and that was about it that I can remember. Once you learned that stuff, that was about all there was out there. I had that down in a couple of days, so I was sort of on my own from that point on. I listened to a lot of piano players. McCoy Tyner was a big influence on me.

As far as other guitarists who influenced me, most of the great guitarists were lead guitarists, but in the Grateful Dead I've always had the role as a rhythm guitarist or a structural guitarist. My biggest influences have probably been piano players or horn sections or string sections. That's the kind of stuff that I listen to and I try to evoke that kind of stuff from the guitar. Probably, you can hear the piano influence most readily.

When I was growing up in the Bay area, we were blessed with really diverse music on the radio. We had country stations, a couple of rock 'n' roll stations, a couple of R&B and soul stations, a jazz station, and a couple of classical stations. There was plenty of music to grow on, and grow from, when we were coming up and we listened to all of it. We had all the stations programmed into our car radios, and we'd just play the buttons on the radio. I guess after a few years of that — of listening to a country song after a jazz tune, after listening to some classical music, the way that all fit together in our heads — we came up with our own little view of what music amounted to, particularly American music.

Sometimes we build songs in the studio and sometimes we've been playing them live for years. It happens in any and every conceivable way. Usually, I just pick up the guitar and start hammering away and see if that opens up a crack in the sky for something to fall through. Really, my best writing has been done through any and all conceivable combinations of events: the music first, the lyrics first, at the same time, all by myself, with people.

What I prefer to do with Ratdog — and we were actually starting to do with the Grateful Dead before Jerry checked out — is to gather everyone together in the same room at the same time, hopefully, with a lyricist as well — myself or anyone in the band who has something to say — and we just start kicking ideas around. We use a sort of one-two-three-go approach, and we'll find a key that we'll settle into and a rhythm that we'll settle into and start kicking that around. Then we'll see if we can start lining up some contour, taking it in a few directions. That way, everyone is involved in the writing, so everyone has an emotional investment in it and an artistic investment in it. I like that approach.

With the improvisation that we did as a band [Grateful Dead], it was a matter of playing until a few gems fall out. That's pretty much how it happens; you practice with your instrument but your instrument is your band and your PA and everything. We got a lot of playing time in playing together through big PAs and stuff like that and so we developed an ability to improvise pretty freely, and, from night to night, we did hit some pretty high notes.

I'm not looking to create a very tightly-structured band sound and go out and perform a note for note set, night after night. That would drive me nuts. I don't think I'd make it through a short tour with that. The way I prefer to play is just loose and everybody adding and camping on what everybody else is doing and then somebody comes and camps on you — the rock 'n' roll Dixieland approach. It keeps things interesting and fun.

But I don't think of myself specifically as a songwriter or a musician. I think of myself as '*music*'. When they say occupation on a form that you're filling out, I always write, 'music'. I write it, I sing it, I perform it, I arrange it, I produce it... whatever it takes. I've just gotta have it, so I'll do anything.

I love simplicity. I view myself as a structural guitarist more than a rhythm guitarist. I like to build the house the song lives in. You need strong, clean lines to hold that kind of stuff up. My old pal Joe Campbell referred to me as a conjurer, and I guess it kind of stuck. My role within the group was that of a conjurer trying to make stories or musical themes palpable and real vivid to our audience.

We have Chuck Berry's old piano player Johnny Johnson in our group [Ratdog], and, in some ways in those early days, he was almost as important to the music as Chuck was. If you listen to all those old records, Chuck Berry was one hell of a guitar player. In his heyday, he was just amazing. He really expanded the bounds of electric guitar. He played one of these [ES335], I think, but at the same time he learned a lot from playing with Johnny Johnson, who was as busy creating rock 'n' roll piano as Chuck was creating rock 'n' roll guitar, taking it from the blues and R&B, and pushing it more to a late 20th-century kind of place to be.

:| |•|•|

This is a Gibson 335, made in 1959, which has two patent-applied-for humbucking pickups. It's kind of a collector's item, I guess. I got it used back in the early '70s for 300 bucks or so. They're worth a lot more than that now. This was a good little buddy to me for a long time, so I keep it around. I love to play this guitar and always have. There was a while where I got tired of the sound of the pickups, but you don't take these pickups out and put some other kind of pickups in this guitar, so I just left them in and just never plugged it in; I just played the guitar for fun. Now I'm starting to like the sound of the pickups again.

I played an SG for a while and I played this guitar [ES335] for three or four years, I think, back in the '70s. After a while, I sort of burned out on the sound of double coil pickups and went to single coil pickups for a while and now these are starting to become more attractive to me again. I guess you just go through phases.

Sometimes, you'll get to a point where you hit a wall with your guitar playing and what you have to do then is bang your way through it or take a week or so off and then bang your way through it. Sometimes, you're just getting tired. People get tired no matter what you're trying to do. You have a lot of energy sometimes and you have your peaks and valleys and so sometimes you take a little time off and then come back at it and you may hear things in a different way. Otherwise, you can take a flying run at it and see if that works.

It's not only important to play with other good players on your own instrument but it's important, to my way of thinking, to play with different instruments and get their way of hearing things and seeing things in your head. You hear things differently when you play with different instruments.

I never related to another musical instrument like I relate to the guitar. A guitar holds a lot of mysteries for me. Quite often, when I'm playing, the guitar will suggest something to me, a direction to go. I'll just hear something in a mistake I made or I'll just hear something when I'm playing a new way, and that doesn't happen to me if I'm trying to play another instrument. I don't have that much facility on another instrument, so it's not surprising. I have a fair amount of facility as a singer, but I get the most surprises from the guitar. I guess I have a sort of a mystical connection with the instrument.

Hank Williams Jr.

Randall Hank Williams Jr.
Born May 26, 1949
Shreveport, Louisiana

:|Hank Williams Jr.|·|·|

*H*ank Williams Jr. first drew breath a couple of weeks before his father, country music legend and pioneer, Hank Sr., made his triumphant debut at the Grand Ole Opry in Nashville on June 11, 1949. A little more than four years later, Hank Sr. died of heart failure in the back of a Cadillac on the way to a New Year's Day gig in Canton, Ohio. He was only 29 years old and the most successful country artist of his day.

For the young Williams, whom his father had nicknamed Bocephus, reportedly inspired by the name given to Grand Ole Opry ventriloquist Ron Brasfield's dummy, these were big shoes to fill. Hank Jr.'s mother, Audrey Sheppard Williams, herself a country singer of some note, was instrumental in guiding his early career, which saw him master a wide range of instruments, including the guitar, banjo, fiddle, piano, drums, and harmonica, and debut on the Grand Ole Opry when he was only 11. By the age of 14, he had his first hit record and soon after signed a blockbuster record deal with MGM Records.

Initially, he was nothing more than a clone of his father, but it wasn't long before Hank Jr. found his own voice, influenced in equal parts by his country music roots and the more rebellious sounds of Southern Rock as popularized by groups like The Allman Brothers, The Marshall Tucker Band, and Lynyrd Skynyrd. Following a few major crises in his life in the mid-'70s, including an attempted suicide and a near fatal fall while mountain climbing, he emerged in 1975 a new man. His major career breakthrough came in 1979 with the release of the albums FAMILY TRADITION and WHISKEY BENT & HELL BOUND, which would see him rack up some impressive album sales through the '80s. His dynamic live shows led to a string of Entertainer of the Year awards from both the Academy of Country Music (ACM) and the Country Music Association (CMA) during this period.

In the late '80s, he used some new recording technology to allow him to sing a duet with his late father on the old track, *There's A*

278| •| •| Hank Williams Jr. |:

Tear In My Beer, as well as on the accompanying video. He won a Grammy for the duet in 1990. His profile was raised enormously, beginning that same year, as Williams composed and performed the theme for the highly-rated ABC *Monday Night Football* program, for which he won four consecutive Emmy Awards beginning in 1990.

We spoke to Hank Williams Jr. at his Hank Williams Jr. Enterprises office in Paris, Tennessee, about 100 miles west of Nashville, where he pulled out a couple of his favorite Gibsons — his signature SJ-45 Southerner Jumbo and a Les Paul — to noodle on during our conversation.

*D*addy had a Gibson guitar that I always liked, which is in the Alabama Archives now. Later on, when I wanted Gibson to make a Southerner Jumbo model, they said they didn't make them anymore. I said, 'Gosh, I'd love to have one like Daddy's, with the parallel pearl inlays in the fretboard and the sunburst finish, which I always liked — not too loud. This model has been a long time in the making, but they make them now and they do have the original plastic keys, exactly like Daddy's. We have a picture of Daddy on one of the old Hadacol tours [promoting a medicinal compound] back then, and it is this guitar exactly. I think that picture was in '51. The only change we've made to this guitar is in the keys for the rough treatment of the road where they don't stay tuned. This one doesn't sit in the corner; it's used on stage. It's been a long process, because they had to find an original to start with. I really like it. When I write songs, it means a lot to me which guitar I use.

They have to be deep and resonant for me. That bass has to go 'Baaaaaa…' — on and on and on. I want it to have a lot of deep resonance and a lot of sustain, though that's usually a word that you use with electric guitars. I want my acoustic guitars to sustain, even though I don't have a signal to chime or do it with. I want the bass note to sustain. I drive my sound crew crazy with boomy guitars like this because they will feed back a little bit. The bottom end is what I like about it. [Demonstrates] It sustains and that's good. We both have a lot of bottom end and I like that. [Laughs] No tinkley guitars for me.

I don't remember the first time I picked up a guitar, but there's a picture of me and Daddy where he's sitting there with his wonderful suit on and I have a ukulele. Actually, we are now in the process of trying to find the little three-quarter Gibson that they ordered through Hank Snow's Music Shop and had made for me. That was my first one. The one that I have on loan to the Country Music Hall of Fame in Nashville is one of Daddy's real early Gibson acoustics. I forgot about that one. That was important, too. Those are the ones in my memory. The one that was made for me and the one that we donated to the Hall of Fame, they're the ones that stick out in my mind. That was the only one of his that I had. The rest of them are behind glass. The one I wanted was behind the glass in the Alabama Archives, but now I've got it here.

When I write songs, I might get the words in my mind, but I've got to have the guitar. I think I did, believe it or not, *All My Rowdy Friends* on a piano, but that's probably the only one ever. It's much easier on the guitar because you've got the notes in your mind — you want it to sound like this. You might have the words, but you need the guitar. There again, I want that big bottom. If I want to get Delta blues, I just tune down to open G. [Demonstrates] With *Whiskey Bent And Hell Bound*, I remember, I opened it in G and I wrote it in 10 minutes. I had just tuned to the old open G and more or less the tuning made me write the song.

Some of the Allman Brothers had asked me, 'How do you go about writing that stuff?' And I said, 'What's the difference between a rock song or a country song? It's got to be about a good woman at home, who thinks I've done no wrong, and you've got to have some love affair in there or something about drinking, and that's how I wrote *Whiskey Bent And Hell Bound*.' Good old Gregg [Allman] and Dickey [Betts] had just showed me a lick on *Come And Go Blues*. They inspired me. I said, 'God, these guys are heavy. I've got to come up with something myself.' And that's how I wrote that. [Laughs]

Open tunings are beautiful because you don't have to fret the guitar very much. A guy named Bo Diddley made a pretty good career out of just tuning it in G and he held 'em all down at once. [Laughs] He did alright.

My number one blues influence is Lightnin' Hopkins. [Plays a few bars in Hopkins' style] That's all I played, Lightnin' Hopkins and Jimmy Reed. People say, 'Man how did you get into Ray Charles and all this blues stuff?' And I said, 'That's what I like.' I went through a bluegrass period when I wanted to play every fiddle and every five-string banjo. I camped out at Earl Scruggs's house. I was a guy that played all the instruments and I just liked the open tuning. A lot of pickers are this way. When they sit down in a room they say, 'Hey, let's do a John Lee Hooker song!' It doesn't matter if it's The Rolling

Stones, Keith Richards, or Billy Gibbons, we all come back to that same spot, 'Hey, let's play some blues!' And the other side to that is, 'Hey, let's do a Hank Williams song!' We don't show off with all the trills we can do, we just… [Plays and sings a few bars of a blues song] When pickers get into it, you can tell, that's what they're going to do. Eddie Van Halen, the first time we met, he steps on the bus and walked over to Merle Kilgore [Hank Jr.'s manager] and said, 'How do you do *Ring Of Fire*?' [Laughs] So you never know who someone's heroes are.

I don't play guitar everyday. Heavens no! Are you kidding, as much as I've played in my life? I try to play with a 44 or a 45 or a Land Cruiser or a Four-Wheeler or a shotgun, but not a guitar. These fingers got toughened up… I'll never forget soaking them in lemon juice when I was eight years old. That was the smart thing to do back then in 1957. 'Stick 'em in lemon juice!' they said. And I had my little three-quarter Gibson and I was going, 'Oh god, it hurts so much!' I was holding those strings down. So, no, I don't play every-day. I wouldn't want to make a guess on how many shows I've played. But, when things are done and I'm writing a lot of songs, it would probably come down to every other day, through the year of playing, if you include all of the shows and the rehearsals, the recording and interviews, like we're doing now.

I got to where I thought I was a pretty hot guitar player back in the '70s with good teachers like Gregg Allman and Dickey Betts, some of the guys from Lynyrd Skynyrd, and, of course, Toy [Caldwell] from the Marshall Tucker Band. Some of that's got to rub off on you, but I was in a great position. Here I am at a house where Fats Domino and Jerry Lee Lewis and everybody were showing up and you're a little, bitty boy. There were also people like Chet Atkins and Earl Scruggs. I decided I had to play five-string banjo. That took me a while; that's pretty hard. I had all these wonderful people to look up to, and they knew I was serious about it. There was Doc Watson. Man, I bought every Doc Watson record there was. We're all cut from the same cloth as far as what we like to listen to. I'd go through a fiddle craze and then a rock 'n' roll piano craze, five-string bluegrass and then back to the blues things again. And you end up right back here [Taps on the Gibson Southerner Jumbo he's hold-ing]. One of those fiddles can make you sound really bad if you screw up on it.

Duane Allman was incredible. He never had to work at it. He's like certain great football players. He never had to practice; he was absolutely born with it. He was fantastic and clean and very soulful… and Dickey Betts, too. Those two together, as far as I'm concerned, boy, they were something. They had a different sound from Ed King [Lynyrd Skynyrd], actually. There were two different kinds of Southern Rock, I think. It's sort of like that deal, 'If you don't like Hank Williams, you can kiss my rear!' I'd kind of go the same with a Duane Allman, the same deal. If you don't like that, there's something wrong here. We're not talking about the same thing then. He was fantastic. He probably had the most natural God-given talent. This [Holds up guitar] was nothing to him; it was simple. To a lot of the rest of us, we might have to say, 'Now wait a minute, we've gotta work on this a little bit.' Those are the best ones, the ones that are just effortless; those are the best players.

The whole Southern Rock thing just happened in the late '60s — 'Rebel Metal'. The bands would go to Frisco and New York and Central Park and people said, 'Hey this is pretty cool!' and it was. 'Jaimoe' [Jai Johanny Johanson of the Allman Brothers] on the drums back there is something different. It was great. And every single hillbilly, they were into it too, if they're in my age group. It was a very big thing that happened in the South, but also happened everywhere else. They sold out in New York and they sold out in Frisco. Later on, for me to be touring with those same people in the mid-'90s was pretty neat, too. Those bands and that music has a lot of longevity to it.

:| |•|•|

I have a white Les Paul with 'f' holes and you can get pretty warm on it. [Plays a few licks on the Les Paul] They play themselves, I swear. Speaking of effortless, I remember the first time I started working with this particular one and with a certain SG and, God, they're just so easy. When you've been on what I call the big boards all your life and your fingers are like bricks… these are really a lot easier to play than bluegrass and stuff like that. They almost play themselves and there's lots of tricks and sustain and all. It's a whole other world. And I'm rough on 'em on stage. I beat them up and throw them around, but [Raps on the guitar] they hold up good. I like that. [Laughs]

This 'f'-hole is pretty rare. I don't think there are a lot of 'f'-hole Les Pauls. I don't customize a lot. We changed the keys on this and that's pretty good. So, all we changed on the Gibson acoustic were the keys, as well as on this one, just because of the rough treatment it takes when I'm on stage jumpin' around. This one [Les Paul] has been around for a while, but it looks good, sounds good, plays great and you can raise the roof with it if you want to. We get hog wild sometimes with these things.

I first started playing electrics back in a combo called Rockin' Randall and the Rockets back in '60 or '61. Hell, I played a lot back then. That was all I did back then — lots of Jimmy Reed licks like everybody else. I even recommend to kids… I say, 'Okay, start them on an acoustic but electric's a lot easier. Just get them a little electric and a little amp. It really is easier. They'll pick it up quicker and they'll get better faster.'

To me, the main difference between a Gibson Les Paul and a Gibson SG is that the SG has a much faster neck and a little more sound up on the top. I think it's because of the way it's cut away. The strings are closer together, maybe that's why, but to me it's faster. The sustain king is the Les Paul, and has been for quite a while. When you've got a big outdoor thing to play and you're trying to do something, you look over to the guys and say, 'Give me the heavy artillery!' Well, here's the big medicine. [Holds up the Les Paul] The little medicine is the SG; the big medicine is the Les Paul.

I've played some slide guitar, but we've got two hot guitar players in the band anyway, and we have a steel guitar player, who's really good, so we have three, and I'm standing up there, too. I've fooled with slide. It's fun. Now, I like to play dobro style, that's how I really like to play in a dobro tuning — G. Dickey [Betts] spent a lot of time with me, but it just kind of wore off, and I said, 'Okay. It's great, but we've got four guys up there playing guitar. People are hearing lots of guitar going on. We have a slide mania on one song, but how many slides can you take at once?'

Steve Winwood

SPENCER DAVIS GROUP, TRAFFIC, BLIND FAITH, STOMU YAMASHTA'S GO

Steve Winwood
Born May 12, 1948
Birmingham, England

: Steve Winwood ·|·|

There hasn't been a decade since his recording debut with the
Spencer Davis Group in the mid-'60s that Steve Winwood hasn't had
an impact as a recording artist. It was a youthful Winwood who
joined his brother Muff as a member of the Muff Woody Jazz Band in
the early '60s. Shortly after, playing at a local club in Birmingham,
they were both recruited by Spencer Davis for a musical project
that bore his name. Winwood took a brief hiatus during this period
to work with the group Powerhouse, which also featured Eric
Clapton and Jack Bruce, before returning to The Spencer Davis
Group, which had a number of international hits in 1966 and 1967
with *Gimme Some Lovin'* and *I'm A Man*, among others.

Seeking to expand his musical horizons, Winwood took his leave
from Spencer Davis and formed the group Traffic with Dave Mason,
Jim Capaldi, and Chris Wood, which had almost immediate success
in the wake of their debut album MR. FANTASY. The group would stay
together until 1974, though Winwood would spend time during this
period in short-lived 'super-groups' — Blind Faith, with Eric
Clapton, Ginger Baker and Rick Grech; and Ginger Baker's Air Force.
By the early '70s, Winwood was at work on a solo album which
would ultimately evolve to Traffic's fifth and most successful album,
JOHN BARLEYCORN MUST DIE.

In 1976, creatively restless once more, he joined keyboardist
Stomu Yamashta and drummer Michael Shrieve in the group Go,
which recorded a couple of albums before calling it a day as
Winwood embarked on a solo career in 1977. After a disappointing
self-titled debut sales-wise, Winwood regrouped in 1981 to record
ARC OF THE DIVER, an album on which he collaborated with lyricist
Will Jennings but produced and performed on all the tracks himself,
including the subsequent chart-topper, *While You See A Chance*.

1986 was a banner year for Winwood as his third solo album,
BACK IN THE HIGH LIFE, on which he worked with musicians like Joe

Walsh and James Taylor, produced four hit singles and a Grammy for Record of the Year. The follow-up, ROLL WITH IT, became Winwood's first Number 1 album in the United States.

A rekindled interest in Traffic resulted in Winwood and Jim Capaldi reuniting to record a new Traffic album, FAR FROM HOME, and to launch an associated tour, which included an appearance by the group at Woodstock II. Following a brief hiatus, 1997 saw the release of Winwood's latest solo project, JUNCTION SEVEN.

Initially intending to meet Steve Winwood at the Randolph Hotel in Oxford, England, we ultimately received an invitation to his estate in the English countryside a short drive from town — he also has a home in Nashville — where he was doing some recording. We spoke to Winwood, Gibson Firebird in hand, on a chilly September evening that was threatening rain.

There were always musical instruments in the house when I was growing up. There wasn't a guitar, but there were all kinds of banjos, mandolins, and a piano. I started picking tunes out on the piano. I have a brother who's five years older than me and he got a guitar. Like any younger brother, I wanted a guitar as well.

In 1956 or '57, when I was about eight, I got hold of my first guitar. I've no idea what it was. It could have been some kind of European or German or Austrian model. They kind of copied some of the Gibson models. There were companies like Hofner and Framus. Of course, there were a lot of American guitars, but I don't think a lot of them came to Europe in those days, so it was all acoustics. They had metal strings, though, with a round hole.

Rock 'n' roll was everywhere, but even for an eight or ten year old, because I had an older brother, that tends to influence your ideas. It brings you on a bit with your musical ideas, which it did for me. But there were guitars everywhere. There was Elvis and Carl Perkins and blues came later. There was a thing called 'skiffle' here in England, where a lot of musicians took bluegrass and rockabilly music and gave it its own sound.

Playing guitar was more appealing to me than playing piano because you stood at the front of the band and you kind of gyrated around. When you played piano in those days, it was always some kind of out of tune piano and you were at the mercy of the house really and the damp proofing or whatever it was that had been spilt down on the pianos. So there was no question about it for me. At that time, I was pouring my energies into being a guitar player rather than a keyboard player. It wasn't until the Hammond organ came along that it liberated a lot of keyboard players who had been piano players up till then. That was the case with me.

I started off playing much more guitar in the Spencer Davis Group, then towards the end of the life of the band when we got a Hammond organ, we began to be more keyboard/organ-based on songs like *Gimme Some Lovin'* and *I'm A Man*. But the Spencer Davis Group marked our discovery of blues at the time. Blues was a big influence on a lot of music in England at that time. A lot of bands and a lot of musicians came out of that era.

With Traffic, I did play a lot of guitar on songs like *Dear Mr Fantasy* and *Pearly Queen*, though I played keyboards as well. In Traffic, we used to switch around and play different instruments, but I played the majority of guitar in that band. I played the guitar on *Forty Thousand Headmen* as well. Later, the band went into a more jazzy phase in the early '70s with THE LOW SPARK OF HIGH-HEELED BOYS, which was more keyboard oriented.

When I played in Blind Faith with Eric Clapton, it was important to play a supporting role with keyboards, but we did a lot of things with two guitars like *Can't Find My Way Home*, where we played two guitars.

:| |•|•|

I went on to do various other projects in the '70s, but it was during the early days of Traffic that I first went to the Gibson factory in Kalamazoo, Michigan and picked out a guitar. It was a Firebird, but they made several versions of the Firebird. The Firebird looked a bit odd the way they first made it. It looked like it was back to front or should be played left-handed, but then they made it the right way round. It was a 'right-way-around' one with two pickups that I got from the factory. That would have been about 1969.

It was a very precious guitar to me, and as often happens when something is very precious, it got lost or it got stolen, never to be seen again, from inside a truck in the East Village, parked outside what was known then as The Academy of Music. I've tried many times since to get one, but I think there were so few of them made, that I don't think there are any. I've made several inquiries to fairly serious collectors and tried to circulate word on the grapevine if there is one, but they are very hard to find. Mine was kind of green-colored. I have a picture of me playing the Firebird at Steve Paul's

Scene club in New York, which was a famous club at the time. People like Dr. John, Jimi Hendrix, and Buddy Guy used to play down there. Traffic played there as a trio. It was small, but a great place to go and see music and to play. I don't have too many photographs of that Firebird and that shot turned up. If anybody who is reading this has the Firebird, perhaps we can talk.

The Firebird had a rawness, and in the days when amplifiers didn't have built-in overdrives or built -in sounds, you had to try and draw the sound out of the amplifiers as much as you could. Some guitars did that much better than others. Now, I know nothing about electronics, but it looks to me that the Firebird is a very simple guitar. The pickup looks very simple. I'm sure there's a lot of complicated stuff going on under there, but it looks like a simple instrument and it seems to have a rawness to it that I like very much. I think it may have been very similar to the Flying V that I played on a couple of occasions. This particular Firebird was around the same era as the Flying V and it seemed very similar. It was a different shape, but that also had a rawness about it. Maybe it's the body being solid like that. The Les Paul was also a great guitar, but somehow it seemed a little more sophisticated, a little more of a precision instrument, whereas the Firebird had some basic elements to it that I really liked. John Entwistle, who lives just up the road from here, is one of the major guitar collectors in the world. He's got a big attic with the most amazing selection of guitars. I've gone through his guitars with him to see if I could find a similar guitar but with no luck.

Every guitar is different. Each one has its own character. It's made of natural materials largely. Each neck is different and then, consequently, each one will sound slightly different and certainly feels very different. You can go to a guitar-maker, as I have, and say, 'This is the guitar I love. Can I have one exactly like it?' They all say, 'Yes,' but of course, it never is. Each one is a one-off and I think that's the nature of the guitar. Perhaps, in the days of computer measurement and so on, it's a little easier these days to match them, but in the present time, each one is very slightly different.

When I write, I use both guitar and keyboards; I can't say it's either one or the other. Writing is a thing that can happen in so many different ways, in fact, my friend Leonardo and I have just finished writing some songs and I don't think I played any keyboard at all. I played guitar most of the time. It's hard for me to narrow down what happens with writing. It can be anything; whatever the situation calls for. Sometimes, it maybe just because the guitar is leaning up against the wall and you happen to pick it up or because you're nearer to the keyboard or the drum kit or the bass. It may also be a sound you are looking for. Some songs obviously lend themselves to guitar — acoustic guitar particularly.

There are a lot of good guitar players around but, having said that, it's not for me to do any rating really at all. I just try and play guitar the best I can. Perhaps the fact I play other instruments as well, people think of me perhaps as a guitar player or a singer or a keyboard player or something else. In fact, I played a lot of guitar on the Traffic tour a few years ago and a lot of people came up to me and said that they didn't even know I played guitar.

Ron Wood

JEFF BECK GROUP, THE SMALL FACES, THE FACES, THE ROLLING STONES

Ron Wood
Born June 1, 1947
West Drayton, London, England

:|Ron Wood|·|·|

For every star in the rock 'n' roll firmament, there's always that story of humble beginnings and amateur jitters. Ron Wood of The Rolling Stones is no different in that regard, and he'll tell you about his early music experience with his school's madrigal choir and his first big break in the music business at the age of nine, when he played the washboard in his brother's band at the local movie theater between two Tommy Steele films. "I almost peed in my pants," is his recollection of the momentous occasion.

Though he dabbled with other instruments in those early days, the guitar became his passion as he joined his first band, The Birds, which actually had a promising start under the management of British impresario Robert Stigwood. Stints with groups like Santa Barbara Machine Head and The Creation, as well as an offer to join The New Yardbirds — later to become Led Zeppelin — followed, before he formed The Jeff Beck Group with ex-Yardbird's guitarist, Jeff Beck, featuring vocalist Rod Stewart. That's Wood playing bass on the group's THE TRUTH and BECK-OLA albums. In 1969, Wood replaced Steve Marriott in The Small Faces, who subsequently shortened their name to The Faces with the addition of Rod Stewart as vocalist. The group became one of the biggest draws of the early '70s before breaking up in 1975.

Wood became a Rolling Stone in 1975 following Mick Taylor's departure the previous year, though he would later find out that the opportunity had been open to him back in the late '60s. 'The strange thing that few people know is that I could've — and would've — joined The Stones a lot earlier than I did,' Wood explains in his book *The Works*, on which he collaborated with Bill German and which is illustrated with his own paintings and drawings. (Wood is a classically-trained artist specializing in silk-screen portraits.) 'It was in '69, about the time Brian Jones died. Ian Stewart phoned up the studio where The Small Faces were rehearsing and got Ronnie Lane on the line. 'Now that Brian's gone,' Stu told him, 'do you think Woody would be happy with the job?' If I had answered the phone — I was in the other fuckin' room! — I would've said, 'Is sixty seconds too late to show up?' But Ronnie Lane, fully aware of the fact, answered, 'No thanks, I think he's quite happy where he is.' It wasn't until five or so years later that I found out this story, and by then, I was a fuckin' Rolling Stone!' Wood's first public appearance with 'The World's Greatest Rock 'N' Roll Band' was playing *Brown Sugar* with the group on the back of a flatbed truck, cruising down 5th Avenue in New York as publicity for the Stones' 1975 tour.

Don Was, who handled the lion's share of the production on The Stones' 1997 BRIDGES TO BABYLON CD, characterizes Wood as "a really versatile and creative musician," in talking to the Net's www.rockn-world.com. Was continued: "He brings so much color to the record just in terms of picking up the mood of a song and then finding a texture from the various instruments that he's proficient on. He played some beautiful dobro stuff and this kind of moody, David Lynch-like guitar line on the chorus to *Already Over Me*."

Wood has released a number of solo albums, including NOW LOOK (1975), GIMME SOME NECK (1979), and SLID ON LIVE: PLUGGED IN AND STANDING (1993).

In 1997, Wood, who's an avid collector of vintage guitars, took delivery from Gibson of the prototypes of his signature Firebird VII; a J-200, based on his 1957 J-200; and a special gold-plated Model 90 Dobro.

We spoke to Ron Wood one evening in the garden of his home in Richmond, the London suburb where the first incarnation of The Rolling Stones played some of their earliest club gigs in early 1962 and where Wood first saw the group live at the Richmond Jazz Festival two years later.

*W*hen I was a little boy about seven, I was given, or so I thought, this guitar by this guy, who I saw only a few weeks ago at one of my son's gigs. Jesse, my boy, has got a band called Wood Spirit, and I went to see them and this guy was there, who, when I was in short pants, was friends with my brothers and my mom and dad. He gave me my first guitar. It was an acoustic guitar; a cheap, old thing, but I learned my first chords on it. Then he got called up to the army and he had to take the guitar away, so I was very sad for a few years until my brothers saved up and bought me my own guitar. That was also a cheap, old acoustic, but at least it was something to keep my E and my A and my B7 chords all going. And then I saved up and bought myself a Rogers guitar. It was a semi-acoustic and cost £ 25. That's what I played my first gigs with.

I used to have an old Dance-ette 45 and LP record player in my bedroom, and Carlo Little, a friend of my brothers, Art and Ted, was a drummer with Screaming Lord Such, who used a leopard skin drum set. He also had import records from America on the old Chess and R&B labels — the red and yellow label. I used to get Chuck Berry singles. He got me one on a blue label, too — *Blue Feeling* by Chuck. I really liked that. That was my first introduction to that kind of chord shape. Carlo used to get me imports and so did the guy who used to head Carlin Music at the time, Franklin Boyd. He used to be up in Saville Row. I got some amazing Motown stuff from him.

What I used to do at night was listen to guys like Jimmy Smith with Kenny Burrell and Jimmy McGriff with Grant Green — all the organ players along with their guitar players — and Wes Montgomery. Big Bill Broonzy was my first 'proper' man I wanted to play like, and I'm still trying to this day to sound like him. [Laughs]

When I was growing up, everybody was playing like The Shadows, and they didn't understand it when I didn't really want to do that, so I got put on the back burner. 'He's not cool! He isn't into synchronized guitar playing!' I used to laugh when I was little and ask why are those guys all dressed the same and all moving so silly? But that went hand in hand with local success. All the bands in my neighborhood, when I was growing up, all wore suits. For a start, they could afford a suit — a big plus — and they could afford these guitars and proper amps. In my first band, we had one amp — a

Bird amp — with the vocals, the bass, and two guitars going through it. The only thing that wasn't going through the amp was the drums. Funny enough, you used to be able to get the clarity, but no wonder not many people came to our gigs. [Laughs]

I think that a breakthrough happens when you least expect it. I thought I'd gone as far as I could go on guitar, then when Jeff Beck left the Yardbirds, we got together. He asked if I would consider playing bass. I said, 'Yeah, that would be fantastic! It would give me another angle on things.' So I played bass for a few years and really enjoyed it. And then, when I did go back to the guitar, I came back playing the slide with the Duane Allman influence.

I never met some of the earlier influences I mentioned, but I did meet Ry Cooder, who played on some of the Stones' sessions like *Love In Vain*. I recently saw some footage of Big Bill Broonzy. It's incredible to actually see his hands after trying to learn from records. When you see his hands and how simple those chords were... But to string them together like he did was absolutely wonderful. And then there's the other dizzy-heights kind of player like our gypsy friend Django Reinhardt and I also love Jimmy Reed.

When the Stones did the CD-ROM — I've got one, but I still can't work it — we went through all of this archive stuff. It's amazing. I've got this footage of Big Bill, Howlin' Wolf, Muddy Waters, and all kinds of players, that I hadn't seen in certain circumstances, that were just incredible. Did you ever see that original Newport Blues Festival when Muddy played? I think it was the mid-'60s. It's incredible, the stuff he was playing.

When I first saw the Stones in one of their first publicity shots, they were all by the River Thames with all their hair blowing everywhere and all dressed different. It seemed like a statement, and I thought, 'Yeah, I like this band! I'm going to be in that band one day!'

I used to hang out at Steve Marriott's house. He had a flat in Chiswick, and I used to wait there for them to get home from the *Top of the Pops* (a popular British TV music show). Steve would come in like, 'Wheee!' — Jack the Lad. They were all this high [Indicates with his hand their lack of height] and they were like the workers from Willie Wonka's Chocolate Factory coming home; these four little guys buzzing — Ronnie, Kenny, Mac, and Stevie. Steve would come in and we'd immediately put on Booker T and the MGs and all the soul stuff. We used to just dig all of the American stuff. They were only together a couple of weeks, but they were suddenly number one so they had money and contacts and records and I'd just hang there. One of my crowning glories was when I did a Bob Dylan tribute at Madison Square Gardens a few years ago. I did

Bob's song, *Seven Days*, and I had Steve Cropper, Booker T. Jones, and Duck Dunn — we don't have Al Jackson, unfortunately, anymore, our favorite drummer apart from Charlie [Watts]. It was just marvelous for me to have Booker T. and the MGs. It was like a dream realized. That saying, 'Less is more,' as far as sound is concerned, almost originated with them. I've always thought that approach is much better than fiddly-diddly.

When I joined the Stones, we first did IT'S ONLY ROCK 'N' ROLL just up the hill here in Richmond when I had The Wick, which Pete Townshend has just bought, by the way. Back in '74, we did IT'S ONLY ROCK 'N' ROLL there and I joined in '75. I'm just working with the guys again that I worked with then — Willie Weeks, who used to play with Donnie Hathaway and Aretha [Franklin] on bass, and drummer Andy Newmark, who used to be with Sly and the Family Stone. We got back together to the day; I think July 7, 1974 was the last time we played, and on July 7, 1996, we got back together again, and it was like no time had passed by. And Bob Dylan just came over and we've been doing some stuff as well.

It's wonderful the way things developed and matured between Keith [Richards] and I. It's an unwritten thing. We call it an ancient form of weaving. We listen back to playbacks and I go, 'Oh yeah, I like what I did there!' and he says, 'It wasn't you, it was me.' And I go, 'It was fuckin' me!' And we'd fight a little, but, nine times out of ten, we don't really know who's doing what. It just magically fits into place

:| |•|•|

I always liked the Fender Stratocaster, but anytime I had an acoustic, it was always a Gibson — the J200. I have some marvelous examples of 'Gibos' in Ireland where I keep most of my collection when the Stones aren't touring. I don't store them at SIR in New York. When I finally get them all back home, I've got this great old 'Cowboy' Gibson. I call it the 'Cowboy' one because it's like the one that Elvis played on in that film where he did, 'I just want to be your Teddy Bear.' He had a single scratch plate, where mine's got a double, but it's exactly the same coloring, the same wood, everything. That's a real special guitar of mine. I had a Gibson from the 1920s or '30s. That was when you used to send away for the guitar in the Sears-Roebuck catalog. It was the L100 model and it was $29.95. About 15 years ago, I bought one for 15 grand. They used to send them out from Sear-Roebucks mail order, but they used to send these fragile, wooden, acoustic guitars off in a cardboard box, so, if you got one sent to L.A. or New York, it would arrive as a bunch of wood chips. I suppose that's why they're so rare. [Laughs] It also had the name 'Gibson' stenciled on the top.

In England, in the early days, these guitars from the States were gold dust. We used to have to settle for a Burns Black Bison. That was top of the line. They had these huge horns on it. That was like state of the art then. The Futurama was fantastic. It had these push-button things and it was like your affordable Fender or state of the art guitar. You could pick them up quite cheap. They had a good sound and a tremolo arm.

I don't personally tinker with my guitars too much. I have my trusty guitar techs. There's 'Chuch' Magee, who has been with me for God knows how long — perhaps, 25 years. There's Alan Rogan. He's very good. He has whole storerooms with stashes of amps and guitars and all kinds of effects. There's also Pierre DeBeauport. Pierre is a wonderful technician. I could say, 'I don't like this fret here and the electrics have gone,' and he'll have it done in a New York minute.

As far as favorite guitars go, I do have my 1955 Stratocaster, which has been with me for many years, and, I suppose, he's my main man. Then again, I've got my Emmons pedal steel, which I love. It's a single deck. I have a Sho-Bud, too, which is wooden with two decks, but I like my Emmons. I have an incredible collection of Gibsons and Epiphones, either acoustic or semi-acoustic. I do love Dobros and National Steels. On the bass side, I still have my original Fender Jazz, which is still performing perfectly. I also have a wonderful Gretsch White Falcon, in mint condition, and I have a lovely Les Paul, a black one, that Slash gave me for my birthday last year. He'd lent it to me for the VOODOO LOUNGE tour and he realized he wasn't getting it back. He said, 'I've got a great present for you!' And I said, 'Is it what I think it is?' and he said, 'Yeah. It's your Gibson Les Paul.' Unlike Mick Taylor and Jeff Beck and people like that, I've never really been a Les Paul man but this one sounds very comfortable.

And I met the man himself once — Les Paul. It was a marvelous experience. I was in a studio in New York with him — he's a lovely old man — and he's sitting there and he's says, 'What do you think of this studio, Ronnie?' I tell him it's marvelous what they can do today in the recording studio. We were in the control room looking at the console and he said, 'I invented that. I invented this. See that console? That's one of my original modules that I invented.' All the outboard stuff; its amazing. I didn't know this. He invented 80 to 90 percent of everything that's used in the studio today.

My guitars are indispensable to me. I would hate to be without my precious ones. There's a precious one to me in every range, whether it be a pedal steel, a lap steel, a hollow neck Weissenborn — now that's a weird guitar; they're great, very rare too — my acoustics, my basses. In a way, I'm very hardened to not relying on them as the only ones because, through the years, I've always had my favorite guitars stolen. Tony Zemaitis, who made lots of my favorite guitars — he's an exceptional craftsman, this man. He makes everything himself, except for the carving on the silver plating and stuff. Tony made some really fantastic, number one guitars for me, but they kept getting stolen. Each time, he'd make me another one. He never makes two the same. I'm now on my fourth guitar of this particular six-string, lead, electric guitar with a silver front. These are the ones that are probably up in some old ladies' attic somewhere, but they've got my name all over them and they can't do anything with them. I just wish they hadn't stolen them. I had a guitar with a mother-of-pearl mosaic inlay and the guitar actually sounded great because I would design every guitar and he would ask what pickups I wanted. Along with his and my early Gibson and Fender guitars that I used to rely on getting stolen, I've got a little hardened to not relying on one in particular.

Acknowledgements

In the making of *Wired for Sound: A Guitar Odyssey*, the television program and home video, Hallway Entertainment would like to thank the following for their collaboration with us during the time we spent in pre-production, production, and post-production in England, the United States, and in Montreal, Canada. A power chord of thanks goes to Paul Cadieux and W. Douglas Hall, Executive Producers; Dave Goard, Editor; Gordon Judges, Director of Photography; J.W. Whitten, Associate Producer; Kristen Topping, Production Associate; Bill Mather, Post Audio Engineer; Bob "The Iceman" Segarini, Narration; Walter Carter, Technical Advisor; David Cairns, Location Manager (U.K); Jack Lawrence and Matt Coale, Camera Operators; "Damon" Phil Jones, Location Sound/Transit Van Racer; Sal Grimaldi and Dean Allen, Assistant Engineers; Chris Wallace, Colorist; Stephane Boudreau and Josee Trottier, Assistant Editors; Clearcut, Licenses & Clearances; and Walter " Six Strings, Nine Lives" Rossi, Closing Theme — RIPDAD from his self-titled Aquarius Records album, produced by George Lagios and Michel Pagliaro.

Hallway Entertainment would also like to express their gratitude to the following people for their goodwill and assistance during the shooting of *Wired for Sound*: Jayne Andrews, Ralph Baker, Maryellen Benenati, George Betts, Luke Burland, Coran Capshaw, Steve Church, Brigitte Cottu, Nicholas Cowan, Fine, Dan Griffin, George Gruhn, Karel Hannak, Monty Hitchcock, Mike Keys, Merle Kilgore, Mary Klauzer, Paula Krafton, Mark Lazare, Lori Lousararian, Tom Maher, Tim McCausland, Michael O'Driscoll, Bob Pridden, Catherine Reed, Mark Ryman, Chris Scott, Sidney Seidenberg, Jeff Smith, Steve Smith, Paula Szeigis, Sharon Tapper, Ron Weisner, Kris Wilkinson, John Willis, PJ Winkelman, and William and Erin Taylor.

At Gibson USA, a special thanks goes to Henry Juszkiewicz, Joe Aniello, Wayne Beavers, Carl Hansen — and Orville H. Gibson [1856-1918].

The authors would like to express their gratitude to the unaccredited collaborator on this book, Greg Hall, whose behind-the-scenes work on this TV and book project, as president and co-founder (with Mark Hall) of Hallway Entertainment, saw this project through from conception to broadcast to publication. A tip of the hat also goes to Bob Hilderley and Susan Hannah at Quarry Press for the fine job done in the production of this book. And to the 38 artists we spoke to for this project, thank you for your words, your enthusiasm and your gracious hospitality.

QUARRY MUSIC BOOKS

Celtic Women:
Profiles of the Life and Career of Over 20 Celtic Women Artists
Maireid Sullivan
$21.95 CDA/$16.95 USA

Country Women:
Profiles of the Life and Career of Over 20 Country Women Artists
Jim Brown
$21.95 CDA/$16.95 USA

George Jones: The Same Ole Me
Doug Hall and Martin Melhuish
$21.95 CDA/$16.95 USA

Chicago: Feelin' Better Every Day
Edo van Belkom
$21.95 CDA/$16.95 USA

Celtic Tides
Martin Melhuish
$21.95 CDA/$15.95 USA

The Real Patsy Cline
Doug Hall
$21.95 CDA/$15.95 USA

Straight Shooter: The Mamas and The Papas
Doug Hall
$19.95 CDA/$15.95 USA

Wired For Sound: A Guitar Odyssey
Martin Melhuish and Mark Hall
$21.95 CDA/$15.95 USA

The Other CD Guide:
Extraordinary Music for Everyday People
Raffaele Quirino
$34.95 CDA/$26.95 USA

For What It's Worth:
The Story of Buffalo Springfield
John Einarson
$21.95 CDA/$15.95 USA

Don't Be Denied: Neil Young
John Einarson
$21.95 CDA/$15.95 USA

American Woman: The Story of the Guess Who
John Einarson
$21.95 CDA/$15.95 USA

Magic Carpet Ride: John Kay and Steppenwolf
John Kay and John Einarson
$21.95 CDA/ $15.95 USA

The Hawk: Ronnie Hawkins and The Hawks
Ian Wallace
$21.95 CDA/$15.95 USA

The Legend and the Legacy: The Story of Dick Damron
Dick Damron
$21.95 CDA/$15.95 USA

Superman's Song: The Story of Crash Test Dummies
Stephen Ostick
$21.95 CDA/$15.95 USA

Building A Mystery:
The Story of Sarah McLachlan and Lilith Fair
Judith Fitzgerald
$21.95 CDA/$15.95 USA

Falling Into You: The Story of Celine Dion
Barry Grills
$21.95 CDA/$15.95 USA

Ironic: The Story of Alanis Morissette
Barry Grills
$21.95 CDA/$15.95 USA